Audiovisual Translation across Europe

New Trends in Translation Studies

Volume 7

Series Editor:
Dr Jorge Díaz Cintas

Advisory Board:

Professor Susan Bassnett
Dr Lynne Bowker
Professor Frederic Chaume
Professor Aline Remael

PETER LANG

Oxford • Bern • Berlin • Bruxelles • Frankfurt am Main • New York • Wien

Audiovisual Translation across Europe

An Ever-changing Landscape

Silvia Bruti and Elena Di Giovanni (eds)

PETER LANG

Oxford • Bern • Berlin • Bruxelles • Frankfurt am Main • New York • Wien

Bibliographic information published by Die Deutsche Nationalbibliothek.
Die Deutsche Nationalbibliothek lists this publication in the Deutsche National-
bibliografie; detailed bibliographic data is available on the Internet at
http://dnb.d-nb.de.

A catalogue record for this book is available from the British Library.

Library of Congress Control Number: 2012954353

ISSN 1664-249X
ISBN 978-3-0343-0953-0

© Peter Lang AG, International Academic Publishers, Bern 2012
Hochfeldstrasse 32, CH-3012 Bern, Switzerland
info@peterlang.com, www.peterlang.com, www.peterlang.net

Printed in Germany

Contents

SILVIA BRUTI AND ELENA DI GIOVANNI

Revisiting audiovisual translation research

The aim of this publication is to cast light on the expansion of audiovisual translation (AVT) studies and practices within European institutions, universities and business domains. The contributions from researchers and practitioners from a host of different countries and backgrounds collected in this volume reflect the rapid pace and the complex nature of this expansion.

Europe is formed by many languages and cultures. What for some is a negative and costly problem, for others is considered a wealth, since there is much research to be carried out and an increasing amount of work opportunities are available for translation professionals. This multi-language social reality is, these days, a recurrent topic of research in AVT Studies. Evidence of this is amply provided by an increase in the number of films where different languages are spoken in order to portray a complex, but rich, reality. Some such examples are present in this publication, accompanied by case studies and insightful comments.

The language/culture tandem is also an important factor, one that, ironically, is increasingly more pertinent as the unifying financial force of globalization advances. While an increasing number of products, and even traditions, seem to be capturing global interest, more attention than ever is being paid to local languages and their associated cultures. No matter how widespread and vital dialects and ethnic varieties are, they have a recognized social status of their own for what they represent within a given community. This is, for example, reflected in the attention that international organizations such as UNESCO and the European Union grant to endangered languages, i.e. those languages that run the risk of not being passed on to younger generations. Should this happen, these 'vanishing voices' (Nettle and Romaine 2000) will no longer represent the cultural identity of a specific ethnic group. In a critical, and sometimes inevitable, panorama of disappearance and extinction, languages are nowadays considered a wealth and a key social identifier, a fact which is bound to be reflected in all artistic representations, including films and the translations which make them travel the world. The power of audiovisual texts and their translation is thus also one of language and cultural 'ecology', which implies preserving and revitalizing the voice of communities of speakers that are being marginalized.

Europe is not only unified by the disparity of languages and cultures, but it also forms a united front in the defence of social rights, such as access to audiovisual content by all its citizens. It is important to remember that, in the information and communication society, images and sounds, integrated in tactile mobile screens, have taken on the role of a repository of information, the role played by books and paper in previous cultures. The risk of being excluded from access to audio and visual materials is high for those who have sensorial differences. As a consequence, the European Commission has issued a series of directives to ensure that all EU citizens will be included in a diverse society which seems to be increasingly driven by technology and its financial gains. As a discipline, Audiovisual Translation Studies (AVTS) have also taken on this challenge and numerous scholars in this growing domain have started and propelled a new field of research, i.e. media accessibility. This field requires special attention, since many issues beyond language and mode of translation are also at stake. Social issues and human rights are interwoven with it, as well as the numerous market forces involved in the provision of subtitling for the deaf (SDH), audio description (AD) and the many possible combinations of these modes for the benefit of the sensory impaired. The vast array of available formats for the distribution and consumption of audiovisual material, added to the sheer amount of available content, also poses a challenge.

The first films date from the late nineteenth century so that, when compared to books and their origins, cinematic art may seem almost newborn. However, while books had a relatively low social popularity – among other reasons because of the levels of social literacy – everyone can read images, irrrespective of their age or the language they speak. Technology has also helped immensely and, thanks to the increasing diffusion of media-related technologies, users have turned into producers of content which can be made available across the globe thanks to web portals and social networks. Many research projects now focus on finding alternative ways to facilitate the viewing experience for those who encounter communication barriers, be they due to language, sound or visual impediments.

All the issues which have been raised so far are explored in this book, in which essays have been organized in two sections. The first section revolves around the multiple relations and intersections of AVT and culture. Since the famous 'cultural turn' in translation studies back in the 1990s, the complementary nature of the two domains at stake, cultural studies on the one hand and translation studies on the other, has come to the fore. In Torop's words 'the understanding of the cultural value of a translation text has grown deeper, especially in respect to the importance of translations for the identity of the receiving culture' (2002: 593). As intimated above, the homogenizing force of globalization has made it necessary for any society wishing to foreground its specificity to prioritize the consideration of cultural identity. The term 'culture' addresses three salient categories of human experience: the 'personal', in that we, as individuals, think and function as such; the 'collective', in which we act in a social environment in which we share certain features (e.g. belong to a particular group); and the 'expressive', as there are several ways in which society expresses itself, giving vent to its voice. These three constitutive pillars are touched upon in the papers grouped in the first section, sometimes more than one at a time because examining one often implies considering the other. For example, the representation of identity through linguistic and verbal stereotypes involves the personal, the collective and the expressive at the same time: the personal, because a character is constructed as a unique being through her/his verbal and nonverbal behaviour; the collective because each individual is also affiliated with one or more groups, with which s/he is identified; and the expressive, as values are more or less overtly conveyed through language.

Most of the contributions in this section address the idea that translation is particularly conditioned by the (in)correct perception and codification of cultural values, both in dubbing and subtitling. In 'The transposition of cultural identity of Desi/Brit-Asian in Italian dubbing', Veronica Bonsignori studies the transposition of linguistic varieties in dubbing, a very challenging task, which is very often tackled by levelling out diatopic variation. This is particularly true in the case of varieties like Desi/Brit-Asian, which reflect their own cultural ideologies and a certain sense of belonging and identity. This article sets out to identify the most salient linguistic traits of Desi/Brit-Asian within a small corpus of films which portray the multilingual and multicultural society of South-Asian immigrant communities living in the UK and the USA and, above all, the clash/encounter between different linguistic systems – i.e. English and non-English – that gives rise to a sort of 'hybrid language'. In her analysis, Bonsignori compares these features to their rendering in Italian dubbing and pinpoints the most common strategies employed, especially when the target language does not offer efficient translating solutions. This is a preliminary step to ascertaining how translation affects the perception of the identities that are portrayed in the films. Finally, the solutions adopted in the dubbed version are contrasted with the linguistic strategies that have been employed for the construction of Indian identity in an original Italian film, namely *Oggi Sposi* (Luca Lucini, 2009).

In '"I do what I like, and I don't have to go to work every day": The *status quo* of audiovisual translators in Poland', Anna Jankowska offers a very interesting overview of the profession of the audiovisual translator in present-day Poland. As she makes clear, Poland reflects the status of AVT in Europe, at a time when it has finally entered universities in most European countries. The job of an audiovisual translator is often regarded as elitist, partly because people think that it is almost impossible to get started without contacts in the industry and partly because they are convinced that it is well paid. Informal discussions with her students prompted Jankowska to explore the situation further, with a view to shedding more light both on the status of audiovisual translators and on market conditions. Her data was mostly collected from a web survey promoted by the Polish Association of Audiovisual Translators (STAW) through their intranet forum and Facebook page and was later supplemented with comments posted on professional forums and personal interviews with students. Some of the most interesting and perhaps surprising results concern the difference between the situation of novice and experienced translators, which varies considerably, especially in terms of remuneration and royalties.

Paradigm shifts regarding global culture is the topic of Alice Casarini's chapter 'XOXO: *Gossip Girl* and dubbing in the age of "Net lingo"', where she discusses the impact that the new media have been having on language over the past decades. The younger generations in the USA, born and raised in a world of cutting-edge technologies and instant communication, offer an exclusive environment in which to study linguistic and cultural evolution. This contribution focuses on *Gossip Girl*, a popular teen television series created in 2007 and narrated by the eponymous (and anonymous) blogger and self-proclaimed 'one and only source into the scandalous lives of Manhattan's elite'. Computers, cell phones, webcams and all other technological devices are not only crucial for narrative purposes within this series (the information posted on *Gossip Girl's* website causes multiple storyline developments), but also prove fundamental in shaping the language of the new Upper East Side brat pack. Starting from establishing the linguistic identity of the original, Casarini proceeds to evaluate the shortcomings of the Italian version. The fact that many Italian viewers have perceived and criticized the limits of the dubbing of *Gossip Girl* (and did so over the internet) is due to the revolutionary impact that the internet has had on viewing experience. This newly acquired attitude shows a significant evolution within the Italian audience which may offer useful insight towards a reconsideration of AVT quality assessment (House 1977, 1997) and methodologies. In the specific case of *Gossip Girl*, the research shows that genre-based homogenization is strongly rejected and the loss of the show's original flavour in dubbing – to be ascribed not only to lip-synching purposes or lack of equivalent terms, but also to the unnecessary generalization of specific technological references – is heavily criticized.

The translation of dialects in interlingual subtitling is the topic of Mariagrazia De Meo's chapter 'Subtitling dialects: Strategies of socio-cultural transfer from Italian into English'. The author examines how culture-bound language varieties such as dialects, ethnolects and socially connoted language are translated in the English subtitles of two films by the Sicilian director Emanuele Crialese: *Respiro* (*Grazia's Island*, 2002) and *Nuovomondo* (*Golden Door*, 2007). The three most significant features of dialects, i.e. their non-standard grammar, specific lexical features and distinctive accent, are embedded in a regional and social group and represent a complex dynamic system. The translator/subtitler seems to walk a tight-rope trying, on the one hand, not to include too much linguistic variation that could impede communication and, on the other, not to mutilate the original too much, thus losing the socio-cultural nuances of the source language. In this chapter, the author argues that, as subtitling relates to a polysemiotic construct, the co-presence of the different semiotic channels offers a certain degree of intersemiotic redundancy that contributes to the transfer of culture-specific information through nonverbal channels. In films, where the referential function of the verbal code is ancillary to that of the visual one, the most frequently employed translation strategies are not necessarily those of condensation and omission, as cultural transfer often necessitates expansion. It thus emerges that the 'intrusiveness' and 'visibility' of subtitles are in need of a redefinition and subtitles become an independent form of hybrid text which, despite being written, often borrows features from oral and colloquial speech.

In her contribution entitled 'Lost in subtitling? The case of geographi-cally connotated language', Adriana Tortoriello bases her approach on the fact that subtitling as a mode of audiovisual translation yields a mul-timodal target text characterized by the addition of an extra layer – the subtitles – onto the invariant part of the original text, i.e. the images and the soundtrack. In her opinion, the subtitler aiming to preserve the same degree of cohesion as that of the original text cannot avoid taking into account the information that is conveyed by the nonverbal codes present in the original, most notably, the kinesic and the paralinguistic. This situ-ation is rendered yet more problematic when the original audiovisual text is characterized by the presence of geographically connotated language, be it in the form of regional or foreign accents. The author then proceeds to her analysis of several scenes taken from two Italian films subtitled into English for the DVD market in order to illustrate the strategies available to and/or activated by the subtitler.

The centrality of the interplay between different codes is also dealt with by Nathalie Mälzer in 'The functions of dialogue in feature films', where the author focuses on the importance of considering film dialogues as part of multisemiotic mediatexts. She also discusses the implications of the fact that in Germany – a dubbing country – the rough translation that serves as a basis for the dubbing director is generally made by a translator who has not seen the movie and does not know how the dialogue is embedded in the mediatext. By analysing extracts from two films, *Mauvais sang* (Loes Carax, 1986) and *Citizen Kane* (Orson Welles, 1941), which involve two different language pairs (French to German and English to German respectively), Mälzer shows that slight alterations in dialogue actually reduce its function to a mere mimesis of orality but irreparably obliterate all intra- and inter-textual allusions and ambiguity. She thus argues for more time to carry out the translation and full access to the AV programme, which would allow the translator to consider the interplay between the various semiotic codes.

The translation of ethnically and socially marked language is the object of Denise Filmer's chapter, entitled 'Ethnic epithets and linguistic taboos: Offensive language transfer in Clint Eastwood's *Gran Torino*'. Controversial and politically loaded, the lexical field of ethnophaulisms has been debated in various disciplines, from sociology and discursive psychology to studies on ideology and discourse analysis. However, from the point of view of translation studies, the issues raised in attempting to render these often culture-bound epithets in the target language (in this case Italian) is an area of study yet to be exploited to its full potential. This chapter opens up the debate on the politically correct stance regarding race talk, contrasted with the point of view that ethnic humour can be justified. Filmer analyses both the Italian dubbed and subtitled versions of *Gran Torino* (2008) to unveil the strategies behind the linguistic transposition of the loaded meaning potential of racial slurs and ethnic epithets. She also reports on a pilot survey she carried out with some undergraduate students on their perception of connoted language, claiming that the perception of 'what constitutes a linguistic taboo or verbal offense is not static within a community ... let alone across cultural boundaries'.

Along the same lines, in her contribution titled 'Racial stereotypes on screen: Dubbing strategies from past to present', Serenella Zanotti examines how representational practices such as stereotyping are dealt with in dubbing. As a case study, she investigates the norms presiding over the choices made in the dubbing of African American Vernacular English into Italian. Starting with an ample review of the narrative functions fulfilled by dialects and racist stereotyping in audiovisual texts, and reflecting upon the vibrant debate over translating diastratically marked varieties, Zanotti discusses some interesting case studies, that is, the two dubbed versions of *Gone with the Wind* (Victor Fleming, 1939), one of which was never commercialized, *Casablanca* (Michael Curtiz, 1942) and the more recent *Bamboozled* (Spike Lee, 2000). Her insightful analysis proves how dubbing elaborates, absorbs, comes to terms with, and sometimes even represses racist discourse and representation practices.

In 'Italians and television: A comparative study on the reception of subtitling and voice-over', Elena Di Giovanni explores the Italian viewers' explicit and non-explicit preferences for non-fiction TV products as they emerge from a survey carried out with forty individuals. After describing the new role taken on by TV in an age of media proliferation and the different tastes and preferences of the audience, Di Giovanni reflects on the specific TV genre of documentaries. She shows how they are perfectly in line with the overall tendency towards specialization which is visible in television (e.g. the restructuring or creation of specialized TV channels, especially by private broadcasters) and describes the current situation in Italy. Most of the documentaries aired on television are translated and, despite the fact that Italy has traditionally been a dubbing country where for a long time documentaries were mainly voiced-over, subtitling is now becoming an alternative translation strategy, thanks to its lower production costs. More recently, the remarkable increase in viewers and TV channels, and consequently in revenues, have favoured a return to the 'preferred' mode of voice-over. The second and most extensive part of the contribution explores the attitudes of viewers towards subtitled and voiced-over documentaries through an empirical experiment in which responses to two clips from different documentaries on cooking, similar in structure and content, are elicited.

The second part of the book is devoted to new perspectives on media accessibility. As this relatively young sub-domain is the object of a constant increase in interest from scholars, marketing agents, broadcasters and audiences, new avenues are being explored as a result of synergies between researchers from different fields and, most significantly, between the providers and receivers of accessible media services. Although within the realm of AVTS media accessibility has traditionally been conceived as a pool of services destined for the sensory impaired, the attention it has attracted and the activities it has set in motion have led to a positive expansion of its scope, whereby accessibility is now seen both as an asset and a universal right. The four contributions contained in this second section are in line with this positive trend, highlighting the importance of increased accessibility to all media contents for all receivers. Ranging from the exploration of the educational impact of audio description for children to the function of surtitles and the provision of subtitles for the deaf in France, the chapters included in this section provide a comprehensive portrait of the latest developments in this rich and expanding domain.

In the first contribution, titled 'Audio description and translation studies: A functional text type analysis of the Dutch play *Wintervögelchen*', Nina Reviers embarks on the study of AD as a new text type, grounding its research within the vast field of translation studies. The definition of AD within the domain of AVT is relatively problematic: on the one hand, AD is a practice that translates the visual elements of the source text into a verbalized target text, something which somehow clashes with the general purpose of AVT as a translation of the verbal code of a source text into another verbal code in a target language. A second crucial point is that AD, subtitling and dubbing are conceived of and designed for different intended audiences, even though none of them necessarily excludes other kinds of potential spectators. The functional analysis of the Flemish theatre play *Wintervögelchen*, which is grounded in a pragmatic, non-normative approach, accommodates AD in traditional translation theory. AD is, thus, a multimodal text type, which combines audio verbal description of visual elements of the ST with verbal and nonverbal aural elements of the ST. By transferring ST functions from the visual to the audio verbal mode they are made accessible to a blind and visually impaired audience. The detailed analysis of the play also reveals a number of challenges for the audio describer, such as how to describe an abstract, unnatural world using concrete vocabulary or how to convey visual humour in words.

The chapter 'Text-to-speech audio description of educational materials for visually impaired children', by Agnieszka Walczak and Agnieszka Szarkowska, focuses on AD and its manifold applications. The two Polish scholars report on the results of a reception study of AD delivered through text-to-speech which was applied to an episode from an educational animation series entitled *Once Upon a Time ... Life*. The results demonstrate that this way of delivering AD has the potential of becoming an educational tool for children with vision impairment. The feedback provided by the participants shows that more than half confirmed the educational value of the AD and expressed positive opinions on the use of text-to-speech software. This is the first experiment of its kind and shows potential for further application of this technology in the AD of other audiovisual programmes and genres. While speech synthesis software may not be the ultimate solution for feature films with many speakers, it may be satisfactory for documentaries and educational material.

The priority given to the functions of audiovisual texts is pivotal in Anika Vervecken's contribution on surtitles, 'Surtitles: Types and functions'. Vervecken starts out with a reflection on the hybrid nature of audiovisual texts as new art forms – or new ways of communication – that combine different semiotic systems. She emphasizes the fact that surtitles do not constitute the translation of the script but of a performance, taking into account both verbal and nonverbal auditory signs along with the visual ones. Thus, surtitles need to adapt to the 'uniqueness' of every performance and interpret the signs within the context. The author then proceeds to analyse surtitles in all their forms and functions, offering a very useful and comprehensive overview on an AVT mode that, despite its ever-growing popularity in opera houses and theatres, has not had much research devoted to it in specialized literature.

In 'Subtitles for deaf and hard-of-hearing people on French television', Tia Muller delves into subtitling for the hearing impaired in France, offering an outline of the state of affairs on French television at the end of the first decade of the twenty-first century. The chapter presents an overview of the French audiovisual landscape and the historical and legislative contexts of SDH in France, followed by a discussion of SDH conventions and an analysis of a sample of SDH output broadcast on French television and selected from four days over 2009 and 2010. This comprehensive survey helps to dispel some of the complexities surrounding subtitling conventions and their impact on D/deaf and HoH audiences and suggests that the production of SDH needs to be further investigated both from a quantitative and a qualitative point of view.

Bibliography

House, Juliane, *A Model for Translation Quality Assessment* (Tübingen: Gunter Narr, 1977).

—— *Translation Quality Assessment: A Model Revisited* (Tübingen: Gunter Narr, 1997).

Nettle, Daniel, and Suzanne Romaine, *Vanishing Voices* (Oxford: Oxford University Press, 2000).

Torop, Peeter, 'Translation as Translating as Culture', *Sign System Studies* 30.2 (2002), 593–605.

PART I

Audiovisual translation across cultures and languages

VERONICA BONSIGNORI

The transposition of cultural identity of Desi/Brit-Asian in Italian dubbing[1]

1. Introduction

Previous studies (Pernigoni 2005; Taylor 2006; Bonsignori and Bruti 2008; Bonsignori 2009a, 2009b; Federici 2011) have shown that the transposition of linguistic varieties in dubbing always raises several problems, which often lead to standardization in the target language. However, regional dialects and accents strongly contribute to the definition of the identity of characters in a film and, therefore, they should be taken into account in the translation/dubbing process. An interesting case is represented by Desi/Brit-Asian, a variety of English spoken by South Asian immigrants in the USA and in the UK respectively. More specifically, it is a hybrid variety born from the encounter between two different linguistic systems – i.e. English and non-English – as described by Balirano (2007) and Balirano and Vincent (2007). It is characterized by linguistic creativity at all levels and it is used as an expression of identity and sense of belonging to a certain socio-cultural and ethnic background. Carter (2004: 199) states that 'creativity in language is not unconnected with the search for and expression of identities. [...] Identity is multiple and plural and is constructed through language in social, cultural and ethnic contexts of interaction'. Such a bond between language, creativity and identity is well represented by Desi/Brit-Asian. A parallel could be traced with Vernacular Indian English, the non-standard variety of English widely spoken in India,

---

1   This paper stems from and develops the analysis carried out in Bonsignori (2011).

which reflects its own cultural ideologies and 'represents the "Indianness" of English' (Bhatt 2008: 546) and with which, as a matter of fact, Desi/ Brit-Asian shares many features. The transposition of such sociolinguistic and cultural values in Italian dubbing represents an extremely challenging and difficult task at all levels.

This paper intends to identify the most characteristic linguistic traits of Desi/Brit-Asian represented by a small corpus of four films, namely *East is East* (Damien O'Donnell, 1999), *Bend it like Beckham* (Gurinder Chadha, 2002), *Ae Fond Kiss* (Ken Loach, 2004) and *The Namesake* (Mira Nair, 2006), which portray the multilingual and multicultural melting pot in today's society of South Asian immigrant communities living in the UK and the USA, constituting the so-called 'new diaspora' of the twentieth century (Bhat 2000). The next step in this analysis is to verify whether or not these features have been rendered in the Italian dubbing and, if so, to pinpoint the most common strategies employed as well as the potential strategies used for compensation when the target language cannot find efficient translation solutions. Most importantly, particular attention will be paid to checking the success of the dubbed version in expressing a character identity that is congruent with the original. Finally, one further goal is to verify whether the same linguistic strategies are actually employed for the construction of Indian identity in an original Italian film, namely *Oggi Sposi* (Luca Lucini, 2009), thus comparing Italian dubbed language with original Italian filmic speech.

2. The corpus

A few comments on the sociolinguistic variation that characterizes the corpus of films in this case study are in order, since it is important to bear in mind the multifaceted status of Desi/Brit-Asian, which renders the translator's task even more challenging.

In regard to the three films set in the UK, in *Ae Fond Kiss* (FK), the Khans are a Pakistani family speaking Punjabi and living in Glasgow, Scotland. In *Bend it like Beckham* (BILB), on the other hand, the Bhamras are an Indian family also speaking Punjabi but living in London. Finally, in *East is East* (EE), the Khans are Pakistani, speak Urdu and live in Salford, Greater Manchester. In this last case, reference has been made to the syntax of Pakistani English (Mahboob 2008) and to Balirano (2007) in order to trace the most characteristic traits of Brit-Asian speech in this film, while for the other films under consideration, reference has been made to Bhatt (2008) and Balirano (2007). The only film set in the USA is *The Namesake* (N), which tells the story of a Bengali family, the Gangulis, who move from Calcutta to New York. This is the only case of adaptation from a novel – Jhumpa Lahiri's *The Namesake* (2003) – while the film directed by Ken Loach, *Ae Fond Kiss*, is not based on an original written script and the actors were free to improvise, so that the dialogues are even more realistic. This is a general trait in the films of Ken Loach, who also usually chooses non-professional and thus more 'genuine', actors (Taylor 2006: 37).

Another important factor that characterizes the films analysed, and also reflects on the language used, is the generational and cultural gap between parents as first-generation immigrants, strongly tied to Indian/Pakistani traditions and cultural values, and their offspring, born in the USA or the UK, who conversely find themselves in between and strive to find and express their own identity. As a matter of fact, Lahiri (2002) uses the initialism 'ABCD', standing for 'American-born confused Desi', to describe the state of second generation Indians living in the USA, thus highlighting the cultural chaos they usually experience. Such differences are mirrored also in the languages chosen to communicate, that is English on the one hand and heritage languages on the other, which are transmitted and taught to younger generations by their parents, mainly to preserve their ties to their countries of origin. As is shown in the study carried out by Barn (2008: 200) in the UK, the transmission of heritage languages is related to the fact that language, ethnic identity and culture are strongly intertwined; see also section 3.4 devoted to code switching as a faithful representation of real life scenarios.

Finally, the Italian film *Oggi Sposi* (OS) is set in Rome and tells the story of four weddings, one of which is between Alopa Prassad, the Indian Ambassador's daughter, and Nicola Impanato, a policeman of humble origins from the south of Italy. In this case, the ethnic and socio-cultural differences between the two protagonists are highlighted and mirrored also in their way of speaking: on the one hand, Nicola – interpreted by Luca Argentero, a famous Italian actor who comes from Turin, in the north of Italy – speaks with a marked regional accent from Puglia, while, on the other hand, Alopa and the Prassad family in general tend to use stand-ard Italian, as foreign and educated people belonging to high society are expected to do. Of course, some specific linguistic features are traceable in the language of this Indian family, which contribute to the construc-tion of their identity, even though, quite interestingly, non-Indian actors were chosen to interpret the roles of Alopa – interpreted by Moran Atias who comes from Israel – and her father the Ambassador, Jadip Prassad, – interpreted by Hassani Shapi, from Kenya. As regards Alopa's mother, Amira Prassad, no additional information could be found, except for the name of the actress in the film credits.

3.   Analysis

In what follows, a general overview of the most distinctive features of Desi/ Brit-Asian speech as used in the films under investigation is given at various linguistic levels – i.e. morphological, lexical and syntactic – analysing both the original soundtrack of the films and their dubbed version in Italian. Moreover, if the same linguistic feature appears in the Italian film also, it will be analysed in the appropriate section, in order to verify whether or not there is correspondence between original Italian filmic speech and Italian dubbing for the construction of Indian identity.

3.1. *Morphology*

In terms of morphology, the linguistic creativity of Desi/Brit-Asian is mainly represented by compounding, reduplication and conversion (Balirano 2007, Bhatt 2008, Mahboob 2008), namely the creation of new words by a change of word class without any alteration of the word itself. Generally, hyphenated compounds undergo explicitation in Italian dubbing, as shown in the following example, where the compound adjective is rendered with a noun phrase followed by a prepositional phrase:

> (1) ZAID: You *cow-worshipping* bastards! (EE) > Bastardi *adoratori di vacche!* [Bastard *worshippers of cows!*]

When it is not possible to find a suitable correspondent in the target language, a wide set of strategies for compensation is employed, ranging from the deletion of the determiner to variations in word order as happens in (2) with reference to the apophonic reduplicative with vowel gradation 'tickle-tackle':

> (2) MR KHAN: Is everything alright? *Tickle-tackle* all gone? (EE) > *Tutto è andato* bene? Ø *Prepuzio* non c'è più? [*Everything has gone* well? *Prepuce* isn't there anymore?]

In this case, the standard construction of the first part of the utterance in the source text is rendered with a non-standard sentence affecting word order in the Italian dub, since the inversion of verb and subject would be required in this case, resulting with '*è andato tutto* bene?'.

Another interesting feature is the reduplication of adjectives, as 'small small skirts' and 'juicy juicy mangos' in BILB which are respectively translated as *quelle minigonne oscene* [those obscene mini-skirts] and *due bei manghi maturi* [two beautiful ripe mangos] in Italian dubbing. In this case, the reduplicative undergoes normalization and paraphrase, with the use of additional adjectival forms instead of employing a phenomenon that is actually available in the target language too (Bonsignori and Bruti 2008). As a matter of fact, in *Oggi Sposi* the reduplication of an adjective is used at least once and represents the only outstanding feature at morphological level:

(3) INDIAN AMBASSADOR: Bè, forse come casta è un *poco poco* inferiore, no?
(OS) [Well, maybe as caste, it is a little little inferior, right?]

Finally, there are also cases of conversion. An example is the word *gora/ goree*, which has the function of adjective in Indian/Urdu, while in Desi/ Brit-Asian it is used as a noun to refer to fair-skinned western people. Generally, such a term is never maintained in the dubbed version, but is translated with substantive adjectives like *bianco/a* [white], *bionda* [blond], as in (4) and (5) below:

(4) MR KHAN: Don't let a cheap *goree* come between us! (FK) > Non lasciare che *una bianca* si metta tra noi! [Don't let a white (woman) come between us!]

(5) INDIAN GIRL: Hey! Who's that *goree* watching her? (BILB) > Ehi! Chi è *la bionda* che la sta guardando? [Hey! Who is the blond that is watching her?]

In BILB, there is a case in which a swearword is used instead – i.e. *stronza* [arsehole]. However, if on the one hand this translating option succeeds in expressing the belligerent attitude of the speaker, on the other it irreparably causes the loss of its racial connotation, which is fundamental in films which revolve around racial conflicts (Bonsignori and Bruti 2008).

3.2. *Lexicon*

On the lexical level, in the original English soundtrack we can observe cases of borrowing and appropriation, that is, the use of borrowed Indian/ Urdu terms with English inflectional morphemes. For example, the plural of *chapatti* [unleavened flatbread from the Indian subcontinent] in (6) and of *dak name* ['call name' used by family members before choosing the official name used in legal documents] in (7) is constructed by the addition of the English inflectional suffix for the plural -*s*:

(6) MRS BHAMRA: What family will want a daughter-in-law who can run around kicking football all day but can't make round *chapattis*? (BILB) > Quale famiglia vorrebbe una nuora che corre tutto il giorno appresso a un pallone ma che non è capace di cucinare *le chapatti*? [What family would want a daughter-in-law that runs after a ball all day long but that can't cook the *chapatti*?]

(7) ASHIMA: Some of my cousins were not named until they were six years old. Until then they were called by their *dak names*. (NS) > A cugini miei hanno dato Ø nome a sei anni. Prima erano chiamati con Ø loro *dak name* e basta. [To my cousins they gave name at the age of six. Before, they were called with their *dak name* and that was it.]

As can be observed, in the Italian dubbed version, only the borrowing is maintained, with the use of the foreign word in its simplest and original form, thus producing the effect of code-mixing (see section 3.4.). In such cases, when only a partial mapping is possible, compensation strategies may be used – i.e. the choice of the regional and colloquial word *appresso* [behind] in (6), and the deletion of the determiners and the use of non-standard word order in (7), instead of the correct *ai miei cugini*. The same trend is observable in the Italian film, as can be seen in the example below, where the name of the Indian dish *tandoori* is used, then followed by the mispronounced *orecchiette* [short, ear-shaped pasta from Puglia]:

(8) INDIAN 1: Allora, io propongo una mediazione. Pollo *tandoori* come *entrata*, dopo, le 'ricchiette'. (OS) [Well, I suggest a mediation. Tandoori chicken as appetizer, then, ricchiette.]

In addition, we can also notice a case of calque. Here the word *entrata* actually stands for *antipasto* or *entrée* and is therefore a calque from French.

3.3. Syntax

On the level of syntax, Desi/Brit-Asian is characterized by the use of the tag 'innit', ellipsis, the elision of the article or other determiners, topicalization and other phenomena related to word order, such as the lack of inversion between subject and auxiliary in interrogatives (Balirano 2007, Bhatt 2008, Mahboob 2008).

The tag 'innit' is diatopically marked, in the sense that it is typically used in the London area (Andersen 2001) and, as a matter of fact, it is present only in BILB. Moreover, 'innit' has also strong socio-cultural meanings, since it is used only by Indian and black² characters, thus becoming a strong marker of ethnicity and posing several problems in dubbing. See the examples below:

> (9) PINKY: I want the choli more fitted! That's the style, *innit!* (BILB) > Io il choli lo voglio attillato! Va così, *vero?* [I, the choli, want it fitted! That's the fashion, true?]

> (10) PINKY: Jess, don't you want all of this? I mean, this is the best of your life, *innit!* (BILB) > Jess, non la vuoi una festa così? Questo è il più bel giorno della vita, *no?* [Jess, don't you want a party like this? This is the most beautiful day of your life, no?]

> (11) PINKY: Yeah, well, they look the bloody same to them, *innit!* (BILB) > Eh – sì, *ma tanto* sembrano tutti uguali Ø! [Eh – yeah, but they all look the same!]

In (9) 'innit' is translated into Italian with the neutral expression *vero* [true], thus losing the sociolinguistic meaning implied, which is in some way compensated by the use of a left dislocation. An alternative translating option for 'innit' in this film is *no*, as seen in example (10). But, of the ten occurrences in the ST, in five cases this tag is totally omitted in the dubbed version, thus showing the extreme difficulty in finding a suitable correspondent in the TL and in rendering the diatopically marked linguistic and sociolinguistic meaning expressed by this tag (Bonsignori 2009a, 2009b). Finally, as shown in examples (9)-(11), Pinky's frequent use of the non-standard tag 'innit', if compared to her younger sister Jess who never uses it, becomes indexical of her cultural identity and her attitude towards Indian traditions. More specifically, the contrast between Pinky and Jess, who conversely wants to become a professional footballer and is romantically involved with her Irish coach, thus going against her own parents' wishes, is highlighted here by Pinky's use of 'innit' which expresses the fact that her ties to family and traditional heritage are the stronger. Unfortunately, this difference cannot be identified in the Italian dubbed version.

---

2   'Innit' is considered a characterizing feature of West-Indian English (Wright 1981) and of Jamaican Creole (Hewitt 1986) spoken in London, which has then influenced the speech of white adolescents in London.

Another characteristic feature of Desi/Brit-Asian is the use of elliptical constructions, and more specifically the use of the ellipsis of the subject and verb, which could be either the lexical verb or the auxiliary. Of course, the difficulty in rendering the ellipsis of the subject is quite clear, since Italian is a pro-drop language, so generally various compensation strategies are used when possible, such as other types of ellipsis, ungrammatical constructions or even the overt subject, which is a marked choice in the TL, as shown in the two examples below:

> (12) MR KHAN: Why Ø *you no listen*? Ø *You* stupid? (EE) > Tu non Ø ascolti? Tu Ø stupido? [You don't listen? You stupid?]

> (13) MR KHAN: *His name* Ø Mr Shah. [...] Ø *Been* this country 25 years. (EE) > Si chiama Mr Shah. [...] Ø *Stato* in questo paese 25 anni. [His name is Mr Shah. [...] Been in this country 25 years.]

In OS we can find cases of ellipsis of the verb, as in (14), and of personal pronoun particles, as the proclitic particle *ci* and the second person singular *ti* with indirect object function, respectively in (15) and (16):

> (14) ALOPA: Papà! Nicola [Ø (è)] già un ispettore stimato! [Dad! Nicola already an esteemed police inspector!] (OS)

> (15) AMIRA PRASSAD: Forse [Ø (ci)] *siamo visti* all'opera? [Maybe we have seen at the opera?]

> (16) INDIAN AMBASSADOR: [Ø (ti)] *Dispiace* se mi informo su questo ragazzo? [Mind if I inquire after this guy?]

The elision of determiners is generally maintained in Italian dubbing. Let us take EE as an example. Of the thirty-eight cases of deletion of the determiner in the original, twenty-nine are maintained in the translation, while in six cases we find unmarked solutions and in the remaining three cases the use of the determiner, as shown in the first and second part of the following example respectively:

> (17) MR KHAN: [...] Go change Ø *bloody clothes*! Leave Ø *pucking fish*! (EE) > [...] Va' a cambiarti e posa *il* pesce! [Go change and put down the fish!]

The deletion of the determiner also takes place at some other points in the dub as a compensation strategy, balancing the number of occurrences in the two versions. The elision of determiners, especially of the definite article, seems to be a widespread device also in OS:

> (18) INDIAN AMBASSADOR: (to ALOPA) Ø *Tuo cuore* vede più della mia mente. [...] (OS) [Your heart sees more than my mind.]

Topicalization is maintained in dubbing whenever possible. Here is an example where the adverbial of time is in the initial position:

> (19) TEETU'S MOTHER: Well, our Teetu also! *For days* he has eaten nothing and drunk nothing! (BILB) > Proprio come il nostro Teetu! Capisco. *Per giorni* non ha mangiato né bevuto niente!

Otherwise standard constructions or other compensation strategies are used, for instance direct questions with no subject-verb inversion, a syntactic construction which is not present in the TL. In the following example (20) the deletion of the definite article is used instead, while (21) displays a standard and unmarked construction:

> (20) ASHIMA: *You don't have time for one cup of tea, Gogol?* (N) > Non hai tempo per offrirle Ø tazza di tè? [Don't you have time to offer her cup of tea?]

> (21) MR KHAN: Listen, dear, there are four or five universities in this bloody city! *What the community is gonna say?* (FK) > Senti, tesoro, ci sono quattro università in questa benedetta città. *Che cosa dirà la comunità?* [Listen, dear, there are four universities in this blessed city! What is the community going to say?]

The same trend is observable in OS, with a marked positioning of adjectives in contrast with what standard Italian would actually require. This is the case of the adjective *sacri* [sacred] in the example below, which should actually follow the noun *animali*:

> (22) AMBASSADOR: Oh, ferma, ferma, ferma! Non voglio disturbare *questi sacri animali*. Continuo a piedi. (starts singing in Hindi) (OS) [Oh, stop, stop, stop! I don't want to disturb these sacred animals. I continue on foot.]

3.4. Code-mixing and code-switching

Code-mixing (Auer 2007) is very frequent in Desi/Brit-Asian and it entails the insertion of an Indian/Urdu word in a sentence in English. More specifically, these foreign words generally pertain to the semantic domains of food and terms of address – a trend also observable in the Italian film OS. As regards their transposition in Italian dubbing, an interesting trend has been observed for names of Indian traditional dishes, such as *aloo gobi, achar, paneer tikka,* and spices, which are maintained in the dubbed version, since they contribute a great deal to the portrayal of South Asian culture and its traditional heritage (Bonsignori and Bruti 2008). On the contrary, in the case of vocatives, different solutions can be adopted: the term can be deleted, translated into Italian or maintained in its original form. For instance, the word *putar* is either translated into *figliolo/a* [son/daughter] or rendered with the same foreign term, though in the majority of cases it is totally omitted in the Italian dub. Deletion is also often employed with words formed by the proper name of the addressee to which the suffix *-ji* is added, an honorific in Indian culture to denote respect – i.e. *Massi-ji* in the following example:

(23) PINKY: Yes, *Massi-ji,* mum's making the *samosas!* (BILB) > Sì, *ma certo!* Mamma prepara le *samosa!* [Yes, of course! Mum's making the samosa!]

Such a suffix is frequently used in the Italian film *Oggi Sposi,* either in isolation or attached to the colloquial term for 'father', *baba,* with which Alopa usually addresses her father:

(24) ALOPA: *Ji?* Cosa vuoi dire? (OS) [Ji? What do you mean?]

(25) ALOPA: *Babaji.. Babaji,* per rispetto alle tue tradizioni, Nicola mi ha chiesto di sposarlo con rito indù. (OS) [Babaji.. babaji, to respect your traditions, Nicola asked me to marry him with Hindu rite.]

On the other hand, the Indian ambassador generally uses the vocative and hypocoristic *beti* to address his daughter Alopa.

Desi/Brit-Asian is also characterized by code-switching, in this case between English and Indian/Urdu, respectively associated with the 'they-code', the majority language, and the 'we-code', the ethnic specific and minority languages (Gumperz 1982: 95). The problem of code-switching is tackled in different ways in the four films analysed. In EE, utterances in Urdu, which is the language mainly used by Mr Khan and by first generation immigrants, are left unchanged in the dubbed version of the film, without any kind of translation. In BILB, the use of Punjabi seems to be gender-related, since the principal users are Mrs Bhamra and Indian immigrants – especially women – of the first generation. In this film, Punjabi in the original soundtrack is either maintained in the dubbed version or dubbed into Italian, as in the two examples below:

(26) MRS BHAMRA: You've ruined your sister's life! [Punjabi]! Happy now? > Hai rovinato la vita a tua sorella! [Punjabi]! Sei contenta ora?

(27) MR BHAMRA: The dinner's ready? > La cena è pronta? [The dinner's ready?]
MRS BHAMRA: [Punjabi] > *Quasi*. [Almost.]

In FK, on the other hand, Punjabi is always translated into Italian, either with subtitles or dubbing. As seen in the example below, the Italian version is usually characterized by standard and unmarked constructions, because the lines are translated from the English subtitles that appear on the screen and show a standard variety. The only exception is the first line uttered by Mrs Khan with the use of a double indirect object and the wrong pronoun – i.e. *gli* for the masculine instead of *le* for the feminine:

(28) CASIM: [Punjabi: I can't get married]. > Io non posso sposarmi. [I can't get married.]

MRS KHAN: [Punjabi: How can I tell your aunt?]. > Eh? *Che gli dico a tua zia adesso? Sembravi così contento ...* [Eh? What shall I tell your aunt now? You seemed so happy ...]

CASIM: I can't go ahead with it, mom. > Non posso farlo. [I can't do it.]

MRS KHAN: [Punjabi: This is not good. What will Jasmine do? This will shame us]. > Non ci si comporta così. E Jasmine, che cosa farà? La vergogna cadrà su di noi! [You can't behave like this. And Jasmine, what will she do? Shame is going to fall on us!]

CASIM: I'll sell the car. I'll give you all the money back for the extension. I can't go ahead with it. > Venderò la macchina, vi ridarò tutti i soldi che avete speso per la casa, ma non ce la faccio. [I'll sell the car. I'll give you the money back you spent for the house, but I can't do it.]

As noted by Monti (2009), the use of code-switching in this film is more related to ethnicity than to gender. As a matter of fact, Punjabi is always used by Mrs Khan, a Pakistani woman firmly attached to her traditions and cultural background, but in the first part of this exchange her son Casim also uses Punjabi to describe his feelings about the decision imposed by his parents concerning an arranged marriage with his cousin Jasmine. Then, when Casim has to talk about his own choice, which is in opposition to traditions, he switches to English. Unfortunately, the function performed by code-switching is completely lost in the dubbed version, since the translation into Italian 'neutralises the socio-cultural implications conveyed in the original version' (ibid.: 171).

Finally, in NS Hindi/Bengali speech is translated with subtitles both in the original soundtrack and in the Italian dubbed version. In this way, the content of the dialogue exchanges are accessible to the audience, without losing realism or credibility, as characters express themselves fully. At a given moment, Ashoke uses code-switching to talk to his wife Ashima, as they have recently moved to America, and mentions that:

(29) ASHOKE: Once you are settled, I will take you to my department and introduce you to my professor here. You won't believe it. [Bengali: In comparison to the professors here, even our *street vendors* dress well.]

> Appena te la senti, ti porto in facoltà e ti presento il mio professore qui. Non ci crederai! [Bengali: I nostri *conducenti di risciò* vestono meglio dei professori di qui.] [As soon as you feel up to it, I'll take you to faculty and introduce you to my professor here. You won't believe it! Our rikshaw drivers are better dressed than professors here.]

The translation of 'street vendors' in the subtitle as *conducenti di risciò* [rik-shaw drivers] is quite interesting, since apparently the only reason for such a change in the Italian version is that this is a more stereotypical image of Indian people for the Italian audience.

Interestingly, in OS there are only two scenes where code-switching is used and both refer to situations of intimacy: one is the wedding itself, where the dialogue is not even subtitled, and the other is when Alopa cries in her bedroom because she has broken up with Nicola as a consequence of continuous fighting over the organization of the wedding ceremony – mainly caused by their parents, who seem incapable of facing the cultural clash:

> (30) AMBASSADOR: Vai, vai! Dille del gemellaggio, mi raccomando! [Go, go! Do tell her about the twinning!]
>
> MRS PRASSAD: È la terza volta, piantala! [It's the third time, stop it!]
>
> ALOPA: (crying) [Hindi: Non dire niente, mamma –] [Don't say anything, mom –]
>
> MRS PRASSAD: [Hindi: Chi dice niente?! Alopa, tuo nonno, il padre di tuo padre, mi era antipatico e *pure* lo zio Kapali e quella pettegola di zia Archita. Io *la famiglia di tuo padre* non *la* sopporto. Per questo l'ho convinto a fare il diplomatico, per stare lontano da quelli!] [Who's gonna say anything?! Alopa, I didn't like your granddad, the father of your father, and even Uncle Kapali and that gossipy aunt Archita. I can't stand your father's family! This is why I convinced him to be a diplomat, to stay away from them!]
>
> ALOPA: [Hindi: *Pure* nonna Dhara?] [Even granny Dhara?]
>
> MRS PRASSAD: [Hindi: Uff! Non me ne parlare ...! Una tirchia prepotente –] [Uff! Don't tell me about it! So stingy and overbearing!]
>
> AMBASSADOR: Prepotente è tuo padre, che mi diceva: 'Tu non farai mai strada!' [Overbearing is your father, who always told me: 'You won't make your way!']

In this example, Hindi is subtitled and interestingly the use of colloquial and regional terms like *pure* [anche] and syntactic constructions, such as dislocations, are meant to reproduce an intimate and ordinary talk between mother and daughter.

4. Conclusions

The present paper has focused on the linguistic creativity of Desi/Brit-Asian speech and the difficulty it presents when translating into Italian. Various choices have been made according to the linguistic phenomenon to be transposed in the TL. On the morphological level, explicitation with a certain amount of creative license seems to be the preferred option, although there are cases of levelled solutions – see the conversion of the term *gora/goree* in examples (4) and (5) – which also apply on the lexical level, sometimes producing the effect of code-mixing.

As for syntax, the tag 'innit' undergoes total normalization, while verbal ellipsis is generally reproduced in the same way, as well as the elision of determiners. On the contrary, due to the impossibility of reproducing the ellipsis of the subject in Italian, other linguistic items may be deleted or the subject personal pronoun is explicitated, a marked case in the Italian language.

Finally, different strategies can be adopted to deal with code-mixing and code-switching. In the first case, the solutions consist in translating or omitting foreign words, or maintaining them in the dubbed version. In the second case, the options range from leaving South Asian speech untranslated, to subtitling or dubbing it.

At this point, it is important to evaluate the effects of such choices in Italian dubbing, and more specifically to verify whether or not they succeed in expressing the socio-cultural values implied. The use of strategies aimed at levelling out causes the loss of diatopic variation, but these are counterbalanced with the use of compensation strategies by morphosyntactic and lexical means, particularly when a certain linguistic phenomenon cannot be reproduced in the same way in the TL. Another approach is the attempt at reproducing ethnic variation by making South Asian characters speak Italian with an Indian/Pakistani accent, a strategy that was not actually tackled in the present paper since the phonological level was not taken into account, but which is worth mentioning. Finally, as regards code-switching, subtitling has proved to be the most efficient strategy, allowing South Asian characters to express their identity, thus avoiding the risk of stereotyping and the ridiculous effects generated by dubbing. Table 1.1 provides a schematic representation of how the various characterizing features of Desi/Brit-Asian are rendered in the Italian dub in comparison with how they are presented in films originally shot in Italian:

Table 1.1 The representation of Desi/Brit-Asian in Italian dubbing
and original Italian filmic speech

Linguistic levels	Features in Desi/Brit-Asian	Italian dubbing	Original Italian
Morphology	Compounding		
	Reduplication		✓
	Conversion		
Lexicon	Borrowing and Appropriation		
	Calques		✓
Syntax	Tag Questions (*innit*)		
	Ellipsis	✓	✓
	Elision of determiners	✓	✓
	Word order	✓	✓
	Code-mixing	✓	✓
	Code-switching	✓	✓

As far as the construction of Indian identity in original Italian filmic speech is concerned, this case study has shown that the linguistic strategies used by South-Asian characters are just the same as those employed in Italian dubbing at all levels. As pointed out in the analysis of OS, the only difference is in the use of calques, but other strategies are adopted too, such as the mispronunciation of certain words or the use of non-standard syntactic constructions. Indeed, the present analysis cannot lead to definitive conclusions, because of the limited set of available data: the few films of Italian production with Indians as protagonists demonstrate an undeniable difficulty in the study of this topic. This is probably due to the fact that the immigration of Indians to Italy is relatively recent and, in comparison with other foreign communities in this country, not relevant enough to affect film production.[3] On the other hand, the creativity of Desi/Brit-Asian and the various strategies both for representing it in film scenarios and translating it in dubbing have clearly emerged.

Bibliography

Andersen, Gisle, *Pragmatic Markers and Sociolinguistic Variation: A Relevance-theoretic Approach to the Language of Adolescents* (Amsterdam: John Benjamins, 2001).

Auer, Peter, 'Mobility, Contact and Accommodation', in Carmen Llamas, Louise Mullany and Peter Stockwell, eds, *The Routledge Companion to Sociolinguistics* (Abingdon: Routledge, 2007), 109–15.

Balirano, Giuseppe, *The Perception of Diasporic Humour. Indian English on TV* (Loreto: Tecnostampa, 2007).

—— and Jocelyn Vincent, 'Migrating English in Postcolonial *Trans*-lation: Brit-Asian/Desi as the Source/target of Diasporic Representations', *Paper presented at the XXIII AIA Conference 'Migration of Forms – Forms of Migration'*, Bari, 20–22 September 2007.

Barn, Ravinder, 'Indian Diaspora in the United Kingdom: Second-Generation Parents' Views and Experiences on Heritage Language Transmission', in Parvati Raghuram, Ajaya Kumar Sahoo, Brij Maharaj and Dave Sangha, eds, *Tracing an Indian Diaspora. Contexts, Memories and Representations* (New Delhi/London: SAGE, 2008), 191–209.

Bhat, Chandrashekhar, *Contexts of Intra and Inter Ethnic Conflict among the Indian Diaspora Communities*. Occasional Paper, University of Hyderabad: Centre of Study of Indian Diaspora, 2000.

Bhatt, Rakesh M., 'Indian English: Syntax', in Rajend Mesthrie, ed., *Varieties of English. Africa, South and Southeast Asia* (Berlin: Mouton de Gruyter, 2008), 546–62.

---

3   According to the last ISTAT report (2009), Indians are ranked tenth among the other foreign communities living in Italy.

Bonsignori, Veronica, 'Invariant Tags Migrating from the UK to Italy and Back', in Domenico Torretta, Marina Dossena and Anna Maria Sportelli, eds, *Forms of Migration, Migration of Forms (Vol. 3, Language Studies), Proceedings of the 23rd AIA Conference* (Bari: Progedit, 2009a), 305–21.

—— 'Translating English Non-standard Tags in Italian Dubbing', in Michela Giorgio Marrano, Giovanni Nadiani and Chris Rundle, eds, Special Issue: *The Translation of Dialects in Multimedia, InTRAlinea* (2009b), <http://www.intralinea. org/specials/article/1709> accessed 30 October 2012.

—— 'Desi/Brit-Asian in Italian Dubbing', in Gabriella Di Martino, Linda Lombardo and Stefania Nuccorini, eds, *Papers from the 24th AIA Conference. Challenges for the 21st Century: Dilemmas, Ambiguities, Directions*, Vol. 2. Language Studies, Proceedings of the 24th AIA Conference, Rome, 1–3 October 2009 (Rome: Edizioni Q, 2011) 141–9.

—— and Silvia Bruti, 'A Linguistic Analysis of Dubbing: the Case of *Bend It Like Beckham*', in Marcella Bertuccelli Papi, Antonio Bertacca and Silvia Bruti, eds, *Threads in the Complex Fabric of Language. Linguistic and Literary Studies in Honour of Lavinia Merlini Barbaresi* (Pisa: Felici Editore, 2008), 509–21.

Carter, Ronald, *Language and Creativity. The Art of Common Talk* (London: Routledge, 2004).

Federici, Federico M., ed., *Translating Dialects and Language Minorities. Challenges and Solutions* (Oxford: Peter Lang, 2011).

Gumperz, John, *Discourse Strategies* (Cambridge: Cambridge University Press, 1982).

Hewitt, Roger, *White Talk Black Talk* (Cambridge: Cambridge University Press, 1986).

Lahiri, Jhumpa, 'Intimate Alienation: Immigrant Fiction and Translation', in Rukmini Bhaya Nair, ed., *Translation, Text and Theory. The Paradigm of India* (New Delhi/ London: SAGE, 2002), 113–20.

Mahboob, Ahmar, 'Pakistani English: Syntax', in Rejend Mesthrie, ed., *Varieties of English. Africa, South and Southeast Asia* (Berlin: Mouton de Gruyter, 2008), 578–92.

Monti, Silvia, 'Codeswitching and Multicultural Identity in Screen Translation', in Maria Freddi and Maria Pavesi, eds, *Analysing Audio-visual Dialogue. Linguistic and Translational Insights* (Bologna: CLUEB, 2009), 165–83.

Pernigoni, Arianna, 'Varietà Substandard e Doppiaggio: il caso di *East Is East, Bend It Like Beckham* e *Monsoon Wedding*', in Giuliana Garzone, ed., *Esperienze del Tradurre. Aspetti Teorici e Applicativi* (Milan: Franco Angeli, 2005), 157–75.

Taylor, Christopher, 'The Translation of Regional Variety in the Films of Ken Loach', in Nigel Armstrong and Federico M. Federici, eds, *Translating Voices, Translating Regions* (Rome: Aracne, 2006), 37–52.

Wright, Peter, *Cockney Dialect and Slang* (London: Batsford, 1981).

Filmography

Ae Fond Kiss (2004), Ken Loach, UK, Belgium, Germany, Italy and Spain.
Bend it like Beckham (2002), Gurinder Chadha, UK and Germany.
East is East (1999), Damien O'Donnell, UK.
Oggi Sposi (2009), Luca Lucini, Italy.
The Namesake (2006), Mira Nair, USA and India.

ANNA JANKOWSKA

'I do what I like, and I don't have to go to work every day': The *status quo* of audiovisual translators in Poland

1. Introduction

For many years, most publications concerning audiovisual translation (AVT) started with the trite statement that 'audiovisual translation has been overlooked for a long time'. However, AVT has apparently become the trend, both in terms of research and teaching. There has been a vast amount of newly published research on dubbing, subtitling, voice-over, audio description (AD)', subtitling for the deaf and hard-of-hearing (SDH), etc. Moreover, AVT has triumphantly made its way into most European universities.

Poland is no exception. Firstly, AVT was discussed in BA and MA dissertations and PhD theses. Then, universities started to offer free elective courses on AVT to MA and BA students. Since 2009, there have been three universities running postgraduate programmes devoted exclusively to AVT.[1] Additionally, the Polish Association of Audiovisual Translators (STAW), together with the Association of Polish Translators (STP), organize special workshops on dubbing, subtitling, voice-over, AD and SDH.

We no longer overlook AVT: we research its theoretical and technical aspects, we organize international conferences and, last but not least, we train students to become audiovisual translators. But what do we actually know about the business that we train them for? Can we answer sincerely if the students ask 'How much will we earn?' or 'Is it easy to get a job?'

---

[1]   Adam Mickiewicz University in Poznań, Warsaw School of Social Sciences and Humanities and Tischner European University in Krakow.

The *status quo* of audiovisual translators and the Polish AVT industry seems to have become the terrain of myth and legend. According to popular belief, the job of an audiovisual translator is highly elitist both in terms of financial remuneration and access to the profession. It is generally considered almost impossible to become an audiovisual translator without having contacts in the industry. However, do those who manage to break into the industry, enter a *land* flowing with *milk and honey, where jobs are amazingly interesting, well-paid, easy and not too time-consuming?* These popular convictions, the questions asked by my students and personal experience have led me to engage inresearch on the status of audiovisual translators in Poland and on market practices which, up until now, seem to have been a no-go area for researchers. In the present article, I will outline some of the findings from a survey carried out among Polish audiovisual translators.

2. Procedure and questions

The data was collected online through a web survey open from November 2009 to April 2010. It was promoted by STAW through their intranet forum and Facebook profile. It was also advertized on translators' social networks such as ProZ and GlobTra.

The survey consisted of twenty-six questions, out of which twenty-three were multiple choice and three open, to give the participants a chance to express their own opinions about the industry and profession. There were two different sources of inspiration behind the questions in the survey, namely similar research conducted among its members by the French Association of Audiovisual Translators (ATAA) and by the questions about the profession asked by students in class and novice translators on internet forums. The questions in the survey covered topics such as place of residence, wages, education, training, type of audiovisual translation, control over the translated text, recruitment and job satisfaction.

3. Sample

A total of forty-eight translators participated in the survey. According to the information provided by STAW, at the time of data collection, there were eighty STAW members and the estimated number of active audio-visual translators in Poland was 200.

For the purpose of this survey, the participants were divided into three categories according to seniority: translators with less than five years' experience (56 per cent), referred to as novice translators; junior translators with five to ten years' experience (19 per cent); and senior translators with more than ten years professional practice (25 per cent).

What follows is a detailed analysis of the survey results with special attention given to seniority, allowing for conclusions to be drawn on how experience apparently influences some aspects of the profession.

4. Place of residence: 'Does it matter if it's subtitling or voice-over?'[2]

The AVT landscape in Poland is dominated by voice-over, widely used on television, and by subtitling, the most frequent form of translation for the cinema. Both methods are also in use on DVD/Blu-ray discs and on the internet. Dubbing is used practically exclusively in children's programmes, animated films and some feature films for younger audiences.

The assumption that the shape of the AVT landscape would be reflected in the type of work accepted by translators proved to be correct after analysing the data. The findings showed that 42 per cent of translators participating in the survey prepare voice-over versions, 38 per cent subtitles, 17 per cent dubbing, and only 3 per cent work on AD or SDH.

2   Section titles are quotations from survey participants' comments.

The survey proved that translators do not tend to specialize in just one type of AVT. While 32 per cent of the respondents declared that they work in just one of the AVT types, 68 per cent work in two or more. Among professionals specializing in just one technique, the majority focus on sub-titling (60 per cent), followed by voice-over (27 per cent), dubbing (6.5 per cent) and AD and SDH (6.5 per cent).

In the group of translators working in two AVT types, the most fre-quent combination is voice-over and subtitling, indicated by as many as 75 per cent of respondents, who also declared that they usually produce subtitles based on their own voice-over version or the other way around. All the respondents specializing in three techniques work in voice-over, subtitling and dubbing, whilst translators who work in four translation types added AD and SDH to their list.

Looking at the data provided in Table 1.1, it is difficult to establish an obvious link between the type of AVT and professional experience. However, it does show that translators with more than ten years' experi-ence are slightly less likely to work in subtitling and more likely to work in AD, SDH and dubbing (see Table 2.1).

Table 2.1 Types of translation work

AVT	< 5 years	6–10 years	> 10 years
Subtitling	42%	39%	32%
Voice-over	42%	39%	36%
Dubbing	13.5%	22%	21%
AD	–	–	4%
SDH	2.5%	–	7%

This was explained by one of the translators, who stated that 'the dubbing folks are the *crème de la crème*' among the audiovisual translators and argues that, since there are relatively fewer jobs in dubbing, it takes much more effort to get one if you are not a professional with an 'established name'.

5. Place of residence: 'You wouldn't make it to the recording'

It is widely believed that one can only be an audiovisual translator in Warsaw. An irrefutable argument I was once given during a conversation with a translation coordinator in one of the studios was that there were 'problems with passing on AVT materials and completed translation, and – in the case of dubbing and voice-over – difficulty in attending the recording sessions'.

In the digital era, making audiovisual content available seems to be fairly easy, if not too easy for that matter, so that the above comment seems rather inadequate. When asked, some of the translators participating in the survey remembered times when they had received material on VHS tapes, later to be replaced by CDs and DVDs, but they also stressed that, nowadays, audiovisual materials are practically always delivered via FTP servers, and completed work is sent back through email. In the light of this, the place of residence ceases to be an important issue.

The findings presented in Table 2.2 show that the vast majority of respondents (90 per cent) do indeed live in Warsaw and its suburbs. A small group of translators indicated Krakow (9 per cent) and Opole (1 per cent) as their place of residence.

Table 2.2 Place of residence

Years of experience	Warsaw	Outside Warsaw
<5 years	81%	19%
5–10 years	89%	11%
>0 years	100%	0%
Average	90%	10%

33 per cent of the translators mentioned that their presence is always required at the recording sessions, stressing that this is the case for the public, and not the private, broadcasters. If they are unable to be present,

translators are obliged to find a substitute. As for the rest, 23 per cent declared that they had never been asked to go to the studio, 27 per cent rarely and 17 per cent sometimes. The translators admitted that, at the beginning of their professional career, it had been advisable to attend a few recordings to 'get a general idea of what is going on there, because it helps to work out the script better', whilst, at the same time, highlighting the fact that 'once one gains experience and knows how to prepare the script, going to the studio is simply a waste of time'. What is particularly interesting is the fact that some translators are not asked to attend any recording, even though their contracts officially require them to do so.

Before conducting the survey and, after talking with representatives of media providers, who stated that a translator must be present at the recording of a dubbed or voice-over version, I assumed that the findings of the survey would reveal differences in the types of translation work carried out by translators depending on their place of residence. The hypothesis was that professionals based outside Warsaw would be more likely to receive commissions for subtitling jobs whilst translators from the capital would focus on dubbing and voice-over. The findings of the survey have only partially confirmed this. On the one hand, translators living in the capital work on dubbing more often than others: 17.5 per cent for Warsaw-based respondents and 10 per cent for those from other locations. On the other hand, more than half (56 per cent) of translators from outside Warsaw prepare voice-over versions as opposed to 40 per cent of those living in the capital. Respondents from Warsaw (36 per cent) prepare subtitles more often than their colleagues from other parts of the country (25 per cent).

There also seems to be a link between place of residence and years of professional experience. All the translators with more than ten years' experience, and as many as 89 per cent of the respondents with five to ten years' experience, live in Warsaw. The findings also clearly show that translators, who have worked in the profession for less than five years, account for the largest proportion (63 per cent) of respondents based outside of the capital.

6. Translators' education: 'I'm not a philologist'

Taking into account the dominant position of the English language in audiovisual productions, it comes as no surprise that it is the main working language of the translators surveyed. A total 89.5 per cent of respondents indicated that they translate from English. However, as many as 49.5 per cent declared that they can also work with other language pairs, including Russian and German (17.5 per cent each); French (15 per cent); Swedish and Spanish (8.5 per cent each); Arabic, Danish and Italian (6 per cent each); and Bengali, Czech, Hindi, Slovakian and Hungarian (3 per cent each). Around 10.5 per cent of all respondents indicated language pairs excluding English, the most frequent combination being Polish with Russian (50 per cent), followed by Swedish, French and Spanish (16.6 per cent each).

The linguistic quality of audiovisual translations is often questioned and this is why the survey included questions concerning the translators' language skills. This part of the survey consisted of multiple-choice questions and, based on the answers selected, the respondents fall into two main groups: translators who graduated with a degree in language studies (70 per cent) and those without a language degree (30 per cent). So far, translation studies have not been officially recognized as a field of study by the Polish Ministry of Higher Education and to study languages students tend to specialize in philology which does not always include any training in translation.

As seen in Table 2.3 (p. 42), translators with a degree in language studies can be further divided into those who have completed university studies, have additionally polished up their culture and language skills during stays abroad or language courses, and have sometimes combined stays abroad with language courses.

Looking at all groups we can easily notice that it is among the translators who have worked in the profession between five and ten years where the proportion of translators with a language degree is largest (77 per cent of the entire age group).

Table 2.3 Translators with a degree in languages

Years of experience	Language degree				
	Degree only	Stay abroad	Language course	Stay abroad and language course	Average for age group
< 5 years	33%	19%	7%	7%	66 %
5–10 years	33%	11%	33%	0%	77%
> 10 years	33%	25%	8%	0%	66%
Average for all groups	33%	18.5%	16%	2.5%	70%

As seen in Table 2.4, audiovisual translators without a language degree account for 30 per cent of all the respondents, stating that they have learned foreign languages during language courses and/or long-term stays abroad. One of the translators without a language degree commented: 'I don't have a philological education, but I think the most important thing is the ability to feel the atmosphere of the film or story you translate and, well, you need to have some literary talent'.

Table 2.4 Translators without a language degree

Years of experience	No language degree			
	Language course	Stay abroad	Stay abroad and language course	Average for age group
< 5 years	12%	11%	11%	34%
5–10 years	11%	11%	0%	22%
> 10 years	9%	17%	8%	34%
Average for all groups	10.5%	13%	6.5%	30%

Interestingly, the highest percentage of respondents without a degree in philology is found among translators who have worked less than five years or more than ten years in the field (34 per cent each). As far as novice translators are concerned, this may be explained by the increasingly good knowledge of foreign languages among young people. Translators who took part in the survey stressed that media distributors give priority to 'translators' who can produce 'natural and trendy' translations even if they only have a basic knowledge of foreign languages. It is apparently not an uncommon practice to hire secondary school students for the translation of films and series for teenagers. Media distributors claim that their translations suit their peer audiences better.

The situation among senior translators is more complex and should be viewed from a historical perspective. The Polish AVT market is relatively young and, up until the 1990s, it was limited to two state-owned television channels (Filas 1999: 43). The first private television broadcasters appeared only at the beginning of the 1990s, creating an urgent demand for people who knew foreign languages irrespective of whether they had a language degree or professional experience in the field of translation.

7.   Translators' skills: 'A friend trained me'

In Poland, the AVT industry is considered prestigious and it is often thought that becoming an audiovisual translator would be impossible without any previous experience and preparation. Indeed, the results (Table 2.5) show that a majority of audiovisual translators, 86 per cent, had vast (20 per cent) or some (66 per cent) previous experience in translation before they started working in the area of AVT. Only 14 per cent of respondents declared that they had no translation experience when they received their first AVT job.

Table 2.5 Previous experience

Years of experience	Vast experience	Some experience	No experience
<5 years	15%	78%	7%
5–10 years	44.5%	55.5%	–
>10 years	–	64%	36%
Average	20%	66%	14%

As shown in Table 2.5, the translators with the greatest experience before entering AVT are junior translators, closely followed by novice translators, of whom 93 per cent declared experience in translating prior to working in AVT. It seems that a large percentage of respondents (64 per cent) who have worked the longest in AVT had little experience in the field of translation before they entered the AVT market, with 36 per cent of them declaring that they did not have any prior experience in translation before their first AVT job. This is most probably due to the rapid growth of the Polish AVT market in the 1990s and the urgent demand for people with foreign language skills at the time.

Audiovisual translation jobs not only require familiarity with a foreign language and with the Polish language, but they also require knowledge of certain translation techniques and limitations specific to each of the AVT methods and, in the case of subtitling, knowledge of specialist software. In the survey, respondents were asked whether they had received any training in AVT before their first AVT job. The answers are presented in Table 2.6:

Table 2.6 Technical training

Years of experience	Training	No training
<5 years	52%	48%
6–10 years	78%	22%
>10 years	55%	45%
Average	61.5%	38.5%

Over half of the respondents (61.5 per cent) said that they had been trained before taking on the work. In 50 per cent of cases, the training was provided by the employer, while 8 per cent of respondents trained independently or were introduced to the world of AVT by experienced friends. A large percentage (38.5 per cent) had no training in the area of AVT before they started work. Among the respondents with no training, the prevailing categories included translators with the fewest and the most years of experience.

8.   Entering the market: 'Getting a job was a nice coincidence'

Entering the AVT industry in Poland is one of the toughest challenges facing a novice translator. This is because, on the one hand, it is considered very elitist and attractive and, thus, off limits for many, while, on the other, the general feeling is that many people make their way into the profession accidentally. This situation, which might sound like a paradox, is aptly described by one of the experienced translators who acknowledges that she 'got in' because someone randomly found her on an internet forum. Under normal circumstances, it is very difficult to 'get into the industry without any contacts unless you work for a pittance for a studio that looks for suckers'.

The general sense of the inaccessibility to the profession is compounded by the fact that Polish media distributors do not seem to follow a standard recruitment system. Some of the translators pointed out that very few Polish studios have websites and, when they do, in most cases, the only contact information provided is a web contact form or a general e-mail addressed to the marketing department.

Experienced AVT translators complain about the lack of of a standardized system of recruitment, which in their opinion usually means that a job is often given to people with little language competence, who also lack the knowledge of translation and AVT specificity.

The survey shows that the vast majority of translators (67 per cent) started working in the field after being recommended by a friend. Approximately 15 per cent of the respondents declared that they themselves found their employers, and 'managed somehow to get an answer to their application letters'. Only 10 per cent admitted that they have been recruited by employers, after having been found through internet forums or answered an ad published by the employer. The remaining 8 per cent entered the field in different ways, such as by volunteering in projects for independent film festivals.

9. Calculating the payment: 'It's a nice second job'

In Poland, payment is calculated per minute of programme, per subtitle or per 10-minute unit of AV material, known as 'act'. For example, a 90-minute film is counted as 9 acts and a 92-minute film is counted as 10 acts. The findings of the survey confirm (83.5 per cent) that translators tend to be paid per act. A much smaller group, just 17 per cent of the respondents, indicated that they are paid per minute or fraction of a minute. A subtitle represented a unit of payment for 6 per cent of the translators surveyed. Other systems, such as a flat rate – i.e. getting paid per film – were indicated by 12.5 per cent of respondents.[3]

It must be noted, however, that the practice of paying per minute or fraction of a minute is much more widespread among translators who work on dubbing (33.5 per cent) than on subtitling (14 per cent) or voice-over (12 per cent). The client's country of origin is also a factor: 30 per cent of translators working for foreign agencies get paid per minute, as opposed to 12 per cent of translators working for Polish companies.

---

3   The translators were able to choose more than one answer. Therefore the total percentage does not add to 100%.

10. A few words about the rates: 'It's better to lay tiles'

Another issue frequently raised on internet translation forums is the rates paid to audiovisual translators, which in the AVT business have been shrouded in mystery. Lack of access to information on rates and on the way of calculating payment has given many people an unrealistic idea about the income that can be expected. At the same time, this lack of information has led to the lowering of rates as novice translators, not knowing how much to charge, end up accepting very low rates.

According to the data provided by STAW in their Standard of Good Practice,[4] the current Polish rates are no more than a tenth of the average European rate, and range between EUR 35–45 per act for dubbing, EUR 15–20 per act for voice-over, and EUR 20–30 per act for spotted subtitles and voice-over. STAW emphasizes that the rates have significantly dropped in recent years and, according to their information, in the 1990s translators could expect payment at the rate of EUR 50–60 per take for dubbing and around EUR 50 per take for spotted subtitles and voice-over.

Sadly, the comments provided by some of the translators are not very encouraging: 'We used to work normally, for reasonable rates, today it's probably better to lay tiles for a living, because to survive in the field (and pay contributions) you practically need to work at two full-time jobs'. Another one commented that she was providing data from six months ago, which was when she finally changed her career, discouraged, after more than ten years.

As shown in Table 2.7, the most common rates are EUR 20–40 per act of dubbed version (46 per cent), and less than EUR 20 per act of voice-over (60 per cent voice-over). As for translators engaged in the translation and the spotting of subtitles, the most frequently indicated rate is EUR 20–40 per act.

---

4 <http://www.staw.org.pl/index.php?option=com_content&task=view&id=89& Itemid=51&limit=1&limitstart=4> accessed 10 January 2012.

Table 2.7 Rates according to AVT type

EUR (per 10-min act)	Subtitling	Dubbing	Voice-over
>60	5%	0%	10%
40–60	18%	12%	7%
20–40	48%	42%	23%
<20	29%	46%	60%

It is possible to establish a connection between years of experience and rates received. As illustrated in Table 2.8, junior and senior translators earn more than their novice colleagues, regardless of the translation type. Their average rate of pay is between EUR 20 and 40 per act, while for novice translators it is usually less than EUR 20.

Table 2.8 Rates according to years of experience

Years of experience	EUR (per 10-min take)			
	>60	40–60	20–40	<20
<5 years	5%	8%	27%	63%
6–10 years	5%	24%	52%	20%
>10 years	5%	12%	53%	30%

The translators also mentioned other issues concerning rates. The first is the absence of a practice still commonly applied in the case of written translations in Poland, that is, raising the rate for express translations and charging differently according to the language of the original text. The latter was introduced by the Act of 25 August 1986 on rates for sworn translators, which divided the languages into four groups (English, French and Russian; European languages and Latin; non-European languages of Latin alphabet; non-European languages of non-Latin alphabet) and established official rates per page of sworn translation. The act has been systematically updated in order to adjust the rates to the changing market situation and the division into four groups has remained unchanged and is commonly used by translation agencies dealing with written translations. Therefore, a translator of Italian or Portuguese can expect a higher rate than one translating from English or French.

Audiovisual translators also stressed that the rates are not raised when the script is not provided even though translating by ear can double the working time. The lack of a higher rate for the time-consuming translation of songs and poems is another problem. The most extreme example was provided by a translator of Bollywood productions, who works on films with numerous dance and song sequences in a language included in the fourth and most expensive category in terms of written translation, but receives the same remuneration as for the translation of feature films from English.

11. Working hours: 'Machines operating 24/7'

According to STAW, AVT, especially in the form of subtitling and dubbing, is a difficult and time-consuming task, not least because of the wide range of topics to be covered and the technical requirements. STAW recommends that a translator enagaged in the subtitling of films and the creation of voice-over versions based on subtitles, should work on no more than three titles a month, in accordance with the work load suggested in other countries where there are formal associations of AVT translators, such as France, Canada, Denmark and Germany, where it is assumed that a translator is able to prepare up to two dubbed versions or three subtitled versions of feature films per month.[5] Unfortunately, the responses in the survey suggest that, due to the falling rates, three or even five titles a month do not provide a satisfactory income. Therefore translators are forced to take on more assignments and to work much faster in order to make a decent living. This very often means working over weekends and holidays.

Most translators who took part in the survey indicated that they are given four to seven days to complete a ninety minute job, with four days

5   <http://www.staw.org.pl/index.php?option=com_content&task=view&id=89&Itemid=51&limit=1&limitstart=4> accessed 12 January 2012.

being the most likely deadline. However, the respondents also mentioned the fact that, over the past few years, clients have considerably tightened, and keep tightening, deadlines. Some of them complained that the clients think of them as 'machines operating 24/7' and do not hesitate to commission translations over a weekend and to demand express translations without raising the rate.

12. Wages: 'You have to pore over the computer'

The monthly income of AVT translators depends on many factors, such as rates, number of jobs, and on whether audiovisual translation is their only source of income. As declared in the survey, some translators see it as 'a nice change from other, more profitable types of translation'. Others work on AVT as work that is 'additional to their full-time job'.

Due to these factors, it is extremely hard to estimate the average monthly income of audiovisual translators. According to data provided by STAW, if translators work at the advisable rate of three films per month, their current average monthly income would range from EUR 550 to EUR 775.[6] The average monthly income of an AVT translator in 1994 was estimated at around EUR 1,000 compared to EUR 130 for other professions.[7] For the sake of comparison, the average wage in the business sector in Poland in 2010 was around EUR 850,[8] while the average earnings of a translator reached EUR 1,150.[9]

---

6   <http://www.staw.org.pl/index.php?option=com_content&task=view&id=89& Itemid=51&limit=1&limitstart=4> accessed 12 January 2012.

7   <http://www.staw.org.pl/index.php?option=com_content&task=view&id=89& Itemid=51&limit=1&limitstart=4> accessed 12 January 2012.

8   According to the Polish Central Statistical Office, <http://www.stat.gov.pl/ gus/5840_1630_PLK_HTML.htm> accessed 12 January 2012.

9   According to Salary Report byAdvisory Group TEST Human Resources, <http:// www.raportplacowy.pl> accessed 12 January 2012.

Among the participants who declared translation to be their main source of income and that AVT makes up 75 to 100 per cent of all their translation work, the average monthly wages vary considerably between EUR 200 and EUR 2,000. In this group, 10 per cent of respondents earn up to EUR 200 a month from AVT, 25 per cent earn up to EUR 500, and 35 per cent up to EUR 900 a month. However, the translators whose income falls into the highest bracket stress that to achieve such results they prepare much more than the advisable three films per month and that they work at least ten hours a day, including Saturdays and Sundays. Or, in the more sarcastic words of one of the respondents: 'To earn decent money, you have to pore over the computer. If you don't want to get ill too quickly, you need to practise a sport'.

The average monthly income once again reveals the differences between translators with varying years of experience in the profession. Among respondents earning below EUR 750 a month, as many as 85 per cent have less than five years' experience. At the other end of the scale, the highest earning groups include only junior (33 per cent) and senior (67 per cent) translators.

13. The question of royalties: 'Translators have their rights'

A significant part of the income received by audiovisual translators should be generated by royalties paid out by ZAiKS (Polish Association of Writers and Composers for the Stage). Based on the Act of 4 February 1994 on Copyright and Related Rights, STAW advises that translators should receive payment every time their work is used, including all the repeats on TV and in the cinema, DVD editions and films shown on buses and planes. Unfortunately, all too often, employers abuse the translator's legal rights and do not include royalties in their contracts. In fact, they do not even ask translators to sign agreements of copyright transfer.

In the survey, translators were asked whether they were guaranteed royalties both at the time of signing a contract and in practice. The answers show that 48 per cent do not get copyright royalties and, of those who are paid royalties, 13 per cent always receive them, whilst 77 per cent receive them sometimes.

Receiving royalties seems to be linked to the years of experience in the profession. Table 2.9 shows that a mere 8 per cent of novice translators 'always' receive copyright royalties, compared with 14.5 per cent of those with six to ten years experience and 22 per cent of senior translators. The majority of novice translators (57 per cent) never receive royalties, as opposed to 28.5 per cent of junior, and 33 per cent of senior translators.

Table 2.9 Royalties according to seniority

Years of experience	Always	Sometimes	Never
<5 years	8%	35%	57%
6–10 years	14.5%	57%	28.5%
>10 years	22%	45%	33%

14. Control over the text: 'This translation is not mine'

Although it may be argued that all the final changes to a text should be agreed with the translator, it is different in practice and changes to the translation are often made by editors, technicians spotting the subtitles, or actors during the final recording. When asked if they were sent the final translation for authorization of any modifications introduced, as many as 53 per cent of respondents said this never happened, while 44 per cent admitted that it only happened sometimes. A mere 3 per cent of the translators declared that they always authorized their translations.

15. Job satisfaction: 'I like watching films'

As mentioned previously, the job of an audiovisual translator is widely perceived in Poland as prestigious, well paid and interesting. It would seem that
people who have managed 'to wend their way' into the profession should be
satisfied to say the least. The results of the survey indicate that under half
of all respondents (45.5 per cent) are satisfied with their job, of which 6.5
per cent are very satisfied, and 39 per cent are satisfied. However, nearly a
third of respondents (28.5 per cent) are unhappy with their job, declaring
themselves dissatisfied (22 per cent) or very dissatisfied (6.5 per cent). A
similar group (26 cent) described their attitude as 'neutral'.

In this respect, it is interesting to observe the way in which the level of
job satisfaction relates to the years of experience. Table 2.10 clearly shows
that translators who have worked for a shorter time are more satisfied with
their job:

Table 2.10 Job satisfaction according to seniority

Years of experience	<5 years	6–10 years	>10 years
Very satisfied	8%	–	–
Satisfied	46%	56%	9%
Neutral	23%	22%	46%
Dissatisfied	23%	–	27%
Very dissatisfied	–	22%	18%

Among novice and junior translators, the percentage of 'satisfied' and 'very
satisfied' comprises more than half the respondents, 54 per cent and 56 per
cent respectively. It should be noted, however, that it was only the junior
translators who found their job very satisfying. Among senior professionals, no respondents declared themselves 'very satisfied' and only 9 per cent
ticked 'satisfied'.

The situation is exactly the opposite when dealing with 'dissatisfied' and 'very dissatisfied' translators. A total of 27 per cent of translators with the longest experience said they were dissatisfied, and as many as 18 per cent claimed to be very dissatisfied. The 22 per cent of junior translators describing their job as very dissatisfying seems low in comparison. Among novice translators, 23 per cent were dissatisfied, but nobody was very dissatisfied with their job.

There are varying reasons for the negative attitudes among translators, expressed by the respondents in separate comments. The frustration of novice translators stems from difficulties in getting started in the field and from the low number of assignments available. Experienced translators, however, complained about a steady decline in working conditions, including falling rates, tighter deadlines and not enough attention given to the quality of the translations.

16. The pros and cons of being an AVT translator: 'All day at home'

The survey also included two open questions on the advantages and disadvantages of being an audiovisual translator, offering respondents an opportunity to express their personal opinion in a more comprehensive way. Their rather emotional responses illustrate how involved translators are in their work.

As for the upside of the AVT profession, the respondents emphasized the fact that the job allows for creativity and self-improvement, gives them a chance to show their artistic skill, and develops their linguistic and cultural competence. As one of them commented:

> The job offers self-development, many experiences, emotions and moving moments [...] It's also like a puzzle, which gives you a chance to prove yourself [...] It allows you not just to copy, but to be creative [...] I feel I can improve myself. I get an opportunity to expand my knowledge of culture, it develops my language skills. Besides, I work the hours that suit me best, rather than hours someone else dictates.

Dissatisfaction is mainly caused by the falling job standards, namely reduced rates, tighter deadlines, and commissioning work over weekends and holidays. As one of the translators emphasized:

> It really hurts me that studios and TV stations take part in the lowering of standards. We used to work normally, for reasonable rates, today it's probably better to lay tiles for a living. Customers don't care at all that there are weekends or holidays, and that a translator also needs to spend time with the family or go on a vacation. In their eyes we are machines, working 24/7. I think a disadvantage of the job is that it's very laborious and relatively badly paid. If you apply yourself, watch the film a few times, 'cut' it carefully so that there would be no corrections during layout and recording, then it really takes A LOT of time.

Another problem frequently mentioned was the hermetic nature of the industry, as there does not seem to be a clear recruitment system. Translators also complained that assignments are irregular and their work is undervalued by both clients and audience, who are usually unaware of the limitations and specifics of AVT. They also denounced the fact that there is no system for assessing translations and that they have no control over the text after it has been dispatched to the client. As one of the translators put it:

> It's hard to enter the market, which is frustrating because it's saturated mainly with incompetent idiots with no linguistic sense, who shouldn't even translate instructions on a matchbox. And what bothers me is the irregularity of the jobs, no royalties, unclear grounds for hiring this translator instead of another, and TC editors changing the meaning of the translation.

Interestingly, some aspects of the AVT profession, which were perceived as advantages by some respondents, were considered disadvantages by others. Hence, some translators are pleased to work from home or from any other place they choose, as clearly stated by one of them – 'I do what I like, and I don't have to go to work every day. I like the variety of the topics, planning my time myself, not being attached to one company, always having to practise the language and improve myself' – whilst at the same time others complained about feeling lonely or isolated: 'The unbearable things are working alone, no time off, uncertainty of employment and having to translate stupid and worthless films'.

17. Conclusion

Over the last few years, AVT has received quite a lot of attention from researchers. However it seems that some fields of AVT have received far more attention than others. Many publications present the results of empirical studies – be it in subtitling, dubbing or voice-over – analysed from various perspectives such as idiomacity of the language, semiotic cohesion, forms of address and stylistic figures (Romero Fresco 2006; Tortoriello 2011; Woźniak 2008). Others concentrate on teaching AVT (Díaz Cintas 2008; Matamala 2008; Remael 2004) or learning foreign languages through AVT (Caimi 2011; Danan 2004; Pavesi and Perego 2008). Audience reception studies, although still scarce, also make up a slice of the 'research cake' (Bairstow 2011; Antonini and Chiaro 2009). However, it seems that we know and publish very little about the professional market.

The present paper set out to describe the current professional situation of audiovisual translators in Poland. The findings have confirmed some of the popular views on the profession, and at the same time dispelled some of the myths. The study has also revealed differences between the situation of the novice and that of more experienced translators, especially significant when it comes to remuneration and royalties.

Although further research is needed, this study provides a good insight into the Polish audiovisual market and the working conditions of audiovisual translators. To have a better understanding of the profession in the global society in which we live, it is crucial to conduct similar studies in other countries so that we can map the situation at an international level.

Acknowledgements

This work has been supported by a research grant from the Faculty of Philology of the Jagiellonian University of Krakow and the UNESCO Chair for Translation Studies and Intercultural Communication.

Many thanks to Anna Celińska and Magdalena Balcerek, the president and vice-president of the Polish Association of Audiovisual Translators (STAW), for their help with the distribution of the questionnaire as well as for all their comments on this article. This work would not have been possible without their help. Thanks are also due to Samuel Brean from the French Association of Audiovisual Translators (ATAA) for all his tips on the design of the survey.

Bibliography

Antonini, Rachele, and Delia Chiaro 'The Perception of Dubbing by Italian Audiences', in Gunilla M. Anderman and Jorge Díaz Cintas, eds, *Audiovisual Translation: Language Transfer on Screen* (New York: Palgrave Macmillan, 2009), 97–114.

Bairstow, Dominique, 'Audiovisual Processing while Watching Subtitled Films: A Cognitive Approach', in Adriana Şerban, Anna Matamala and Jean-Marc Lavaur, eds, *Audiovisual Translation in Close-up* (Bern: Peter Lang, 2011), 205–22.

Caimi, Annamaria, 'Cognitive Insights into the Role of Subtitling in L2 learning', in Adriana Şerban, Anna Matamala and Jean-Marc Lavaur, eds, *Audiovisual Translation in Close-up* (Bern: Peter Lang, 2011), 113–32.

Danan, Martine, 'Captioning and Subtitling: Undervalued Language Learning Strategies', *Meta: Translators' Journal*, 49/1 (2004), <http://id.erudit.org/iderudit/009021ar> accessed 12 January 2012.

Díaz Cintas, Jorge, 'Teaching and Learning to Subtitle in an Academic Environment', in Jorge Díaz Cintas, ed., *The Didactics of Audiovisual Translation* (Amsterdam: John Benjamins, 2008), 89–104.

Filas, Ryszard, 'Dziesięć lat przemian mediów masowych w Polsce (1989–1999)', *Zeszyty Prasoznawcze*, 42/1 (1999), <http://www.obp.pl/_zp-teksty-online/RF-10-lat-przemian.pdf>, accessed 30 January 2012.

Matamala, Anna, 'Teaching Voice-over: A Practical Approach', in Jorge Díaz Cintas, ed., *The Didactics of Audiovisual Translation* (Amsterdam: John Benjamins, 2008), 115–27.

Pavesi, Maria, and Elisa Perego, 'Tailor-made Interlingual Subtitling as a Means to Enhance Second Language Acquisition', in Jorge Díaz Cintas, ed., *The Didactics of Audiovisual Translation* (Amsterdam: John Benjamins, 2008), 215–25.

Remael, Aline, 'A Place for Film Dialogue Analysis in Subtitling Courses', in Pilar Orero, ed., *Topics in Audiovisual Translation* (Amsterdam: John Benjamins, 2004), 103–26.

Romero Fresco, Pablo, 'The Spanish Dubbese: A Case of (Un)idiomatic *Friends*', *Jostrans, 6 (2006)*, <http://www.jostrans.org/issue06/art_romero_fresco.php> accessed 12 January 2012.

Tortoriello, Adriana, 'Semiotic Cohesion in Subtitling: the Case of Explicitation', in Adriana Şerban, Anna Matamala and Jean-Marc Lavaur, eds, *Audiovisual Translation in Close-up* (Bern: Peter Lang, 2011), 61–74.

ALICE CASARINI

XOXO: *Gossip Girl* and dubbing in the age of 'Net lingo'

1. Introduction

The creation and the consumption of entertainment products have been deeply affected by the acceleration of all the activities involving communication and data transmission, initiated by the development of the so-called 'information superhighways'. The new media, and especially the DVD and the internet, have had a significant impact on the relationship between television makers and their audiences. Until the introduction of video recorders, television broadcasting operated in a strictly top-down direction, which compelled viewers either to accept the schedule imposed on them by each network or to switch to a different channel if they did not like what they were being shown. Now DVDs and digital dissemination have rewritten the entire process of television consumption, providing spectators with an instantaneous shortcut to bypassing programming choices and to customizing their own palimpsests by choosing from a virtually endless array of audiovisual material.

Production companies are generally trying to keep up with the new rhythms imposed by faster communication and instant access to digital products, offering a wider selection of 'quality' programmes aimed at proactive niche audiences, rather than at an undifferentiated general public. The Italian audiovisual translation industry, however, seems still to be striving with the technology induced audience evolution, and particularly with the idea of an 'involved viewership' (Espenson 2010: 54) ready to work harder to make the most of their favourite shows. Rather than acknowledging such a change and turning it to their own advantage, many Italian dubbing companies tend to maintain a traditional, genre-based, homogenizing approach. The process of translation and adaptation into Italian often flattens the specificity of imported shows and reproduces yet another version of the relevant generic prototype, meant to fit the broadcasting slot vacated by its immediate predecessor.[1]

While this system might still work for casual viewers who are less interested in the differentiation of televised products than in unwinding in front of the small screen, the analysis of viewers' comments posted on popular television-based online forums indicates that an increasing number of Italian spectators have started openly to question the homogenization of foreign programmes and the careless obliteration of language specificity and intertextual references.[2] This reaction, which was previously atypical in traditional 'dubbing countries' such as Italy, is a consequence of the immediate availability of original texts over the internet, which has prompted viewers to make a linguistic effort in order to avoid the delay and the adulteration of the dubbing process. The percentage of viewers who have adopted this new attitude is still limited, since it requires familiarity with new technologies and an active endeavour to obtain the necessary material and to tackle the language barrier, as opposed to the effortless absorption of television broadcasts. Moreover, as the majority of the people who leave comments on the matter subscribe to the new type of viewing process, it is far harder to gauge the position of those who still prefer to watch dubbed series or do not express a particular need to enhance their television experience. Nonetheless, the sheer fact that a limited but increasing proportion of the

---

1   This tendency is particularly evident in the dubbing of the first eight episodes of *The Big Bang Theory* (Chuck Lorre and Bill Prady, CBS, 2007– present), which obliterated most of the wittiest references to geek culture and transformed the show into the umpteenth hormone-driven youth comedy to be produced in the wake of *American Pie* (Paul and Chris Weitz, 1999). Fans' protests prompted the dubbing company Post In Europe to change the entire dubbing team, but the first episodes were never redubbed, earning the show poor ratings for both its first broadcast on the pay-per-view channel Steel in 2008 and its subsequent airing on Italia 1 in 2010.

2   Such as <http://www.antoniogenna.net>; <http://gossip-girl.forumcommunity.net>; <http://www.tvblog.it>; <http://www.serialmente.com>; and dubbing-related facebook groups.

Italian audience questions the dubbing process and declaredly resorts to alternative means in order to enjoy their favourite shows. This bears witness to a revolutionary development in television reception in Italy, which dubbing companies should take into account in order to adjust their policies based on the changing needs of their customers.

The case of the Italian dubbing of the teen drama *Gossip Girl* (Josh Schwartz and Stephanie Savage, The CW Television Network, 2007– present) is a particularly relevant illustration of this evolution. The fast-paced, technology-imbued series suffered a double deceleration as it was deprived of its linguistic specificity and morphed into just another element in a long sequence of interchangeable teen series. Many Italian viewers, however, refused to consume a diluted version of a show that they knew to boast a higher complexity and the peculiar sociolect of the affluent, tech-savvy Manhattan youth, and promptly resorted to the internet to access the original version with the help of fan generated subtitles and to express their opinion on the dubbing process. This paper will thus analyse the show's original linguistic identity and the shortcomings of its Italian version, focusing on the proactive criticism expressed by Italian fans and suggesting possible solutions of responding to the new idea of the viewing process as a participatory experience.

2. The impact of the new media on television consumption

The binding power of television has been evident from the medium's very outset and persists to this day in the ability to provide audiences with 'completely furnished worlds' (Eco 1986: 198) that they can inhabit, share, and even partly transfer into their own daily lives. The type and the extension of the television-generated coalescence, however, have changed enormously since the 1950s, and even more radically over the past two decades. After casting an uncontested magnetic power on both families and countries as a whole for half a century, television had to reinvent its relationship with audiences as the new media and modes of consumption challenged its monopoly. Scaglioni (2008: 199; my translation) underlines the need for television companies to switch from a monolithic 'general public' to smaller, specialized niche audiences:

> when television ceases to be the mass medium we have known for fifty years and enters the age of fragmentation, a post-network era that sees the proliferation of channels and forms of multi-platform supply, a stronger need arises to build narrower spectatorial communities that are loyal to contents/brands.

The multiplication of networks and alternative broadcasting channels has caused a corresponding fragmentation of the originally compact television audience, invalidating traditional strategies aimed at catering to an alleged 'general taste'. All-encompassing programmes are no longer profitable in a scenario of virtually infinite audiovisual supply. The highest and safest revenues are now generated by dedicated *cult* audiences that are not only willing to tune in every week for their favourite 'appointment viewing', but also to purchase video releases and other ancillary products and participate in fan-based activities (Gwenllian Jones 2003: 165). The increased specificity of contemporary shows and the parallel specialization of their audiences have triggered a process of mutual improvement that has proved to be extremely productive in terms of artistic value. As Jancovich and Lyons (2003: 3) state in the introduction to *Quality Popular Television*:

> the shift from networks as facilitators of a national public sphere to a situation in which these organisations are increasingly preoccupied with garnering international niche audiences has also become instrumental in television's acquisition of greater cultural legitimacy.

Quality has become a distinctive and necessary parameter to survive the natural selection intrinsic to the new kind of audience-driven viewing experience. A *good* show will not only attract and maintain regular spectators, but also prove consistent and detailed enough to sustain and encourage the repeated and uninterrupted viewings made possible by the new technological supports (mainly the DVD and the internet).

The DVD has perfected the audience-empowering evolution sparked by the advent of the VCR, optimizing the archiving process and introducing the possibility of watching whole seasons in a row or instantly to retrieve specific episodes for closer analysis. Thompson (2007: xix) observes that:

> unlike the home-video industry, which released small numbers of series episodes, the basic unit of release on DVD is an entire season, sometimes an entire series. Producers now make shows with the knowledge that each episode might be viewed and scrutinized over and over again.

The internet has taken the entire viewing experience to another level by providing instant access to digital material through downloading and streaming websites, thus virtually allowing viewers to watch any show they choose at any given moment and from anywhere in the world, without even needing to retrieve it on a physical support such as a DVD. The web has also fostered the development of active fan communities, often endorsed by producers themselves: 'concerned to hang on to their diminishing and dispersed audience, broadcasters have promoted tie-ins between programmes and the Web, with a proliferation of contests, chat rooms, live interviews with stars web cast' (Seiter 2002: 35).

The new media-savvy audience adopts an interactive, analytical approach that fandom scholars such as Hills (2002) and Jenkins (2006) have compared to that of academics (hence the term 'Aca/Fan', as Jenkins defines himself).[3] *Viewers 2.0* not only absorb the material provided by the shows or by the extra contents on DVDs or websites, but also 'display agency in their everyday media consumption' (McKee 2002: 67), actively responding to the audiovisual stimuli by producing their own material (such as *fan fiction, fan art, fansubs* and other forms of UGC – User-Generated Content) and finding pleasure in cross-referencing and in deconstructing the increasingly complex network of intertextual (and often transmedial) references and connections that transcend the limits of each single show.

Television consumption now functions in an opposite, bottom-up direction, as explained by Gwenllian Jones (2003: 168):

---

3   See Jenkins's blog <http://www.henryjenkins.org> accessed 10 March 2012.

> digital and internet technologies facilitate the production and dissemination of
> [...] fan-produced texts and 'steals' from source texts in ways that were previously
> unimaginable. Digital production and dissemination profoundly alters the unwritten
> contract between the culture industry as the producer and distributor of popular
> cultural texts and fans as merely passive consumers.

The effects of the DVD and the internet have proved to be all the more
revolutionary for the foreign audiences of anglophone products, especially
in countries with a strong dubbing tradition (such as Italy, Spain, France
or Germany). Prior to these technological advancements, viewers were
so accustomed to being spoon-fed by dubbing companies that it barely
occurred to them that what they were watching was an adaptation and
that, as such, it might not only differ from the original version, but possibly
also suffer from significant 'lingua-cultural drops in translational voltage,
[...] such as a cultural reference which is not completely understood, an
unnatural-sounding utterance, an odd-sounding idiom or a joke which falls
flat' (Antonini and Chiaro 2005: 39). Thanks to the instant accessibility of
anglophone material over the internet and to the language selection tool
for audio tracks and subtitles on DVDs, foreign viewers now benefit from
a much higher exposure to the complexity of the original dialogues, often
replete with inter-textual connections, inside jokes, references to popular
culture and all the other markers of each show's specificity.

In Italy the subsequent desire to enjoy the viewing experience to the
fullest has generated an unprecedented cultural change in television consumption. In spite of the country's renowned dubbing tradition, many of
the tech-savvier viewers are now openly denouncing their increasing dissatisfaction with the lower quality, rushed dubbing of television series and are
willing to make a linguistic effort in order to appreciate the specific identity
of each show in its entirety. An increasing number of spectators, including
those with a limited command of English, choose to resort to fansubs –
subtitles voluntarily created by language-skilled fans and available for free
shortly after each US broadcast. In five years of activity (2005–2010) the
main Italian fansubbing community, Italian Subs Addicted (ItaSA, <http://
www.italiansubs.net>) has reached over 220,000 members. While this still
constitutes a niche audience compared to Italy's population of about 60

million people (or even to the 16.5 million Italians aged between ten and thirty-five years,[4] who are more likely to access online resources), the rapid expansion of this phenomenon betokens both a fast growing interest in the 'complete' experience of foreign shows and a newer attitude towards subtitles, traditionally perceived as an irritating display of linguistic affectation and now reappraised as a useful tool with which to evade the protracted dubbing process and instantly access the 'true' version of each episode.

The consequences of this evolution could be deleterious for the entire AVT industry, since the immediate and cost free availability of amateur resources is bound to affect the demand for both professional dubbing and professional DVD subtitling. Many Italian dubbing companies, however, still seem oblivious to this new viewing attitude, especially when it comes to productions that are considered less sophisticated, such as situation comedies or teenage series. The Italian dubbing process traditionally sacrifices the specificity of these kinds of shows to recreate yet another version of the respective generic prototype that will be broadcast in its 'usual' slot to address its 'typical' audience, which is assumed to be constantly wanting more and more of the same formula. This article, however, aims to demonstrate that the rejection of genre-based homogenization and the pursuit of each show's 'original flavour' are common to all the components of the new viewership, regardless of differences in age or programme preferences. An analysis of the linguistic specificity of *Gossip Girl* and of the viewer response to its Italian version will provide an idea of the unprecedented translational awareness of the Italian audience and of the need for a reassessment of AVT practices in order to address the new patterns of television consumption.

4   Source: ISTAT – National Institute of Statistics (http://demo.istat.it).

3.   *Gossip Girl* and the postmodern tech teen

Teenage oriented productions have acknowledged the evolution of the
television audience since the late 1990s, introducing deeper layers of complexity and factoring in a tech-savvy viewership born within the new media
paradigm and accustomed to the postmodern synergic interaction between
different media platforms. Wee (2004: 90–3) explains that:

> in an effort to cater to a teenage market that has access to an ever-expanding range
> of media platforms, the late 1990s' culture industries engaged in focused efforts to
> exploit and franchise any and all teen-oriented property they owned. [...] Having
> recognised the 1990s' teen audience's heightened media and cultural literacy, which
> were built upon an obsession with popular entertainment and movies in particular,
> many [...] teen shows consistently utilised intertextual pop-culture references in an
> attempt to attract and profit from this target audience's interests.

Gossip Girl, created by *The O.C.* authors and producers Josh Schwartz and
Stephanie Savage in 2007, incorporates this multimedia synergy within
its own plot, with its heavy reliance on technology and multiple channels
of communication and the frequent guest appearances of popular icons
from the worlds of music, cinema, and fashion,[5] addressing a culturally
aware viewership that enjoys the show's cutting-edge style and slang and
its numerous puns and intertextual references.

Italian networks were remarkably fast in choosing to acquire the show
for dubbing, based on the successful ratings that the first few episodes had
scored in the US in the fall of 2007. Nonetheless, when the series premiered
on the pay-TV channel Mya (part of the Mediaset Premium package) a
few months later, in January 2008, it became clear that the Italian producers had partly failed to appraise the reasons behind the show's success,
as most of its distinctive traits and engaging references had been lost in
the hastened translation process. The subsequent decision to rebroadcast
Gossip Girl on Italia1, a highly teenage-oriented network, only contributed

---

5   For instance, Lady Gaga (episode 3x10, 'The Last Days Of Disco Stick'); Tyra Banks
     (episode 3x04, 'Dan De Fleurette'); Tim Gunn (episode 4x06, 'Easy J'); No Doubt
     (episode 2x10, 'Bonfire Of The Vanity').

to the widespread perception of the series as yet another unoriginal teen show, apparently devoid of any specificity and requiring little effort from its audience.

Yet the programme's specific location, its format and its distinctive language create a peculiar, innovative product that upgrades *The O.C.*'s representation of the life of the rich and the famous with a much higher focus on accelerated communication and state-of-the-art technology. As opposed to the nondescript, fictitious small towns typically associated with teen drama, such as *Dawson's Creek*'s Capeside, *Veronica Mars*'s Neptune or *Buffy The Vampire Slayer*'s Sunnydale, *Gossip Girl*'s specific Manhattan setting instantly raises the narrative stakes by calling for a higher degree of spatial verisimilitude and setting a diegetic pace based on jam-packed, faster ticking 'New York minutes'. The need for instant communication generated by the metropolitan life in the fast lane is then exacerbated by the high-society Upper East Side environment, where the most glamorous façades conceal the darkest of secrets, and where possessing the right kind of information at the right time becomes the most precious asset.

Technology thus plays a crucial role in the constant, immediate exchange of time sensitive rumours and pictures. The plot unfolds through real-time updates disclosed by the eponymous blogger Gossip Girl, the self-appointed 'one and only source into the scandalous lives of Manhattan's élite'. The other characters not only receive her instant blog updates on their cell phones, but they also contribute their own shocking reports and compromising snapshots, acting as Gossip Girl's voluntary spies. Such virtually instantaneous exchange entails a reduction of the time allotted for message composition. The most practical solution involves conveying the proverbial thousand words with a single, meaningful picture, but whenever it is impossible to send images, instantaneity is achieved through a variety of text condensation techniques. Yet cell phone communication takes up such a conspicuous portion of the protagonists' time that abbreviations, acronyms and simplified syntactic structures end up permeating real-life language as well. The younger tech-savvy characters seamlessly incorporate 'Net lingo' and text messaging slang into their daily conversations, creating a distinctive sociolect that verbally highlights the generation gap at the root of much of the show's conflict.

The abundance of acronyms became such a prominent, recognizable feature of the series that the CW Television Network chose to use it as the core of the entire promotional campaigns for the second and third seasons. The exclusive appeal of the highly controversial, but nonetheless effective, 2008 'OMFG' (Oh My Fucking God) teaser carried on to the slightly tamer 2009 'WTF' campaign, which allegedly stood for 'Watch This Fall'. The audience thus developed the perception of a fast-moving, potentially daring show to access which they would have to be initiated into a whole series of trademark linguistic conventions functioning as a secret code.

Indeed, the show's own acronyms and abbreviations, even though less provocative, are just as relevant a feature when considered as a whole. Female protagonists refer to one another by their respective first name initials, condensing each of their own identities in a single letter (S for Serena, J for Jenny, V for Vanessa, and above all B for Blair, which also allows for the recurrent 'Queen B' puns). Being BFFs (Best Friends Forever), S and B often make plans to see each other 'in the a.m.', on the following morning (episode 1x06), or 'in 10' (minutes, that is; episode 1x08), and BTW (By The Way; episode 1x04), some of the parties they attend are BYOB, meaning that guests are supposed to supply their own alcoholic beverages (Bring Your Own Booze; episode 1x03). Rather than creating a 'kiddie talk' effect, as they would have done in a slower-paced, lower-profile show, the acronyms and abbreviations in *Gossip Girl* add to the fast rhythm of the show and increase the idea of a sophisticated, metropolitan youth leading a busy adult life packed with high-society drama, of which one can only keep track through highly advanced technological means.

4. Manhattan transfer: Issues in the Italian dubbing

The Italian version of *Gossip Girl* conveys a very limited percentage of the characteristic *techno-politan* sociolect of the original. While many of the linguistic changes prove necessary for lip-synching purposes or for sheer lack of equivalent terms, the translation process also seems to be aimed at reproducing a hackneyed idea of televised youth that the Italian audience will recognize as typical and whose distinctive wealth, big-league urban adventures, and technological addiction will appear to be only incidental.

Resorting to a form of 'teen dubbese' is hard to avoid in many of the occurrences in which the show's linguistic identity is most pronounced. For instance, the omnipresent acronyms and abbreviations are almost invariably lost in translation, given that they rarely have a same-length equivalent in other languages. Nonetheless, their replacement with conventional adaptations deeply affects the show's linguistic specificity, as illustrated in the following examples (see Table 3.1).

Table 3.1 Lost in translation: Acronyms and abbreviations

Speaker	Original version	Italian dubbing	Back translation
GOSSIP GIRL (All eps)	XOXO!	Kiss kiss!	Kiss kiss!
GOSSIP GIRL (1x04)	As much as a BFF can make you go WTF ...	Anche se a volte capita che gli amici ci fanno [sic] saltare i nervi ...	Even if it sometimes happens that friends may irritate us ...
CHUCK (1x10)	Don't F with an F-er!	'Chi vuoi prendere in giro?'	'Who do you think you're kidding?'
GOSSIP GIRL (1x16)	Asher Hornsby overheard bragging that Little J swiped her V card at his register.	'Ho sentito Asher vantarsi di aver finalmente colto il fiore della piccola J.	'I heard Asher bragging that he had finally picked Little J's flower.

In the first example Gossip Girl's trademark valediction 'XOXO' (for 'Hugs and Kisses') becomes a far less poignant 'Kiss Kiss', which substitutes the blogger's self irony with a preposterous American flavour and evokes the much shallower image of star-struck, perpetually infatuated teenagers popularized by glossy magazines. The sentence 'Anche se a volte capita che gli amici ci fanno [sic] saltare i nervi ...' does not only contain a grammatical mistake[6] which clashes with Gossip Girl's typical upper-class, sophisticated talk, it also has a much weaker ironic impact than punning on the fact that a 'BFF can make you go WTF' (What The Fuck); while it would have been hard to find two equivalent acronyms, it was still possible to fashion a non-abbreviated pun, given that all of Gossip Girl's lines are uttered in voice-over and thus leave more freedom in terms of lip-synching. Similarly, a creative approach to translating *enfant terrible* Chuck Bass's 'Don't F with an F-er' ('Don't fuck with a fucker') would have done more justice to the character's brazen yet hilarious linguistic wit than the plain solution 'Who do you think you're kidding?'. Since the video clearly shows Chuck mouthing the letter 'F' twice, a rendition based on alliteration – for instance, *Non mi freghi, filibustiere* [You don't fool me, scoundrel/pirate] or even *Non fare il finto tonto* [Don't play silly dumb] – would also have enabled a better synchronization.

The fourth example represents the most relevant case in point. One of the crucial storylines of the first season involves Brooklyn-born Jenny's attempt to climb the social ladder of the prestigious private school she attends with the rest of the main characters. Driven by a weird mixture of steel determination and selective compassion, Little J, who is slightly younger than the rest, often engages in popularity struggles to steal prima donna Blair's Queen Bee status. In episode 1x16, Jenny pretends to lose her virginity to her boyfriend Asher, anonymously reporting the news to Gossip Girl to cover up the (subsequently confirmed) rumours about the boy's homosexuality in exchange for the popularity she acquires by dating him. If Gossip Girl's original line aptly captures the commercial value of the transaction, the Italian version ineffectually chooses to revive an anachronistic flower metaphor, losing not only the original's contemporary teen slang feel, but also its sarcastic hint at the commodification of relationships in a card-swiping world and the reference to Jenny's lower-class background, which is often expressed in terms of 'swiping her MetroCard back home to Brooklyn' (as opposed to using private cars or even helicopters, as the

6   The indicative form 'fanno' should have been replaced with the corresponding subjunctive 'facciano'.

Upper East Siders do). Once again, the fact that Gossip Girl only speaks in voice-over would have allowed translators to compensate the absence of an Italian equivalent for 'V card' with any other witty comment referring to Jenny's attempt to improve her social status.

Specific technological references often undergo an unnecessary generalization as well, as is evident in the following two examples, for both of which direct equivalents would have been readily available (see Table 3.2).

Table 3.2 Lost in translation: Tech talk

Speaker	Original version	Italian dubbing	Back translation
VANESSA (1x06)	We'll deprogram you later.	Dopo ti farò il lavaggio del cervello.	I'll brainwash you later.
BLAIR (1x16)	I'll have Dorota Blackberry everyone an itinerary.	Vi mando una mail con l'indirizzo.	I'll send you an email with the address.

In the first example translating 'to deprogram' as 'to brainwash' would have worked well in most other shows, but in *Gossip Girl* it fails to convey the crucial technological connotation that carries the sociolinguistic meaning of the sentence. As she helps Jenny masquerade herself to secretly attend an upper-class ball to which she has not been invited, Vanessa, another outsider character, hints at the sort of mental software necessary to live the soulless, quasi-robotic existence of the rich and famous; the Italian verb *riprogrammare* would thus have provided a better solution in terms of both semantic value and lip-synching.

Conversely, the Upper East Siders resort to technology to underline their own superiority. In episode 1x16 (second example), Blair emphasizes Jenny's debacle and her own return to power by promising to have her maid Dorota 'blackberry everyone an itinerary' for her multiple location clubbing plans. Her statement contains three different elements aimed at underlining her restored Queen B status: her personal servant ('Dorota'), her ability to organize articulated, unforgettable nights out ('itinerary', as opposed to a single-venue party) and her efficient use of technology (the verb 'to blackberry', which implies that her friends will receive the itinerary directly on their portable devices, eliminating the need to print or write down addresses). A translational generalization ('I'll send you an e-mail with the address') works well in terms of dialogue development, but also discards all three of Blair's status markers. Since the Blackberry is a popular device in Italy as well, translators could have retained the word (especially since Blair faces straight into the camera when she pronounces it) and possibly the other two elements as well: for instance, *Dorota vi manderà l'itinerario via Blackberry* [Dorota will send you the itinerary via Blackberry].

Episode titles involve similar multi-layered references which combine trademark puns on movie or book titles with hints to their own narrative content. While pre-DVD and pre-internet audiences rarely had access to the titles of single episodes, which were superimposed over the opening sequence for a few seconds at best, the new *cult* viewership tends to perceive each episode as both a part of the longer story arc and a full-fledged, self-standing unit and thus pays far more attention to details that were previously negligible. At first, the translators of *Gossip Girl* attempted to address these new spectatorial needs and maintained or recreated both movie puns and crucial diegetic references, but after a few episodes they started to discard either of the two elements, or sometimes even both of them, as illustrated in Table 3.3.

Table 3.3   Lost in translation: Episode titles

Ep.	Original title	Italian translation	References in the Italian version
1x03	Poison Ivy	La mia peggiore amica	Italian title of the movie *Poison Ivy*
1x09	Blair Waldorf must pie!	La torta ti fa bella	Pun on the Italian title of *Death Becomes Her*
1x18	Much 'I do' about nothing	Molto terrore per nulla	Altered Shakespearean title, no marriage reference
2x06	New Haven can wait	Il nuovo paradiso può attendere	Altered movie title, no Yale reference.
3x12	The debarted	Il fantasma di Bart	None

Earlier titles were translated more accurately: episode 1x03, 'Poison Ivy', was renamed 'La mia peggiore amica', correctly quoting the Italian version of the American movie bearing the same name, and episode 1x09, 'Blair Waldorf Must Pie!', adjusted the original pun to a different movie ('La torta ti fa bella', referring to the Italian title for *Death Becomes Her*, *La morte ti fa bella*), but managed to maintain the crucial pie reference (Blair associates the traditional Thanksgiving pie with her faraway father, who has left the family to live with his gay boyfriend and whom she misses deeply; she also has a bulimic past and tends to binge on cake as a means of dealing with familial stress).

As the show progressed, however, the adaptation of episode titles declined ostensibly, either for lack of time or due to deliberate choice. Later, Italian titles often obliterated relevant in-plot references, such as episode 1x18, 'Much "I do" about nothing', deprived of the fundamental marriage reference, or episode 2x06, 'New Haven can wait', the translation of which bore no connection with the crucial Yale application process. Some of the titles did not even include any plays on words, even when the Italian audience would have been able to understand the original reference, as is the case with episode 3x12, 'The Debarted' (a pun on Chuck's deceased father, Bart, and on Scorsese's 2006 movie 'The Departed').

Episode titles, and perhaps many of the other aforementioned examples as well, might not have been a concern for pre-internet spectators in Italy. Analysing the online response of the Italian audience to the dubbed version of *Gossip Girl*, however, proves that new-generation viewers have become increasingly aware of the fact that they are being served an insipid version of the show, which loses much of its unique appeal through inadequate voice casting, insufficient translational solutions and the obliteration of many popular culture references. Even though the responses I have investigated are far from being representative of the entire audience, since they were mainly taken from forum discussions or fansubbing websites and thus implied a stronger familiarity with the internet than might be the norm, they still signal a noteworthy evolution of Italian viewers. Consider the following selection (my italics, my translation):

1. 'I'm awaiting the Italian dubbed version *anyway* to see what kind of *catastrophes* it comes up with!'[7]
2. 'The Italian dubber for Chuck Bass is an *insult* ... I had heard a couple of lines on YouTube and, after two episodes, I can confirm my first impression: *AWFUL*! Moreover, as was easy to foresee since more than half the audience has already seen the show on digital TV or elsewhere, last night the première scored a *mere 2 million viewers*; it will definitely be moved to the afternoon slot. Too bad. But not for me, *I have already watched it all.*'[8]
3. 'The Italian dubbing *belittles* the show. I am watching *Gossip Girl* in English (with Italian fansubs, my English is *not so good yet*) ... And Blair's lines are so much better when spoken in *HER* voice!'[9]
4. 'The Italian dubbing is really *terrible*. And I hate it when they *change the episode titles*, the English ones are brilliant while ours are completely *unrelated* to the show.'[10]

These comments allow for a basic appraisal of the tech-savvier part of the Italian *Gossip Girl* audience. Many of the viewers had already seen the show before it even landed on national television and correctly predicted that this very fact would cost the series its primetime slot; those who had not seen it, or had only seen a few episodes, were still able to realize that they were missing out on much of the show's appeal and were ready to watch the original version even when they did not have a sufficient knowledge of English (in which case they admittedly resorted to fansubs). Most of them had also taken notice of the unsatisfactory rendition of details that dubbers had deemed less significant, such as episode titles.

As previously mentioned, the main reason behind this evolution is due to the higher accessibility of original shows and related material, especially

---

7   <http://gossipgirlvideos.com/chuckblair-quella-che-non-sei> accessed February 2010.
8   <http://spuffy87.spaces.live.com/blog/cns!48D18C55F64FDFCC!2809.entry> accessed January 2009.
9   <http://www.mentedubbiosa.com/blog/2009/09/17/its-a-me-mario/> accessed September 2009.
10 <http://forum.teamworld.it/forum1657/122340-gossip-girl-2.html> accessed January 2009).

over the internet. The opportunity to retrieve untranslated episodes right after they have been aired in the US may increase the audience's awareness of what will be lost in translation. Moreover, the possibility to access a wide variety of information through DVD extras, promotional websites and search engines, but also to interact with other fans, does develop cross-referencing skills and paves the way for a deeper cultural understanding, also functioning as a sort of wake-up call in terms of appraising linguistic and cultural alterations of audiovisual products. Knowing that there is often much more to the shows than filters through dubbing, in turn, prompts fans to expend a linguistic effort in order to preserve most of their viewing experience. This process is also fostered by the emergence of the idea of authorship in television products: even if Josh Schwarz and Stephanie Savage lack the cult following of authors like Joss Whedon or J.J. Abrams, viewers who were already familiar with their style were likely to have specific thematic expectations about their subsequent shows, as *The O.C.* had set a definite standard for high-society teen drama.

Last but not least, the development of participatory culture, especially over the internet, favours an interactive relationship with other viewers and with the shows themselves by way of fan fiction, fan art, forums and fansubbing and raising translational awareness even among fans with a limited knowledge of the English language.

5. Conclusion

Such revolutionary changes call for an urgent reassessment of audiovisual translation techniques, a necessity which many dubbing companies have yet to acknowledge, in spite of the evident symptoms of an 'advanced viewership' and of the experiments conducted by several particularly receptive television networks. Easier access to both videos and corollary materials, the emergence of TV authorship and the overall increased quality and complexity of TV shows have had a striking effect on viewers, leading to an unprecedented mass overcoming of the traditionally untrespassable language barrier (think, for instance, of the remarkable number of people who tuned in at 6 am on 24 May 2010 to watch the last episode of *Lost* broadcast in English on Sky Italy). The consequently increased cultural, authorial, and linguistic competence of the Italian audience implies a stringent need to reconsider the translational approach and the value of previously overlooked details, especially given the redefinition of cult television in terms of an actual spectatorial religion, complete with complex viewing rituals and accurate text exegesis. In the long run, failure to address these issues will probably result in lower shares for dubbed programmes and an increased usage of free subsidiary resources, first and foremost of fansubs, which tend to sacrifice optimal synchronization and readability in favour of cultural explanations, thus promoting viewer comprehension but also damaging professional subtitling.

Viable solutions may either lean towards higher quality dubbing or aim at portraying the foreignness of the original version through better structured, clarifying subtitles. Italy's age-old penchant for dubbed products and its equally long-standing lineage of qualified voice actors might still favour the dubbing market, provided techniques are reconsidered in deference to their newer audience and in spite of the tighter deadlines imposed by the faster acquisition of audiovisual products through satellite TV and the internet. Background research must become crucial to any dubbing job and translators need to gain a far deeper knowledge of each show and of viewer expectations in terms of authorial style, cultural references and intertextual connections.

Alternatively, networks might decide to exploit the newly assessed openness towards subtitling by following the successful experiments attempted by MTV Italy, which broadcast several shows in English with Italian subtitles: *The Hills*, *Next*, *Room Raiders* and *Parental Control*. Many fans appreciated this choice and are even advocating a return to subtitling now that these shows are dubbed, thus signalling an increased willingness to make a linguistic effort. Should this choice be adopted, however, networks will need to resort to professional subtitlers, both to preserve the industry's quality standard and up-to-date techniques and to provide their viewers with well-structured products that are just as enjoyable as they are explanatory, with subtitles that convey the right amount of information but are still synchronized with the original audio and avoid hampering the viewing process.

The choice of either solution is directly linked to the perennial debate on the most appropriate type of audiovisual translation. Yet, whether networks decide to continue to provide viewers with the dubbed products to which they are accustomed or to experiment with less domesticating subtitles, they will still need to fine-tune translational procedures to cater to a new kind of viewer who, in the words of screenwriter Espenson (2010: 54):

> don't just turn on the television faucet, but who actually buy DVDs, tune in for special events, and find their way to the network's web sites for commentaries, video blogs, and downloads – an audience that will go out of its way for [their] cookie.

Bibliography

Antonini, Rachele, and Delia Chiaro, 'The Quality of Dubbed Television Programmes in Italy: the Experimental Design of an Empirical Study', in Marina Bondi and Nick Maxwell, eds, *Cross-Cultural Encounters: Linguistic Perspectives* (Rome: Officina Edizioni, 2005), 39.

Eco, Umberto, '*Casablanca*: Cult Movies and Intertextual Collage', *SubStance*, Vol. 14, No. 2, Issue 47: 'In Search of Eco's Roses' (1985), 3–12.

Espenson, Jane, 'Playing Hard to "Get." How to Write Cult TV', in Stacey Abbott, ed., *The Cult TV Book* (London: I.B. Tauris, 2010), 54.

Gwenllian Jones, Sara, 'Web Wars. Resistance, Online Fandom and Studio Censorship', in Mark Jancovich and James Lyons, eds, *Quality Popular Television* (London: BFI Publishing), 165–8.

Hills, Matt, *Fan Cultures* (London: Routledge, 2002).

Jancovich, Mark, and James Lyons, eds, *Quality Popular Television* (London: BFI Publishing, 2003), 3.

Jenkins, Henry, 'Confessions of an Aca/Fan' weblog, <http://www.henryjenkins.org> accessed 14 November 2011.

McKee, Alan, 'Fandom', in Toby Miller, ed., *Television Studies* (London: BFI Publishing, 2002), 66–9.

Scaglioni, Massimo, 'Fan & the City. Il Fandom nell'Età della Convergenza', in Veronica Innocenti and Guglielmo Pescatore, eds, *Le Nuove Forme della Serialità Televisiva. Storia, Linguaggio e Temi* (Bologna: Archetipo Libri), 199.

Seiter, Eileen, 'New Technologies', in Toby Miller, ed., *Television Studies* (London: BFI Publishing, 2002), 35.

Thompson, Robert, 'Preface', in Janet McCabe and Kim Akass, eds, *Quality TV: Contemporary American Television and Beyond* (London and New York: I.B. Tauris, 2007), xix.

Wee, Valerie, 'Selling Teen Culture: How American Multi-Media Conglomeration Reshaped Teen Television in the 1990s', in Glyn Davis and Kay Dickinson, eds, *Teen TV: Genre, Consumption and Identity* (London: BFI Publishing, 2004), 90–3.

MARIAGRAZIA DE MEO

Subtitling dialects: Strategies of socio-cultural transfer from Italian into English

1. Introduction

This paper will analyse the translation strategies adopted in the transfer of multicultural elements present in dialect, slang, idiolects and similar forms of regionalized communication, which play an essential role in *Respiro* (*Grazia's Island*, Crialese 2002) and *Nuovomondo* (*Golden Door*, Crialese 2007). The success achieved abroad by both films is evidence of the excellent work of their director, Emanuele Crialese, and is also due to the poetic image they project of rural Italian communities, which is particularly fascinating and appealing to foreign audiences. Our intention is to focus on the treatment of the vernacular oral medium in translation. If it is accepted that subtitling enhances the foreignness in translation, as opposed to dubbing, since the original soundtrack remains untouched (Szarkowska 2005), it is also important to consider that, when subtitling dialects and accents, the resources at the translator's disposal can be limited and, at times, inadequate to this multifaceted task.

Dialects may be considered independent languages, not only because of their specific grammar and lexicon, but also in terms of distinctive intonation and pronunciation, which transform the use of standard language into a strongly localized expression of socio-cultural identity, thus enhancing a phatic connotation of speech. It is the language usually identified with ordinary people in society that carries the realistic nuances of popular culture and at the same time the roots of our civilization. Our aim, here, is to observe the features of dialect that are retained in the subtitles and which overcome the rigid constraints of written language.

In subtitled programmes the source dialogue and target text coexist, generating interesting issues of the interrelation between oral and written codes. The general criteria regulating this process of transfer are not only concerned with linguistic features but also with other complex socio-cultural aspects, which define the speaker's identity (Díaz Cintas and Remael 2007). However, subtitling compared to dubbing suffers from the added difficulty that 'the written to be spoken as if not written' language is transformed again to the written mode and cannot totally extricate itself from the canons of written language (Taylor 2006: 47). Evidence that the language of subtitles often transcends the limits of written language will be sought through the observation of a number of instances of non-standard grammatical forms, repetitions, redundancies, and colloquialisms. While recalling features of spoken language, they have the function of compensating for previous simplifications and omissions in the transfer of culturally loaded language. In particular, non-standard interrogative forms will be interpreted as a strategy through which features of accent and intonation are conveyed. We will also consider the role of code-switching in determining the speaker's identity, focusing mainly on the relevance of translation strategies, such as explicitation and addition, both at word and sentence level, in an attempt to compensate for what is lost in the translation of dialect.

When referring to film dialogue, it is commonly accepted that audiences expect a high level of complexity which gives the illusion of spontaneous conversation (Taylor 2006), and, in this respect, it is interesting to consider the contrast in the target audience's expectations of good subtitles, which, on the other hand, are expected to be clear and concise, so that they interfere as little as possible with the other semiotic aspects. However, if we readily accept this distinction, the task of defining transparency in subtitling becomes extremely complex and subjective. In films presenting culturally connotated language, good subtitles are expected to show some evidence of the spoken register through the transfer of some features of oral discourse to the written text. If this distance from strict written norms is taken into account, there will probably be less interference with the recipient's eye than might otherwise be expected, thus generating a more natural assimilation of the written word.

2. Language in Crialese's films

In the films analysed, there are frequent instances in which the language used overcomes its referential function in order to acquire a strong phatic tone through the presence of a mixture of Sicilian dialect and standard Italian. The dialogue is not syntactically and semantically complex but it is generally full of extended pauses, repetitions and phatic discourse markers, so that the visual and auditory channels support the subtitler's task, whose use of reduction strategies such as condensation and omission does not directly involve a loss to the overall effect. Chaume (2004) employs the term 'semiotic cohesion' to refer to the interrelation between text and image, where it is possible to fill a gap in the subtitle with an image on screen.

Respiro tells the story of Grazia, a woman whose free and unconventional behaviour soon becomes a worry for the conservative and secluded community of the small island of Lampedusa where she lives. Set at the beginning of the twentieth century, *Nuovomondo* portrays the journey of a Sicilian family from their desolate village to the New World or rather to its gateway, Ellis Island, where they can observe their destination from a distance without actually reaching it. In both films, dialect is used as the standard form of communication until the deviation from the Italian language becomes explicit through linguistic misunderstandings. Hence, the foreign audience is also made aware of the use of different linguistic codes and of the fact that dialect belongs to a sub-standard and local variety, as a form of utterance with its specific morphosyntactic and phonological system.[1] In *Nuovomondo* the lack of familiarity with the Sicilian dialect means that subtitles are also required for the Italian audience. However, these are used randomly throughout the film and omitted from some key scenes, thus leaving room for interpretation and interfering with the

---

1   This shift between codes is explicitly mentioned in *Respiro* when a policeman, who is not one of the locals, cannot understand the dialect used by another character, while in *Nuovomondo*, during the journey to America, the word Italian is used to refer to the language spoken by other Italians on the ship, highlighting the fact that Sicilian emigrants do not consider themselves as belonging to the same group.

meaning. For example, this occurs in the final and most important scene, when the protagonist Salvatore questions the harsh decision taken by the committee to repatriate his mother and his apparently dumb son. The Italian audience is forced to rely merely on nonverbal features of discourse in order to understand the situation, as is the case in some crowd scenes where Italian subtitles are missing, despite the fact that, when people are shouting all at once, understanding is impeded. In these scenes, the verbal code loses its semantic function, enhancing elements of sound and rhythm, as 'sound is primarily understood as evoking the viewer's "aural" attention to accompany the visual attention, triggered by the visual stimuli' (Baumgarten 2008: 9). Subtitles are much more consistent in translation, showing an overall concern for referential meaning.

3.   Translating orality

In theory, subtitling should try to reproduce the character's intentions and way of speaking, rather than merely referential content, despite the lack of correspondence between the source and target languages. This theoretical objective is certainly demanding when translating a dialect which constitutes a language variety in its own right. In the films under investigation, the distinctive Sicilian accent permeates the dialogue, giving pragmatic and communicative power to utterances, even in cases where the use of the vernacular lexicon is limited. As Taylor (2006: 249) points out, 'oral speech is more of a process than a product', referring to the fact that the character's emotions and attitudes, as well as the communication of his/her socio-cultural status, are constantly present and perceivable through their way of speaking and the use of the prosodic elements of intonation, rhythm and stress that give the specific diatopic variety its unique properties. Clearly, the task of subtitling specific features of oral language, such as accents, is certainly demanding, but it is also difficult to ignore them, as shown in the following example from *Respiro*. Here the misunderstanding between the Sicilian protagonist Filippo and the policeman, who is a newcomer to the island, is entirely based on the fact that Filippo speaks with a broad accent, which is not immediately intelligible to an outsider. In spite of the self-explanatory visuals showing the policeman's puzzled expression, the subtitle presents explicitation, using the word 'accent' to clarify the reason for the misunderstanding. Moreover, the aggressive tone of the oral dialogue, which is suggested through the marked pronunciation of the verb *vuoi* [you want] becoming *buò*, is rendered explicit in the subtitle which omits the repetition, but maintains its force through the choice of the allusive expression 'you want trouble?'

(1)	Original [*back translation*]	Subtitles
FILIPPO	Ma se mia sorella ha a venì cu mìa, che vuoi? [*But if my sister has to come with me, what do you want?*]	She's my sister! You want trouble?
POLICEMAN	Che bò tu, ah? Che buò tu? Non ti capisco. Non ti capisco. Cos'è che ha detto? Cos'è che ha detto? [*What do you want? What do you want? I don't understand you. What did he say?*]	I don't understand your accent. What did he say?

As we have already stated, the purpose of this paper is to focus on the analysis of those ungrammaticalities that, although not typical of the written form, are used as a strategy to convey features of dialect in conversation. In many cases, we have observed that marked dialect intonation is often translated by choosing a non-standard grammatical question form which drops the auxiliary, particularly in the translation of yes/no rhetorical questions, in an effort to maintain the informal and familiar tone of the original soundtrack. Although these non-standard forms are also present in films in which standard Italian is used, their occurrence increases significantly when the source language is a dialect. Table 4.1 shows a higher proportion of yes/no rhetorical questions in *Respiro*, while they are less frequent in *Nuovomondo*, probably because this film is more economical in the use of dialect, especially in the second part, where the immigrants switch to standard Italian and use an interpreter to communicate with American inspectors and doctors.

Table 4.1 Yes/no rhetorical questions

	Total no. of questions	Standard forms	Non-standard forms
Respiro	104	69	35
Nuovomondo	67	49	18

The subtitles contain instances of the use of irregular grammatical forms only to translate dialect. We would suggest that the contrast in the use of non-standard interrogative forms rather than regular ones might constitute an attempt to maintain the phatic value of the oral dialect, recalling incorrect forms that are stereotypically associated with the English language spoken by immigrants. As we can see in the following scenes, where dialect is used in the original dialogue, the yes/no questions are simply rendered with the addition of a question mark and through the strategy of condensation. In example 2 from *Nuovomondo* the auxiliary is not only omitted from the subtitle, but so is the past tense of the original dialogue. The subtitle recalls a form of broken oral language which has been written down, and the strategies of condensation and omission do not depend on the restrictions regulating subtitling since neither film presents elements of lexical density.

	Original [*back translation*]	Subtitles
(2) ROSA	U sentiste che ti disse? [*Did you hear what she said?*]	You hear her?
(3) MAN	Pecché nun glie dici a tua madre di scennere? [*Why don't you tell your mother to come down?*]	Your mum's staying there?
(4) GRAZIA	Non mi cerca chiù? [*Is he not looking for me anymore?*]	He's stopped looking?
(5) MAN	O capisti? [*Did you understand?*]	You understand?

The omissions in the extracts above contribute to the fast rhythm of the dialect in the original. In example 6, the negative intonation of the original dialect is translated using compensation in the subtitle. Thus, Filippo's surprise and dissatisfaction concerning the poor meal presented by his sister is over-translated in the target text.

	Original [*back translation*]	Subtitles
(6) FILIPPO	Ma che mangiare è chisto? [*What kind of food is this?*]	What the hell do you call this?

So far, the analysis shows evidence that the use of non-standard grammatical forms and compensation can be considered strategies aimed at the convincing transfer of some features of dialect and intonation.

4. Code-switching in subtitling

While some authors intend code-switching merely as an intra-linguistic variation in terms of register (Hymes 1974), this strategy will be considered, in the broadest sense, as common practice with a speaker who uses two languages considered to be distinct entities in terms of their morphosyntactic structure and phonological and lexical levels. Therefore, in our case, standard Italian and Sicilian dialect are perceived as totally different languages. According to Giacalone Ramat (1995: 46) 'the choice and the alternation between different languages is triggered by social and psychological factors rather than by internal linguistic factors of the languages involved'. Code-switching also works as a magnifying glass portraying the cultural identity of the characters. Bucholtz and Hall (2005: 587) mention that 'identity is a discursive construct that emerges in interaction'. The shift between standard language and dialect is a natural form of bilingual interaction in specific rural communities where the practice of code-switching mainly exemplifies different levels of the relationship existing between the speakers, expressed through different nuances of formality. 'Code-switching is thus a form of language practice in which individuals draw on their linguistic resources to accomplish [social] purposes' (Heller 1995: 161).

The films under investigation use dialect differently. In *Respiro*, the language of the rural community is more modern and, therefore, the use of dialect is perceived as being mainly related to the close family. When there are external contacts, the characters switch to Italian in search of a more formal register. This happens, for instance, when children address adults, at points of conversational significance or, more generally, when speakers seek reciprocal approval by enhancing mechanisms of adaptation to the other speaker's language. Switching between codes happens quite regularly throughout the film, marking the different social interactions between characters and also acquiring the function of 'an emotional device' (Giacalone Ramat 1995: 52). This practice, so frequent in conversation, is transferred to the subtitles through the use of Italian loan words referring the audience back to the soundtrack. While in extracts 7 and 9, the impatient Filippo cannot restrain the natural flow of dialect, even though he is addressing a lady he does not know, example 8 shows a very formal use of language. In subtitling, code-switching is used as a strategy for conveying the sociocultural aspects of language and, while maintaining some elements of the identity of the speakers, it also manages to lessen the neutralizing effect by reducing the text to standard forms of language (Taylor 2006).

	Original [*back translation*]	Subtitles
(7) FILIPPO	A signò, ma cà niente vinco? [*Madam, don't I win anything?*]	*Signora*, that's not fair!
(8) FILIPPO	Signora, voglio giocare tutto completamente. [*Madam, I want to bet absolutely everything.*]	*Signora*, I want to bet them all!
(9) FILIPPO	Signò, uscì! [*Madam, it came out!*]	*Signora*, I've won! Look!

On the other hand, the kind of dialect spoken in *Nuovomondo* is older and more impenetrable, even to an Italian audience. Its use appears more unconscious and spontaneous, as the majority of characters of the small rural community are illiterate. The island is a world of its own; therefore the practice of code-switching with standard Italian is rare until the Sicilians come into contact with the *foreign* Lucy. In the subtitles, this strategy is limited to the reiterated use of loan words for the titles *Signor/Signora/Signorina* [Mr/Madam/Miss].

In the use of regional dialects, as well as in standard Italian, a strong awareness of hierarchy exists between interlocutors. As every utterance occurs in a context and is delimited by a specific register, linguistic use changes depending on the level of formality. In this way, for instance, a group of children talking to an adult will adopt a more formal register, as when addressing a stranger. In the following examples, this shift in tenor between formal and informal levels is not conveyed, not only because the English language lacks a distinction between the formal and informal use of personal pronouns, but also through the deliberate choice of the translator to maintain the emotional content of the utterance through the use of informal language. Extract 10 shows Grazia speaking to the policeman and, therefore, using the formal personal pronoun *lei*. The loss of formality in the use of the personal pronoun in the subtitle is nevertheless compensated by the choice of a standard interrogative form.

	Original [*back translation*]	Subtitles
(10) GRAZIA	Lei è nuovo, vero? [*You are new, right?*]	Are you new here?

The following examples from *Nuovomondo* show other cases marked by loss of formality in the transition from oral dialogue to subtitles. In example 11 the missing auxiliary in the subtitle gives the impression of a casual offer which does not correspond with the formality of the original dialogue. In the following subtitle, the substitution of the dialect cluster *no loco* [not there] with 'that's good' transforms a negative remark of disapproval into a positive one, omitting any sign of formality. Examples 13 and 14 use reduction and simplification, particularly in the last subtitle, with the omission of the formal request and of the old-fashioned and formal Sicilian word *voscenza*, similar in meaning to 'your majesty'.

	Original [*back translation*]	Subtitles
(11) ROSA	Vuole? [*Do you want?*]	Want some?
(12) SALVATORE	No loco. Si mettesse cà incapo. [*Not there. Take the one on top.*]	That's good. Take that one.
(13) SALVATORE	No, niente. Nun se preoccupasse. [*No, nothing. Don't worry.*]	Don't worry about it.
(14) SALVATORE	Voscenza m'ave a scusare. [*Your majesty has to excuse me.*]	Excuse me ...

While the original dialogue presents elements of formality, as a sign of a structured social hierarchy between the speakers, the subtitle resorts to an informal register. As the above examples are extracts from scenes that are set on the ship to the New World, where the immigrants share a limited space, the contrast between the familiarity of the situation and the formality maintained in conversation is more evident. This shift is completely lost in the subtitles, which convey some elements of informality whilst disregarding the instances where the true nature of dialect is expressed in the original.

5. Culture-bound words in translation

Finally, in my analysis of the main features of dialect, we will focus on the presence of specific lexical words, emphasizing the reiterated use of certain keywords which occur mainly owing to their phatic function rather than to a referential and denotative one. In the following qualitative investigation, the translation strategies observed show a considerable degree of variation without apparent consistency. Gottlieb (2005) argues that discourse on translation strategies refers more to a theoretical rather than pragmatic stage within the translation process. In the practice of subtitling dialect, condensation and omission are frequent, in order to extrapolate what is significant and also to account for time and space restrictions, despite the fact that the subtitle is moving towards standardization. However, the strategies of explicitation and compensation also deserve attention owing to the fact that they aim to clarify the source text through generalization or by providing specifications and substitutions, in order to account for the cultural load embodied in some of the words and expressions. A list of some occurrences of frequently used dialect words from both films and the main translation strategies used are presented in Table 4.2. First of all, it is interesting to observe that the frequently occurring omissions are sufficiently balanced by cases of direct translation, although, in this case, the words are usually translated using the closest semantic equivalent rather than a pragmatic and functional one, losing the actual connotation and the speaker's intended meaning (Baker 1992). The lack of functional equivalence helps to explain the frequent omissions, for instance in the case of *ammuni*, a word used in dialect mainly with a phatic value, in the sense of a strong exhortation rather than in a merely denotative sense.

Table 4.2 Translation strategies at word level

Dialect	Rough translation	Omission	Direct translation	Explicitation
acchianare	get on	2	4	3
ammuni	come on	23	21	1
caruso	young boy	2	3	–
curnuto	someone with horns	1	–	5
picciò	young boy	3	2	–
piccioli	money	1	1	4
picciriddo	young boy	2	1	1
scanto	fear	–	–	2
scantare	to be afraid	–	6	–
talia	look	6	16	–
vatinne	go away	7	4	–

Although the strategy of explicitation is used more rarely than omission or direct translation, it still offers interesting cases of adaptation, which is considered necessary when the socio-cultural load of the source dialogue calls for a more explicit choice of words. For instance, the recurrent swear word *curnuto*, only used to refer to men, has no functional equivalent to render the cultural implications of the offence, which indicates someone sporting animal horns as a consequence of a woman's infidelity. With its negative and deeply offensive connotation within the Sicilian socio-cultural context, it is often self-referential, so that the subtitler needs to provide a more extensive explanation or substitution, as in the translations 'I'm cursed' or 'Damn me', where the source connotation is lost. On the other hand, more referential words such as *talìa* [look] have a more direct equivalent in translation and further explicitation is less necessary.

Moving on from the translation of specific words to an examination carried out at sentence level, a variety of set phrases and colloquial expressions that enrich language with those unique images created by idiomatic expressions, metaphors and clichés are encountered. The strategy of explicitation limits the audience to a mere semantic and denotative level, failing to convey the speaker's intention, so that the illocutionary force is totally missed (Pedersen 2008). The use of idiomatic sentences in the subtitles enhances the pragmatic aspects of communication since, as Moon (1998: 17) points out, 'a pragmatic level of idiomacity is typical of discourse functional approaches according to which fixed expressions and idioms are used as strategies for fostering interaction as well as markers of textual organization'. In the following extracts, the subtitles offer interesting examples of target language creativity, through the use of substitution:

	Original [*back translation*]	Subtitles
(15) MOTHER-IN-LAW	Ne fa uscire pazzi a tutti [*She makes everybody crazy.*]	She drives us mad!
(16) SALVATORE	Preciso spiccicato a mìa. [*Precise and identical to me.*]	He is my spitting image.
(17) SALVATORE	Che è sta cosa? [*What is this thing?*]	Give us a break!

The term 'culture bumps' has been adopted by Archer (1986) to refer to problems generated in intercultural communication by the use of allusive language that depends on a considerable amount of shared knowledge between the author and the recipients, capable of activating effective and immediate interpretation. As Snell-Hornby (1995: 41) points out, 'the translatability of a text depends on the extent to which the text is embedded in its own specific culture and so on how far apart, with regard to time and place, the source and target cultures are'. The following extracts present some examples of allusions. The reference to a popular Italian singer, in extract 18, is not immediately meaningful to the English speaking audience and, therefore, requires substitution with a more generic term. On the other hand, the next example does not present particular problems, as the character of Rambo is well known to the foreign audience. In the latter case, while in the dialogue the reference to the baron's belongings is real, as this person actually existed, the use of a set phrase in translation gives a more generic sense to the utterance.

	Original [*back translation*]	Subtitles
(18) WORKER	Ma chi ti credi di essere, Patty Pravo? [*But who do you think you are, Patty Pravo?*]	You think you're a star?
(19) FILIPPO	Cosa sembri Rambo? [*What, you look like Rambo.*]	You think you're Rambo?
(20) FRIEND	Tutte cose de barone ne sto dando. [*I am giving you all the baron's belongings.*]	These are clothes for a prince!

When substitution moves towards compensation, the subtitle presents courageous examples of linguistic creativity, with a choice of lexicon that appears to be more powerful in terms of cultural reference and connotation than the one found in the dialogue. The purpose is to compensate for previous losses, to stress intonation or to retain the phatic value of the emotionally charged language. In extract 21, the addition of 'you little shits' compensates for the loss of repetition of the dialect word *iativinni* [go away], also translated using the strongly connotated verb 'get lost', while, in extract 22, the problems in rendering *rompiscatole* [pest] determines a radical change in the subtitle with the choice of the pragmatic idiom 'bored shitless':

	Original [*back translation*]	Subtitles
(21) BOY	Iativinni, iativinni, iativinni! [*Go away, goaway, go away!*]	Get lost! You little shits!
(22) FILIPPO	Ma che rompiscatole cà. [*But what a pest here.*]	We're bored shitless here.
(23) MARINELLA	Ma che fai? [*But what are you doing?*]	What the hell?

Linguistic creativity, as a source of language play, is enhanced through the use of compensation, triggered by the search for effective communication and for re-contextualization of meaning (Baker 2006). Mainly following a target-oriented perspective, substitution and compensation are seen here as subtitling strategies, marking a form of independence from the original dialogue, a way of acquiring extra space within the technical constraints of the medium, since 'creativity is clearly contextually framed and conditioned' (Carter 2004: 10).

Subtitling culture-bound language and dialect requires the use of a number of translation strategies that serve the purpose of retaining elements of spontaneous conversation and social interaction. Within the discourse on language creativity, we will suggest that some features of redundancy are maintained in the subtitles to enhance the phatic and emotive value of some scenes, reproducing the repetitions encountered in the oral dialogue. The use of false starts and repetitions is common, particularly at times when the dialogue is not dense with denotative information. The following scenes from *Nuovomondo* provide examples of the communicative power of redundancies that are maintained in the subtitles, where the repetitions serve a purely phatic purpose, since meaning is clearly conveyed through the image.

	Original [*back translation*]	Subtitles
(24) SALVATORE	Ci pare ca me scanto? Ci pare ca me scanto? [*Do you think I'm afraid?*]	She thinks I'm afraid! She thinks I'm afraid!
(25) PRIEST	Riri. Riri. Riri, riri. [*Smile. Smile. Smile, smile.*]	Smile. Smile! Smile!

In extract 25, although the gestures of the priest leave no doubt about the meaning of the word *riri* [smile], the subtitle keeps the repetition in order to convey the dramatic moment of the immigrant's departure from the community. The polysemiotic texture of films allows meaning to be carried over by various intersecting channels of communication that are active at the same time as the visual-verbal one, supporting the subtitler in the task of conveying meaning, even more so when it comes to rendering culture-bound language. However there are cases when, in spite of the semiotic cohesion between image and words, the translator opts for explicitation, as in the following extract where we find that the meaning of the woman's words is immediately clear from her actions rather than from the indistinct sounds uttered:

	Original [*back translation*]	Subtitles
(26) GRAZIA	I morti, i morti. Vai. La morta. La morta a galla [*The dead, the dead. Go. The dead. The floating dead.*]	Let's float. Stop it. Float.

The Italian allusion used to describe Grazia's body floating on water, *i morti* [the dead], requires reformulation because of lack of formal equivalence.

6. Conclusion

'How does one translate the sophistication of spoken language variants into a regimented written form?' (Díaz Cintas and Remael 2007: 185). This question encapsulates the challenge encountered in subtitling, in particular when a language variety such as dialect, embedded in a specific socio-cultural context, is used as the main channel of verbal communication in the oral dialogue. The current analysis of the subtitles to Crialese's films has as its main purpose the highlighting of the presence of linguistic features that move away from the canons and constraints of written language, allowing us to consider subtitles as an independent type of text. We have suggested that the power of the visual elements in these films supersedes the mere verbal component of dialogue, therefore omissions in translation can be considered as a way to drive the target audience closer to the source language(s). At the same time, retaining elements of redundancy in the written subtitle appears to be an attempt to transfer features of spoken discourse. Moreover, some instances of written non-standard grammatical forms were considered to constitute an attempt to maintain some of the expressive power of intonation and accent found in dialect. Despite the complications and well-known problems in translating any form of language variety, particularly into the intersemiotic mode of subtitling, and the inevitable omissions and standardization of the written form, we have attempted to emphasize the meaningful and interesting use of linguistic creativity allowing the target audience an intimation of the socio-cultural complexity and richness of the original dialogue.

Bearing in mind that a classification of the most frequently used translation strategies is in practice very difficult, as this usually implies a sharp distinction between the techniques used, we have tried to give a general overview. It is therefore possible to conclude that, although condensation, omission and simplification are predominant strategies encountered in our analysis, we have also found a number of examples of explicitation and compensation in the target text, necessary in particular as part of the cultural transfer implied in the translation of dialect. The idea that the quality of subtitling is determined by the lack of interference with the image has been challenged by the presence of idiomatic expressions, loan words, non-standard grammatical forms encountered in questions, deictic elements, repetitions and redundancies in the written language. Readability can be enhanced through the presence of elements that are immediately recognized by the audience as familiar and pragmatically effective, even though they overcome the boundaries of written language rules and invade the realm of spoken discourse. Our final point is based on the assumption that subtitles should become more visible, as for any type of translation defined by specific features. As Díaz Cintas (2001: 207) argues, 'subtitling like dubbing has to be understood as an integral part in the process of the artistic creation of a film and not as a mere appendix, subject to market forces'. Considering subtitles as an independent text lays the foundation for further research into the use of language creativity, re-contextualization and relevance in translation, focusing not so much on how to reproduce the source text, but on what to translate.

Bibliography

Archer, Carol, 'Culture Bump and Beyond', in Joyce Merrill Valdes, ed., *Culture Bump. Bridging the Gap in Language Teaching* (Cambridge: Cambridge University Press, 1986), 170–8.

Baker, Mona, *In Other Words: A Coursebook in Translation* (London: Routledge, 1992).

—— 'Contextualization in Translator-and-interpreted-mediated Events', *Journal of Pragmatics* 38/3 (2006), 321–37.

Baumgarten, Nicole, '"Yeah, That's it!": Verbal Reference to Visual Information in Film Texts and Film Translations', *Meta* 53/1 (2008), 6–25.

Bucholtz, Mary, and Kira Hall, 'Identity and Interaction: a Socio-cultural Linguistic Approach', *Discourse Studies* 7/4–5 (2005), 586–614.

Carter, Ronald, *Language and Creativity. The Art of Common Talk* (London: Routledge, 2004).

Chaume, Frederic, 'Film Studies and Translation Studies: Two Disciplines at Stake in Audiovisual Translation', *Meta* 49/1 (2004), 12–24.

Díaz Cintas, Jorge, 'Striving for Quality in Subtitling: The Role of a Good Dialogue List', in Yves Gambier and Henrik Gottlieb, eds, *(Multi)Media Translation* (Amsterdam: John Benjamins, 2001), 199–211.

—— and Aline Remael, *Audiovisual Translation: Subtitling* (Manchester: St. Jerome, 2007).

Giacalone Ramat, Anna, 'Code-switching in the Context of Dialect/standard Language Relations', in Lesley Milroy and Pieter Muysken, eds, *One Speaker, Two Languages. Cross-disciplinary Perspectives in Two Languages* (Cambridge: Cambridge University Press, 1995), 45–67.

Gottlieb, Henrik, 'Multidimensional Translation: Semantics Turned Semiotics', *MuTra 'Challenges of Multidimensional Translation'. Conference Proceedings* (Saarbrücken 2: EU-High-Level Scientific Conference Series, 2005).

Heller, Monica, 'Code-switching and the Politics of Language', in Lesley Milroy and Pieter Muysken, eds, *One Speaker, Two Languages. Cross-disciplinary Perspectives in Two Languages* (Cambridge: Cambridge University Press, 1995), 158–74.

Hymes, Dell, *Foundations in Sociolinguistics: An Ethnographic Approach* (Philadelphia: University of Pennsylvania Press, 1974).

Moon, Rosamund, *Fixed Expressions and Idioms in English. A Corpus-based Approach* (Clarendon: Oxford, 1998).

Pedersen, Jan, 'High Felicity: A Speech Act Approach to Quality Assessment in Subtitling', in Delia Chiaro, Christine Heiss and Chiara Bucaria, eds, *Between Text and Image* (Amsterdam: John Benjamins, 2008), 101–15.

Snell-Hornby, Mary, *Translation Studies. An Integrated Approach* (Amsterdam: John Benjamins, 1995).

Szarkowska, Agnieszka, 'The Power of Film Translation', *Translation Journal* 9/2 (2005), <http://translationjournal.net/journal/32film.htm> accessed 30 January 2011.

Taylor, Christopher, 'Look Who's Talking. An Analysis of Film Dialogue as a Variety of Spoken Discourse', in Linda Lombardo, Louann Harman, John Morley and Christopher Taylor, eds, *Massed Medias. Linguistic Tools for Interpreting Media Discourse* (Milano: LED, 2006), 247–78.

ADRIANA TORTORIELLO

Lost in subtitling?
The case of geographically connotated language

1. Introduction

The 'diagonal translation' (Gottlieb 1994) that is involved in the process of subtitling an audiovisual text – the double switch from spoken source language (SL) to written target language (TL) – yields a multimodal text that is characterized by the presence of an additional layer that has been superimposed onto the original text: the subtitles.

Thus, the responsibility falls to the subtitlers to convey, in a number of subtitles – made of no more than two lines each, and delivered at a reading speed of around 160–80 words per minute – all that they believe is not readily available to their target audience and which they consider essential to a proper fruition of the original text. The choice of the word *fruition* is deliberate, as opposed to understanding, a term which is often, and misleadingly, associated with a mere grasp of the (denotative) meaning of the utterances that make up the dialogue.

Because the verbal utterances of the original are closely and cohesively interrelated to those signs belonging to nonverbal codes, notably the kinesic and the paralinguistic, in the creation of the overall meaning of the audiovisual text (Delabastita 1989, Chaume 2004), the subtitler's task involves a process that goes beyond that of transferring in a one-to-one fashion the verbal utterances of the original and that must inevitably take into account the existence and the role of the nonverbal codes.

This process is more acutely problematized in the case of those films that make use of geographically connotated language; films that, as will be argued below, might well fall under the umbrella definition of 'multilingual films'. Films that rely to a greater or lesser extent on the presence of information conveyed paralinguistically through the use of regional or foreign accents pose a challenge of no easy solution to the subtitler. This article aims to investigate the various strategies activated by the subtitler when subtitling into English, for the DVD market, two Italian films which display a more or less marked geographically connotated language.

2. Geographically connotated language, multilingualism and the definition maze

The debate on heterolingualism, heteroglossia and multilingualism is, and has been now for a number of years, quite topical in (Audiovisual) Translation Studies (Meylaerts 2006, 2012; O'Sullivan 2008; Díaz Cintas 2011). Yet, one thing that can still be observed is a struggle to define just what is actually meant by 'multilingual'.

Starting from the premise that, by definition, no discourse is ever completely monolingual, Meylaerts (2006: 4), in her article on heterolingualism and translation, mentions Grutman's (1997) *hétérolinguisme*, which refers to 'the use of foreign languages or social, regional and historical language varieties', and that in turn is 'reminiscent of Bakhtin's "heteroglossia", which refers to the internal stratification characteristic of any (national) language, i.e. to the social diversity of speech styles within one and the same language'.

Even more important, from the perspective of this study, is the reflection that can be found in an article by Delabastita and Grutman (2005: 15), who argue that, in any discourse on 'multilingualism', the ultimate question hinges on how 'language' is defined. They maintain that the concept of multilingualism should include, above and beyond the so-called 'official' languages, 'the incredible range of subtypes and varieties existing *within* the various officially recognised languages' (ibid.). And therefore, their warning is:

> If habit and convenience may well continue to prop up the conventional distinction between 'languages' and 'language varieties', we would be well advised to keep in mind how shifty and problematic the dividing line really is. [When looking at a text] it matters relatively little in itself whether it is 'national', 'dead' or 'artificial' languages, slang, dialects, sociolects, or idiolects, that make up the multilingual sequences. What matters more is their textual interplay. (ibid.: 16)

In their opinion, what matters the most is the function fulfilled by the different language varieties. This approach is also reinforced by other scholars, such as Corrius and Zabalbeascoa (2011: 115), who suggest that any language, including a language variety such as a dialect, can be considered a 'third language' (L3). Following Grutman (1998), they remark that 'the minimum requirement for a text to be identified as a multilingual text (a text that uses two or more languages) is the presence of at least a single foreign word' (Corrius and Zabalbeascoa 2001: 116). And it is not a matter of whether the L3 in question is an official language, a dialect, or an official language that displays some dialectal traits: 'the concept of L3 stresses the fact that not all voices in a text (e.g. a film or a novel) speak the same language or the same variety' (ibid.: 117).

I shall now illustrate why these reflections are relevant to this study, which looks at the fate of geographically connotated language in interlingual subtitling.

3. The corpus: Fellini and his language

The corpus used in this article is constituted by two films by one of Italy's main film directors, Federico Fellini, in their English subtitled versions for the DVD market, namely *Amarcord* (1973)[1] and *E la nave va* (*And the*

---

1   All the examples are taken, for academic purposes, from the English subtitled version of the DVD *Amarcord*, © 1973 F.C. Produzioni s.r.l. and © 2004 Warner Bros Entertainment Inc. Distributed by Warner Home Video UK Ltd, a Warned Bros Entertainment Company. Subtitles by SDI Media Group. Subtitler not acknowledged.

Ship Sails On, 1983),[2] which offer many revealing insights in the use of geographically connotated language in film. Although much has been said and written on this director and his cinematic work, very little exists on his English reincarnation. Given the nature of Fellini's work, the importance of the visual dimension and the strange love/hate relationship he had with the spoken dialogue, the material offered by his films can indeed be very revealing for the translation researcher.

Fellini loved playing with the actual *making* and *shooting* of the film. This is reflected, amongst other things, in his treatment of the word, particularly the post-synching of the dialogue exchanges of most of his films in a way that at times openly clashes with lip-movements in the original film. In his own words, '[e]verything I do in film is *made*, produced, invented by me. That's why my sea is made of plastic and my sounds are dubbed, postsynched. Postsynching gives the film an added dimension, an even greater range and intensity' (in Cardullo 2006: 194).

Likewise, he prioritized images over words, nonverbal over verbal elements, leaving viewers feeling sometimes that the verbal part is a marginal component of the film, that the dialogue is more a necessary evil than a means of expressing his artistic creativity:

> cinema tells its worlds, its stories, its characters, thorough images. Its expression is figurative, like that of dreams. [...] In cinema words and dialogue, it seems to me, serve the purpose of informing, of helping the viewer follow the plot rationally, and of giving the story some sense of verisimilitude, following the usual criterion of reality; but it is this very operation that, by reflecting on the images some references from the so-called everyday reality, deprives them of that sense of the unreal that is typical of the dreamt image, of the visual language of dreams. (Fellini 1980: 100, my translation)

2   All the examples are taken, for academic purposes, from the English subtitled version that appears on the DVD *And the ship sails on / E la nave va*, ©1982 RAI – VIDES PRODUZIONE – GAUMONT SIM. Licensed by RAI TRADE, Rome, Italy. © 2006 Infinity Media Holdings Ltd. Subtitles by International Broadcast Facilities. Subtitler not acknowledged.

Fellini's interest to rely more on the semiotic environment than on the (verbal) dialogue, in order to convey what he intends to communicate can be noted also in his use of geographically connotated language. The question that inevitably arises at this junction is whether Fellini's films can indeed be considered multilingual. Going back to Delabastita and Grutman's (2005) work, when discussing multilingualism it is very much a case of defining what exactly is meant by language – or language variety for that matter – and, above all, of identifying the actual *function* fulfilled by the different languages and/or language varieties that appear in the film. In this respect, Fellini did resort to a myriad of regional and foreign accents, words, and phrases in his cinematic productions. The aim of this analysis is precisely to ascertain what the functions of these elements are, whether they are kept in the subtitled versions of the films under examination, and if so, how.

As for the use of foreign words and phrases in film dialogue, Chion (1994/1990: 178) observes that a number of directors have aimed at 'relativizing' speech in their films by attempting 'to inscribe speech in a visual, rhythmic, gestural, and sensory totality where it would not have to be the central and determining element'. This, he maintains, can be achieved in a number of ways, one of them being that of resorting to multilingualism. Chion (ibid.) goes on to observe that a number of directors, amongst whom Fellini, have resorted to setting their films in an international environment so that the use of different languages, that are never dubbed nor subtitled in the original, is not conspicuous. The result is that films of this nature 'have relativized speech by using a foreign language that is not understood by most of their viewers' (ibid.: 180).

Such examples abound in Fellini's production, a fact that can hardly be said to be surprising since such 'relativization' is definitely apt for a director for whom words were not his main mode of expression. In several of his films, Fellini resorts to the conscious use of geographical variation in the dialogue, and the message that is conveyed linguistically and paralinguistically by means of regional accents has a bearing on the characters' diegetic profile from a pragmatic point of view.

As Pavesi (2005: 31) argues, dialogue is not just the place where the plot is moved forward, but it is also the place where characters are defined and interpersonal relationships are clarified. It is here that the social and geographic belonging of the characters become evident, and this is achieved by means of socially/geographically connotated patterns of speech. Some of Fellini's films resort to regional variation to a great extent, as noted in Gaudenzi's (2002: 156) study on *Amarcord*, one of the films in which this feature is most apparent. Interestingly, according to Gaudenzi (ibid.), Fellini's use of the Romagnolo dialect in *Amarcord* is the director's way 'to lead the audience away from older, neorealist representations of reality toward a new vision of the world expressed with Fellini's own grammar'.

4. Subtitling geographically connotated language

As argued by Hatim and Mason (1990:40), '[a]n awareness of geographical variation, and of the ideological and political implications that it may have, is [...] essential for translators and interpreters'. In the specific context of AVT, Pavesi (2005: 36, my translation) observes that it is impossible to 'find a geolinguistic correspondent that in the target language takes on the same connotations and the same cultural stereotypes of the geolect or the geolects of the original texts'. Whilst Pavesi refers to a dubbing situation, her reflections are equally relevant in a subtitling context. Yet, it is clear that in spite of all the difficulties, the subtitler cannot (or should not) simply choose to ignore the issue completely, and should avoid producing a version of the dialogue that thoroughly flattens it by levelling out all the paralinguistic nuances that are present in the original. In this respect, the extant literature on multilingualism may be useful for the audiovisual translator and researcher trying to find a way out of the maze when faced with the translation of geographically connotated language.

As discussed by Meylaerts (2010: 227), '[i]f we consider multilingualism as "the co-presence of two or more languages" (in a text, individual or society) while translation is traditionally defined as the 'substitution of one language for another' (Grutman 2009: 182), then translation and multilingualism are inextricably connected'. The question therefore revolves around the issue of how multilingual a translation should be. In order to explore this question, the subtitling of some multilingual instances extracted from two of Fellini's films is discussed below.

For the purposes of the present analysis, geographically connotated language has been classified into the following categories:

1. Regional dialects, including regional accents and dialectal words and phrases.
2. Foreign accents 'proper', i.e. accents indicating that the character in question is a native speaker of a language other than the SL.
3. Foreign languages, including words, phrases and sentences, which are not necessarily meant to be understood by the SL audience.

Each of these three categories fulfils different functions; a fact that should have a bearing on the subtitler's search for the most appropriate translation strategies.

5.   Regional dialects

As Beretta (1988: 763, in Pavesi 2005: 37; my translation), observes in the case of the Italian language:

> Regional variation is still the most evident dimension in the Italian situation: it cuts across all other dimensions and, with the exception of artificial situations, there is no speaker, however cultivated, who will not, in his/her spoken language, display at least some phonetic traits that are diatopically marked.

While discussing a similar situation, albeit in an English-Italian context, Bruti (2009: online) refers to the 'overlapping of regional and social dialects', and to the fact that 'the lower speakers are placed in the social hierarchy, the more diatopic and diastratic variation overlap'. She also observes that, in spite of the translator possibly resorting to morphological and/or syntactic variation, this in itself 'can hardly make up for the loss of all the shades of meaning attached to geographical dialects' (ibid.).

The first examples are taken from the film *Amarcord*, a semi-autobiographical film in which all the characters inhabit a pretty uniform geographical situation, i.e. a fictional town supposedly based on Fellini's hometown of Rimini, in 1930s Fascist Italy. Tellingly, *amarcord* is Romagnolo dialect for the Italian *mi ricordo* [I remember], which emphasizes the autobiographical dimension of the film.

The characters in *Amarcord* all speak with different regional accents interspersed, at times, with actual dialectal expressions. The original Italian audience is made aware of the characters' geographical provenance thanks to, amongst other strategies, the activation of their linguistic variety. The director has made sure that, despite the fact that the dialogue is geographically/socially connotated, the exchanges are at the same time perfectly understandable by all Italians. The result banks on the assumption that Italian native speakers watching the film would be able to establish the correlation that usually exists between social class – and, to a certain extent, age – and the use of dialectal words. Indeed, as mentioned above, the characters in the film are neatly differentiated and those who come from a higher class speak standard Italian with a regional accent, while those belonging to the lower social strata are characterized by the use of odd dialectal expressions.

In Scene 1, a number of people are gathered in the town square to watch a bonfire, the *fogaraccia* in Romagnolo dialect, being lit:[3]

---

3   Because of the alternating in the dialogue, between standard Italian and regional dialect, the words belonging to the Romagnolo dialect have been highlighted in italics.

Scene 1

Original text	English subtitles
DAUGHTER: Adesso, Babbo, vediamo accendere la *fogaraccia* e poi vi porto a casa.	Now, Dad, we'll watch them light the bonfire, then I'll take you home
FATHER: E dicci al dottore che è un *patacca* e io vado a letto quando mi pare a me.	Tell the doctor he's an asshole. I'll go to bed when I please!
BLIND MAN: *Acin passé! È'l mi post quel lè!*	Let me through! That's my place!
BLIND MAN: *Boiazze!*	You creeps!
MAN IN THE CROWD: Giudizio, *ciapa!*	Hey, Giudizio, catch!

As noted above, the whole dialogue is spoken in a regional variation, which incorporates a Romagnolo accent with the use of regional lexis and syntax. However, as can be seen, the English subtitles do not make any attempt at conveying linguistic variation, choosing instead to adopt a standard English throughout. While the original audience is given information not only on geographical, but also on social belonging through the use of non standard Italian, the foreign audience must resort to other sources of information to retrieve the same elements that in the original add to the characterization. In this respect, I would argue that the pragmatic effort required to retrieve them is inevitably greater than in the original since, not having access to the information communicated through the acoustic channel, the foreign viewer will need to rely more on visual clues such as, for instance, those conveyed through the choice of costumes. Information that in the original is redundant, being conveyed visually and acoustically, is only presented visually in the subtitled film.

It may be noted, however, that the subtitler does endeavour to convey, if not the geographical, at least the social belonging of the characters, by resorting to such strategy as the use of colloquial and slang expressions in the target language (e.g., 'asshole', 'creeps'), thereby operating a shift from the paralinguistic to the verbal. Ultimately, to quote Hatim and Mason (1990: 43) again:

the equivalence [...] will be established functionally. The aim will be to bring out the user's social/linguistic 'stigma', not necessarily by opting for a particular regional variety but by modifying the standard itself. The user's status may have to be reflected not primarily through phonological features but through non-standard handling of the grammar or deliberate variation of the lexis in the target language.

6.   Foreign accents and foreign languages

The second category I mentioned was that of foreign, as opposed to regional, accents. This is the case in which the speakers' nationality can be identified because they speak in the source language with a relatively strong foreign accent. Once again, the original audience is usually able to understand the content perfectly, as well as to identify the speakers as having a geographical provenance other than that of the SL country, i.e. Italian.

The third category is that of foreign words, phrases, and sentences, which are inserted in the middle of the Italian dialogue, and which may or may not be understood by the SL audience. In the concrete case of the two films under discussion in this paper, these foreign utterances are not subtitled, leaving the Italian viewer to 'guess' what the words mean.

I will be discussing the second and third categories together because, although distinct in principle, they both appear together in the examples under examination. The various examples analysed below are taken from *E la nave va*, which is the story of a group of characters belonging to the world of opera and classical music who embark on board a luxury liner in order to take the ashes of a famous soprano back to her native island, as per her desires.

In the following Scene 2, the dialogue exchanges take place amongst various guests and both a regional Italian accent and a Spanish accent are interspersed with actual Spanish words and expressions:

Scene 2

Original text	English subtitles
AURELIANO (Romagnolo accent): Chissà se si può avere un bel bicchiere di vino rosso. Waiter (Standard Italian): Ma certo, signore.	– Can I have some red wine? – Of course
SPANISH LADY (Spanish accent; Spanish words in italics): *Es la verdad. La Tetua me diceva siempre* ...	It's true. She would always say ...
SPANISH LADY (Spanish accent; Spanish words in italics): Con Sabatino Lepori, *cantar es* una gioia.	It is always a joy to sing with Sabatino Lepori

In the above examples, we find Aureliano, who speaks Italian with a rather broad accent from the Emilia-Romagna region, and a Spanish lady, who alternates between actual Spanish words and phrases, and Italian spoken with a very strong Spanish accent. The audience relying on the subtitled version, however, are not provided with any of this information as the whole dialogue has been uniformly subtitled into standard English.

In the exchanges from Scene 3, the conversation is taking place among the members of an Austrian Grand Duke's entourage who, supposedly, all share the same language, i.e. German. With the exception of two characters, who speak only German, the exchanges take place in Italian, spoken with a broad German accent:

Scene 3

Original text	English subtitles
AUSTRIAN LADY (speaks German): Als ich einmal krank war, habe ich grüne Gesichte gesehen.	I used to see everyone's faces as green once
PRINCESS (German accent): Ma tutti possiamo percepire i colori della musica.	Everyone can pick up the colours of music
GENERAL (Speaks German): Aber meine Stimme ist halt so.	This is my voice
PRINCESS (German accent): Questo è strano.	It's strange

As can be noted in the examples provided, what happens in the English sub-titles is that both the characters speaking Italian with a German accent and those actually speaking German are treated equally in the English subtitles. The use of this strategy has several implications. Firstly, some viewers may miss the fact that a different language to Italian is actually being spoken in the film and reach the wrong interpretation. Instead of being confronted with language variation and characters representing different nationalities, they may end up with the impression that all the characters are fluent in the same language. Secondly, the subtitled version becomes 'easier' to follow in the sense that even information presented only in German in the original and that may have been cryptic for the source audience is now translated into English for the target audience. Thus a new communicative situation has been created in which the TL audience paradoxically ends up knowing more than the original audience, since the exchanges in German are also subtitled into English.

To some extent, the way Fellini portrays his characters plays with his audience's suspension of disbelief. He chooses to convey the nationality of these characters through both linguistic (foreign words and phrases) and paralinguistic (foreign accents) means, and thus creates a semiotic environment which is idiomatically quite rich and complex. In the English version, on the other hand, all speakers are equally subtitled into English, thus depriving the TL audience of important information on the nature of the characters and the dynamics of their interaction.

7.   Conclusion

As has been seen in the two films under analysis, the information that in the original gets linguistically and paralinguistically conveyed by means of geographically connotated language can be quite diverse. The strategies adopted by the subtitlers, on the other hand, seem rather uniform: very little of this information is kept in the TL version.

My reflections on the matter are as follows. As was observed in the case of *Amarcord*, there might be situations in which the whole dialogue is linguistically quite uniform and indeed the film uses other visual elements to connotate the characters. In this case, I would argue that if the translator produces subtitles written in a fairly standard TL, while, when necessary, resorting to variation in style and register, the pragmatic loss can be kept to a minimum.

According to Díaz Cintas (2001), not much can be done in this respect. Whereas dubbing, which replaces the original soundtrack, can be slightly freer in its range of choices, when it comes to subtitling, where the original soundtrack is kept, viewers must live with this inevitable loss – both in the case of regional as well as in the case of social variation: 'dialectal variations are another of the great [subtitler's] headaches. In dubbing one might opt – arguably – for the replacement of certain accents [with TL ones] but in subtitling this is a strategy that it is impossible to activate' (ibid.: 128; my translation). Starting from the premise that in subtitling it is content, rather than style, that takes precedence when communicating, he states that the result tends to be 'an excessively uniform register, in which class or age differences between characters are hardly marked linguistically' (ibid.: 129–30; my translation).

I do however tend to agree with those authors (Heiss and Leporati 2000) who believe that to some extent the loss can be kept to a minimum, and that at the very least the loss of geographical variation can be compensated by resorting to socially connotated register, e.g. by focusing on the above mentioned correspondence between social belonging and linguistic variety. As stated above, what matters ultimately is that the *function* of these elements is preserved, and in a multimodal text such as an audiovisual text, the possibility exists of activating a strategy that involves the above-mentioned shift from the paralinguistic (the accent) to the verbal (style and register variation).

When, on the other hand, the characters speak in the source language but use a strong foreign accent in the middle of an otherwise standard SL dialogue, then perhaps it would be of help to make the TL audience aware of this fact. I concur with Díaz Cintas (2010) that by now the boundaries between interlingual subtitling and subtitling for the deaf and the hard-of-hearing (SDH) have become somewhat blurred; and I would like to suggest that interlingual subtitling could benefit, in situations like the ones presented in this paper, from resorting to a strategy that is widely used in SDH: that of identifying the speakers or, in this case, their accents, by means of labels. Another alternative open to subtitlers, as has been suggested in some studies on multilingual films (Martínez Sierra et al. 2010), could be to resort to some orthotypographical devices to mark these exchanges, such as the use of italics or of a different colour.

Finally, as concerns the use of a foreign language in the original, one might think of Berman (1985/2000: 289; my emphasis), who, when discussing a series of what he calls 'deforming tendencies' in translation, observes that: 'the power of illumination, of manifestation [...] is the supreme power of translation. But in a negative sense, explicitation [which is inherent in translation] aims to render "clear" what *does not wish to be clear* in the original'.

Indeed, these reflections seem particularly relevant in the case of the introduction of some foreign words and phrases in the dialogue. There may well be instances in which the director might choose to leave a piece of dialogue in a language that is unknown to most of the audience, in order to rely on other elements, such as the intonation or the semiotic environment, to convey what he intends to communicate. I would like to contend that when the original audience are deliberately kept in the dark, i.e. when the characters speak a language that is meant to be unknown to them, then that piece of dialogue should not be subtitled in the TL version as it risks portraying a different dynamics among the various characters on screen.

Going back to what was stated in the introduction, whether these films are to be considered 'truly' multilingual or not, what matters in my view is the *function* that these elements have in the films themselves. If regional accents and dialectal words and expressions serve the purpose of characterizing the film characters in a certain way, be it socially and/or geographically, then this is the function that needs to be kept in translation. If the use of foreign words and phrases in the original dialogue has the function, to return to Chion's (1994/1990) definition, of relativizing speech – and this plays such a crucial role in the cinematic discourse of a director like Fellini – then that ought to be kept in the subtitled version. And if the strategy of mixing foreign accents with foreign words and phrases in a code-switching, intra-sentential manner can be said to be that of foregrounding the director's wish to characterize through playing with his audience's suspension of disbelief, then this ought to be also conveyed in the subtitled version, if we want to avoid that all these nuances be lost in subtitling.

Bibliography

Berman, Antoine. 'Translation and the Trials of the Foreign', in Lawrence Venuti, ed., *The Translation Studies Reader* (London and New York: Routledge, 1985/2000), 284–97.

Bruti, Silvia. 'From the US to Rome Passing Through Paris'. *InTRAlinea Special Issue. The Translation of Dialects in Multimedia* (2009). <http://www.intralinea.it/specials/dialectrans/ita_more.php?id=760_0_49_0_M>.

Cardullo, Bert (ed.). *Federico Fellini – Interviews* (Jackson: University Press of Mississippi, 2006).

Chaume, Frederic. 'Film Studies and Translation Studies: Two Disciplines at Stake in Audiovisual Translation'. *Meta* 49/1 (2004), 12–24.

Chion, Michel. *Audio-Vision. Sound on Screen.* Edited and translated by Claudia Gorman (New York: Columbia University Press, 1994). English translation of *L'Audio-Vision*, Paris: Editions Nathan, 1990.

Corrius, Montse, and Patrick Zabalbeascoa. 'Language Variation in Source Texts and Their Translation. The Case of L3 in Film Translation'. *Target* 23/1 (2011), 113–30.

Delabastita, Dirk, and Rainier Grutman. 'Introduction. Fictional Representations of Multilingualism and Translation'. *Linguistica Antverpiensia NS* 4 (2005), 1–35.

Díaz Cintas, Jorge. *La traducción audiovisual: el subtitulado* (Salamanca: Almar, 2001).

——'The Highs and Lows of Digital Subtitles', in Lew N. Zybatow, ed., *Translationswissenschaft – Stand und Perspektiven. Innsbrucker Ringvorlesungen zur Translationswissenschaft VI.* (Frankfurt am Main: Peter Lang, 2010), 105–30.

——'Dealing with Multilingual Films in Audiovisual Translation', in Wolfgang Pöckl, Ingeborg Ohnheiser and Peter Sandrini, eds, *Translation – Sprachvariation – Mehrsprachigkeit. Festschrift für Lew Zybatow zum 60. Geburtstag* (Frankfurt am Main: Peter Lang, 2011), 215–33.

Fellini, Federico. *Fare un film* (Torino: Einaudi, 1980).

Gaudenzi, Cosetta. 'Memory, Dialect, Politics: Linguistic Strategies in Fellini's *Amarcord*', in Frank Burke and Marguerite R. Waller, eds, *Federico Fellini: Contemporary Perspectives* (Toronto: University of Toronto Press, 2002), 155–68.

Gottlieb, Henrik. 'Subtitling: Diagonal Translation'. *Perspectives: Studies in Translatology* 2/1 (1994), 101–21.

Grutman, Rainier. *Des langues qui résonnent. L'hétérolinguisme au xixe siècle quebecois* (Montréal: Fides, 1997).

——'Multilingualism and Translation', in Mona Baker, ed., *Routledge Encyclopedia of Translation Studies* (London and New York: Routledge, 1998), 157–60.

Hatim, Basil, and Ian Mason. *Discourse and the Translator* (London and New York: Longman, 1990).

Heiss, Christine, and Lisa Leporati. 'Non è che ci mettiamo a fare i difficili, eh? Traduttori e dialoghisti alle prese con il regioletto', in Rosa Maria Bollettieri Bosinelli, Christine Heiss, Marcello Soffritti and Silvia Bernardini, eds, *La traduzione multimediale. Quale traduzione per quale testo?* (Bologna: Clueb, 2000), 43–65.

Martínez Sierra, Juan José, José Luis Martí Ferriol, Irene de Higes-Andino, Ana M. Prats-Rodríguez and Frederic Chaume. 'Linguistic Diversity in Spanish Immigration Films: A Translational Approach', in Verena Berger and Miya Komori, eds, *Polyglot Cinema: Migration and Transcultural Narration in France, Italy, Portugal and Spain* (Berlin: LIT Verlag, 2010), 15–29.

Meylaerts, Reine. 'Heterolingualism in/and Translation. How Legitimate Are the Other and His/her Language? An Introduction'. *Target* 18/1 (2006), 1–15.

——'Multilingualism and Translation', in Yves Gambier and Luc van Doorslaer, eds, *Handbook of Translation Studies* (Amsterdam: John Benjamins, 2010), 227–30.

O'Sullivan, Carol, 'Multilingualism at the Multiplex. A New Audience for Screen Translation?' *Linguistica Antverpiensia NS* 6 (2008), 153–66.

Pavesi, Maria. *La traduzione filmica* (Roma: Carocci, 2005).

The functions of dialogue in feature films

1. The dubbing process in Germany

Germany is a 'dubbing country', and the quality of dubbing is generally regarded as very high. Nevertheless, if we look more closely at the German dubbing process, we can see that it does not always satisfy the requirements of a good translation. I am not referring here to the often evoked expectation that the translated text should be synchronized with the lips and gestures of the actor on the screen, which, as Pisek (1994: 91) shows, is both unrealistic and affords a greater significance than it actually warrants. The problem with dubbing in Germany is rather that the two main factors generating meaning in films are not sufficiently taken into account. On the one hand, the relationship between text and image (Mälzer-Semlinger 2011) should always be analysed by the translator when dealing with an audiovisual text, and, on the other, the function of the dialogue in the film (Remael 2008: 60) should be respected in the translation.

Part of the problem lies in the dubbing process itself and in the fact that, in most cases, economic factors are decisive in the choice of translator or dubbing company (Herbst 1994: 261). As Seifferth (2009: 9) notes, German dubbing studios tend to choose students for the rough translation instead of professional translators. I will, thus, begin by recalling the most important steps of the dubbing process, which is not simply a matter of one person translating a source text (ST) into a target text (TT), as in the case of monomodal texts such as novels, but is divided into several steps carried out by different people working under extreme time pressure.

The first step is generally entrusted to a freelance translator who will provide a rough translation based on the written dialogue of the film. Unfortunately, in some cases translators only have the screenplay to hand rather than the transcript of the actual dialogue (Herbst 1994: 16). They usually receive the pre-production version of the screenplay, meaning that it is still necessary for this version to be compared with the finished movie itself if potential omissions and inaccuracies are to be avoided (Troester 2002: 184). But the differences between the script and the actual film dialogue are not the main problem at this stage. The more significant problem here is the fact that the transcript of the dialogue is sometimes treated as if it were the actual ST, despite it only being one element of the complex multimodal material that is the film. Indeed, in the past, translators were often not provided with the original film (Herbst 1994: 16; Whitman-Linsen 1992: 122). But even nowadays, when reputable dubbing companies provide the appropriate visual material as a matter of course (Troester 2002: 183), translators are still often not given the film or do not refer to it systematically during the translation process if the delivery deadlines are too tight. Although the translation of an audiovisual text only ever constitutes a translation of the verbal components of said multimodal text, the fact remains that these verbal compontents have no meaning in themselves, or, to be more precise, they have a different meaning from the film as a whole. The meaning of the film is produced by the interaction of several semiotic codes – music, image, sound, the words uttered and so forth. For that reason, a reading of the dialogue alone is no substitute for watching and listening to the actual ST. This shows how essential it is to keep in mind that, for film translation, the ST – mediatext A – is the entire film, and the TT – mediatext B – is the dubbed film.

What is problematic in this first stage is the fact that the ST is not only reduced to the verbal part of mediatext A, but also to its transcription of uttered words into a written text. This transformation is always accompanied by a loss of the additional information given by the paralinguistic and prosodic elements of the original dialogue, such as volume, voice quality, intonation, accent, rhythm, and so forth. Thus, in the first stage, we have a double reduction of the ST, which is not only detached from the other semiotic codes of the whole mediatext, but also from the prosodic elements that accompany the verbal text when it is orally presented. The ST is reduced to a more or less precise transcription of the actual dialogue in the film or to the screenplay upon which the film dialogue is based.

Thus, if translators work without referring to the visual material, they miss out on a significant amount of information that would help them interpret fully the dialogue – the interaction between text and image, the interaction between dialogue and sound, and all the prosodic elements closely linked to the dialogue. This makes it difficult for translators to take decisions concerning the actual meaning of the different speech acts, where context or prosody would provide them with crucial information about the intentions of the speakers.

In the second stage of the dubbing process, this rough translation is reworked by the dialogue writer, who watches the film and rewrites the text in order to achieve the highest possible degree of synchronization between the text that will be spoken by the dubbing actors and the lip movements and gestures of the original actors on the screen. At this stage of the dubbing process, dialogue writers have at their disposal a draft version of the dialogue in the target language, accompanied by a copy of mediatext A. These two texts constitute their STs. These will then have to be transformed into a final written version of the TT which respects the speaking rhythm and phonetics of the original when lip synchrony is required. Of course, it is theoretically possible at this point to make up for the information lost in the first step of the process and to eliminate any mistakes in the rough translation that might have occurred. But this only usually happens if dialogue writers notice deviations of meaning or actual mistakes – provided that they are capable of understanding the source language. Even if they are able of doing so, the result of their work sometimes seems to indicate that they only concentrate on their actual task: checking and rewriting all the dialogue exchanges where the actors' lips and gestures can be seen, in order to preserve the illusion that the actor on the screen is uttering the words of a TT spoken by another actor. It is thus likely that the dialogue writer will not notice mistakes or falsifications of speech acts resulting from a 'blind translation' (Krueger 1986) carried out during the first stage.

In the third and final stage, when the written text is spoken by actors chosen by the dubbing director, several difficulties can be encountered. Firstly, the actors will generally not be shown the entire film, but only the scenes where they have to speak their lines (Pruys 1997: 89; Herbst 1994: 13). Although it is true that these conditions are comparable to those faced by the actors in the original film, where the different scenes are never shot in sequence, the actors do have an idea of the plot of the whole narrative, whereas dubbing actors very often do not. In the case of blockbuster productions, the working conditions are even worse and actors will generally only be shown a scratched version of the film, whose details have to be kept secret until its release (Krauss 2010). There is an attempt to make up for this by having the dubbing director give the actors additional information about the plot and the context of each take. Secondly, we once again encounter a shift from written to spoken text that can lead to misinterpretations, as these added prosodic elements are not necessarily the same as in the original film.

The dubbing actors, then, have at their disposal parts of the final written version of the dialogue in the target language, the corresponding parts of the original film and some information provided by the dubbing director about the film as a whole. The recording of the dialogue will of course be followed by several other technical steps before the final dubbed version is complete, but we will skip these details which are described by Maier (1997: 103–14) and Herbst (1994: 13–16), as they do not greatly influence the translation process itself.

2.   Problems related to the dubbing process

I would like to argue that the dubbing process does not seem entirely to satisfy the requirements of a good translation, because it does not attach due importance to the relationship between the dialogue and the other elements of the film. The film is composed of several semiotic levels that interact to generate meaning, such as moving images, music, sound and verbal text. If mediatext A is translated, only the originally spoken verbal text will be substituted. In the case of dubbing, it will be replaced by a new verbal text in the target language spoken by different actors – adding their prosody to the dialogue – while the other elements, such as music, sound and moving images generally remain to a large extent unaltered, except in cases where the international tape is lost, which sometimes happens with older films, and the music and sound have to be recomposed and/or rerecorded. Of course, during the final mixing of the soundtrack a number of changes can occur (Pruys 1997: 118–22). For varying reasons, such as censorship and adaptation for special audiences, different age groups for example, or in order to adapt a movie to the standardized television format of ninety minutes, the dubbed version is often slightly shorter than the original (Maier 1997: 14–24).

The dubbing process does not usually take sufficient account of the fact that the meaning of mediatext A is the result of an interaction between the semiotic levels mentioned above. We must thus expect to encounter translation problems due to a whole host of factors: the rough translation sometimes being based only on the written dialogue, which corresponds more or less to the spoken text in the film; dialogue writers not being always familiar with the source language and using the rough translation as a starting point for their rewritten version, concentrating on scenes that need to be synchronized with the lip movements and gestures of the actors on the screen; dubbing actors not seeing the whole film or, due to the provision of a scratched version, not even the whole image but only the takes which they have to dub; and, last but not least, the two shifts between spoken and written dialogue occurring during the whole translation process, in which prosodic information is lost in a first step and new prosodic elements are added at the end of the process, so that speech acts can easily be altered if the dubbing director is not scrupulous enough.

3.   The importance of the relationship between text and image

To improve this translation process, those involved should keep in mind that the relationship between text and image in mediatext A runs the risk of being altered by the translation in mediatext B if this relationship is not taken into account from the beginning. There are, of course, many different kinds of complex relationship between texts and images, and also a number of interesting attempts to categorize them. Theorists with a linguistic approach, such as Nöth (1990), who distinguishes between illustration, pictoral exemplification, labelling, mutual determination and contradiction, generally concentrate on texts such as print advertising rather than on films. This approach tends to neglect the basic characteristics of film, in which the image is generally a moving image and the text is, for the most part, spoken dialogue (sometimes with voice over narration or lyrics).

Theories informed by film, on the other hand, tend to focus on film as a purely visual medium and there are not many analyses on the relationship between text and (moving) image. One of these is an article by Rauh (1987), who distinguishes between qualitative and space-time relationships between text and image. Qualitative relationships are those of 'potentialization', when image and sound complement each other; 'modification', when they are contradictory; 'parallelism', when there is no additional information given by text or image; and 'divergence', when one comments on the other. Space-time relationships can be either 'asyntopical' or 'syntopical', depending on whether the source of the uttered words or sounds can be seen on screen or not. Rauh also distinguishes between synchrony and asynchrony in reference to the temporal relationship between sounds and their sources. This approach seems more appropriate to the analysis of feature films, as it also takes into account the temporal and spatial relationships between text and image. Zabalbeascoa (2008: 30) puts forward a similar categorization, distinguishing between 'complementarity', 'redundancy', 'contradiction', 'incoherence', 'separability', and 'aesthetic quality'. He also emphasizes that the different types of relationship can be established 'simultaneously, contiguously or separated by a considerable lapse of time' (ibid.).

We can conclude from these theoretical approaches that it would only be possible to produce a faithful translation of the verbal text without referring to the images in the case of a total redundancy/parallelism between the two semiotic levels. In all other cases, however, the analysis of this relationship is essential in order to understand the meaning of a sequence in mediatext A and to provide an adequate translation of the given dialogue. It is obvious that translators have to watch the film in order to know whether the relationship between text and image is redundant or not.

Another important aspect of the relationship between text and image is that a feature film consists of moving images with edited shots. It is, thus, crucial to consider not only the different relationships between simultaneous texts and images, but also between those that are non-simultaneous. Non-simultaneity can occur within the same shot or in the editing of two shots, and of course a text or an image can also refer to a much earlier shot in the film. I would now like to concentrate on the importance of respecting the different functions of dialogue as developed by Remael (2008), who distinguishes between horizontal and vertical functions, following a distinction made by Vanoye (1985: 99–118).

4. The importance of analysing the dialogue function

While the horizontal function of dialogue corresponds to the mimetic one, the vertical function is another denomination for narrative function. The former corresponds to the inner communication system between the characters, while the latter constitutes the outer communication system with the audience and runs the risk of destroying the filmic illusion because it addresses viewers in a more or less overt way, thus piercing the 'fourth wall', to borrow a term from dramatic theory. The vertical function of dialogue does not automatically imply the destruction of illusion, of course, even in those cases where the audience is directly and overtly addressed. But, as Pfister (2000: 397) notes, the vertical function of dialogue in a drama can introduce a new level of illusion. Pfister also points out that the audience addressed is not the real audience, but a fictional one, comparable to the implied reader of a novel. Of course, the dialogue between two characters also addresses the audience, even if it has a mainly mimetic function, because the audience learns something about the characters from the way they speak and the things they say or do not say. But the narrative function of a dialogue is not the only kind of vertical function that addresses the audience. Aesthetic and entertaining functions as described by Rosenthal (1995: 144) should also be included among the vertical functions of dialogue, as they also pierce the 'fourth wall' or, to adopt Pfister's terms, create a new level of illusion.

In terms of the horizontal functions, we must keep in mind that a dialogue in a film (just as in other fictional texts) is not a simple imitation of natural speaking as it occurs in the everyday world, even if the mimetic function in film often seems to be stronger than in other fictional texts. Apart from the fact that it may not be very interesting to hear people talk in the movies as they do in everyday life, it is of course difficult to say what kind of dialogue is 'natural' – so it seems more appropriate to describe the mimetic function of dialogue as an attempt to make it match the expectations of the audience. As these expectations are essentially generated by the film genre itself, we can expect characters in an action movie to speak in a way different from the way they would in a comedy, a romance, a historical drama or a film noir.

In order to illustrate the effect on the translation when the different functions of a dialogue are not taken into consideration, I will now provide a brief example from the German dubbing of the French film *Mauvais sang* (1986), directed by Leos Carax. The scene in question begins at 44.46 and ends at 47.16. Alex and Anna are in a room; she is lying on a bed while he turns the radio on. We hear an old-fashioned love song sung by Serge Reggiani. The DJ then announces the next song and Alex, who has left the apartment – we see him through the glass façade of the apartment – begins to dance and run to David Bowie's song *Modern Love*, with the camera following him in a long travelling shot. He then returns to the apartment, where we see Anna in the bathroom, brushing her hair. In the next shot, Alex is standing in front of the closed bathroom door, where a short dialogue commences between the two of them:

Example 1 (ST)

ALEX: Anna.	[Anna.
ANNA: Oui ?	Yes?
ALEX: Tu crois qu'il existe l'amour qui va vite ... qui va vite mais qui dure toujours ?	Do you think there's the love that is fast ... that is fast but lasts forever?]

In the next shot we see Anna brushing her hair, then she shakes her head. In the German dubbing of these shots, the dialogue has been translated as follows:

(TT)

ALEX: Anna? ANNA: Hm? ALEX: Glaubst du daran, dass die Liebe ganz plötzlich kommt, ganz plötzlich da ist und dann für immer bleibt?	[Anna? Hm? Do you think that love comes very suddenly, is suddenly there and then stays forever?]

Here, as in the rest of the film, we do not have a classic dialogue with a mimetic function where two characters communicate with each other, but rather a kind of collage of different texts, including songs, characters' speech and an ambivalent gesture that is perhaps an answer to Alex's question. Anna's shaking of her head after brushing her hair can in fact be interpreted as a 'no', as a gesture becoming a 'physical dialect' as Manhart (2000: 173) calls it, but it only has this meaning in the outer communication system with the audience, in the vertical function. Alex, who is standing in front of the bathroom door, cannot see her gesture, so it has no meaning in the inner communication system, in which Anna is obviously shaking her head just to do her hair. In this scene, of course, only the characters' speech and the narrator's commentary can be dubbed, while the song and the visual elements are not altered.

As we can see, the German translation does not preserve the ambivalence of the dialogue. In the original version, the dialogue has no simple mimetic function. The characters hardly communicate. As the prosodic elements suggest, Alex is not addressing Anna: his intonation is not that of a question, but rather of a simple statement, as if he were just enjoying pronouncing her name to himself or to the audience (an impression that is reinforced by the fact that he is almost looking directly into the camera). In the German translation, however, the intonation is interrogative, so that there is no doubt that Alex is addressing Anna. And this confers a clear mimetic function to this piece of dialogue. The same goes for Anna's reply. In the French original she says *oui?* while in the translation she just murmurs. Even if it is not clear why the translator has opted to have Anna murmur rather than say *ja* [yes] as in the original, it seems at first sight that the translator has respected the function of the dialogue, preserving the supposed phatic function of her reply. But the problem is that the *oui* in the original allows the audience to relate her answer to the opening text of the film, in which a voice over narrator says: *Il lui a dit 'Tu veux ?' Elle lui a dit ni oui ni non* [He said to her 'You want to?' She told him neither yes nor no], in a direct quote from Charles-Ferdinand Ramuz's novel *L'Amour de la fille et du garçon.*

Anna's murmur in the translation means that we lose the connection with the beginning of the film and the audience misses both the intra-textual allusion to the opening text of the film as well as the inter-textual allusion to Charles Ramuz. So, once again, the function of the dialogue is altered as in the translation it takes on a mimetic function without any ambivalence and loses its aesthetic quality, which lies in the intra-textual and inter-textual allusions. These, in turn, function as a 'sign of marginality, most clearly indicated by the fact that the principal intertexts deal with asocial love' (Powrie 1997: 133).

The translation of Alex's reply also differs from the original: it neither keeps the repetition, nor the exact meaning. The French original allows the audience to relate the words *l'amour qui va vite* [love that is fast] to the long travelling shot in which Alex could be seen running down the street to the song *Modern Love*. The words now give new meaning to the scene, which to the audience had seemed like a kind of dance video, with no other meaning than the aesthetic pleasure of this performance. Retrospectively, however, it becomes an illustration of these words and Alex himself becomes *l'amour qui va vite*. Unfortunately, the German translation makes it nearly impossible to relate the words 'love that comes suddenly, is suddenly there' to the preceding scene, so that these words do not capture the metonymical quality of the original.

While there is a complex weaving of simultaneous and non-simultaneous relationships between text and image throughout the whole original film, and the dialogue fulfils multiple functions, the German translation, which at first glance does not differ so radically from the original, reveals itself to be less complex and to reduce the function of the dialogue simply to a mimetic one by trying to make the characters sound more natural than in the original and by removing all allusions and ambiguity.

Part of the problem we encounter in this dialogue is obviously due to the shifts between written and spoken text during the dubbing process, which has led to the alteration of the prosodic information. But I would also argue that the translation deliberately tried to make the dialogue sound more natural, more mimetic, thus missing the aesthetic function of the allusions and the complex relationships between text and image. Does this mean that the German translation is wrong? From the point of view of the text, setting aside the images and the context, it could seem as if the textual meaning of the original was more or less preserved. But the translation actually modifies the function of the dialogue within the whole film – instead of being vertical, the function becomes horizontal.

The following example, taken from the classic *Citizen Kane* (Orson Welles, 1941), harbours a different problem. The dialogue in the original is clearly mimetic, but the translation risks confusing the audience due to a few changes in the prosody and a typical translation challenge between English and German. The shot begins at 28.36 and ends at 29.02. One of the investigating journalists, Mr Thompson, is sitting at a huge table in a hall of the Walter Thatcher Memorial Library reading a large book, a manuscript containing information about Charles Foster Kane. Behind him stands a man in uniform, Mr Jennings, observing him:

Besides changing the names – the man in uniform is called James, and Miss Simpson is called Jane – the German dubbing introduces slight differences in tone. The discrepancies in meaning between the original and the dubbed versions are obviously due to the shifts in the dubbing process between written and oral dialogue, which have here led to changes in prosody. While in the original, Mr Jennings (alias James) is very stiff and formal when he says 'I beg your pardon', the dubbing makes it seem as if he would like to ask the journalist a question, as if he were really interested in learning something (e.g., what the journalist meant by saying 'oh'). The German audience is thus led to expect James to ask the journalist a question. What is also rather confusing is the following question: *Was sagten Sie?* [What did you say?]. The use of the simple past instead of the present perfect in the German sentence suggests that James is referring to something that was said some time before. The reason for this change in tense is certainly that we can see the mouth of the speaker in this scene, so that the present perfect, *Was haben Sie gesagt?* [What have you said?], could not be used without jeopardizing lip synchrony.

Example 2 (ST)

THOMPSON *(closing the book, disappointed)*: Oh ...
JENNINGS *(coming closer)*: I beg your pardon.
THOMPSON: What?
JENNINGS: What did you say?
The door opens and a woman, Miss Simpson, enters the hall.
SIMPSON: It is 4:30, isn't it Jennings?
JENNINGS: Yes, Madam.
SIMPSON: You've enjoyed a very rare privilege, young man. Did you find what you were looking for?
THOMPSON *(rising tone)*: No ... *(They are all looking at a huge portrait hanging on the wall.)*
THOMPSON: You're not Rosebud, are you? *(He turns to the woman.)*
SIMPSON *(outraged)*: What?
THOMPSON: Rosebud. And your name's Jennings, isn't it?
JENNINGS: Yes, you ...
THOMPSON *(interrupting him, with a loud voice)*: Goodbye everybody. Thanks for the use of the hall.

(TT)

THOMPSON: Oh ...	[THOMPSON: Oh ...
JAMES: Verzeihung Sir ...	JAMES: Excuse me Sir ...
THOMPSON: Was?	THOMPSON: What?
JAMES: Was sagten Sie?	JAMES: What did you say?
JANE: Es ist schon 4:30, nicht wahr James?	JANE: It's 4:30 already, isn't it James?
JAMES: Jawohl Madam.	JAMES: Yes, Madam.
JANE: Ihnen ist eine sehr seltene Vergünstigung zuteil geworden. Haben Sie gefunden, was Sie suchten?	JANE: You've enjoyed a very rare privilege. Did you find what you were looking for?
THOMPSON: Nein ...	THOMPSON: Nein ...
THOMPSON: Du warst nicht Rosebud, hm?	THOMPSON: You weren't Rosebud, were you?
JANE: Was?	JANE: What?
THOMPSON: Rosebud. Und Ihr Name war James, hm?	THOMPSON: Rosebud. And your name was James, hm?
JAMES: Ja, Sir.	JAMES: Yes, Sir.
THOMPSON: Na dann macht's gut. Und vielen Dank für die Zimmerbenutzung.	THOMPSON: Okay well, so long. And thank you for the use of the room.]

Another prosodic change can be found when Thompson answers 'no' when the woman asks him whether he found what he was looking for. In the original, the rising tone marks irony, while in German the tone of his reply remains neutral, preventing the audience from perceiving the tension between the characters. This makes it totally unexpected and unlikely that in the next sentence Thompson addresses Simpson/Jane with the German *du*, the familiar pronoun form. Her outraged answer thus seems more like a reaction to the impoliteness of the reporter addressing her with *du* instead of *Sie* rather than the absurdity of the idea that she could be 'Rosebud'.

In the last sentence of the shot the journalist expresses his thanks for 'the use of the hall', which becomes a 'room' in the German translation, contradicting the image which is obviously showing us a monumental hall and not a room. Again it seems that, because we cannot see the mouth of the journalist while speaking, the rough translation was not counter checked.

The linguistic differences between the original and the translation are, of course, slight. On the paralinguistic level, however, the changes in prosody tend to destroy the mimetic function, because the speech acts seem less coherent. The interaction of the characters is obviously altered in the German dubbing. The politeness of the man in uniform becomes a real interest in something that is not subsequently articulated. The tension between the woman and the reporter is not rendered in the dubbing, where the answer of the journalist retains a neutral tone and then suddenly becomes very impolite. As a result, the German audience may be a little confused by the characters' behaviour in this scene.

5. Conclusion

I hope that these two examples have shown how important it is to be aware of the different functions of the dialogue when translating and of the fact that the dubbing process follows several steps, carried out by different people and involving two shifts between written and spoken text. These shifts can easily lead to an alteration of the dialogue's function. A dialogue can be properly interpreted only if the simultaneous and non-simultaneous relationships between the text and the other semiotic levels of the film – such as images, sounds and, especially, prosodic elements – are taken into account during the entire translation process. I would like to argue, therefore, that the dubbing process can only improve if rough translators are given enough time (and money) to allow them to see and hear the original film, so that they can perceive the relationship between text and image, analyse the functions of the dialogue, and consider the prosodic elements that influence its function as well as its relationship with other elements in the film. It would be ideal to involve translators in the other stages of the process and train them, as Seifferth suggests (2009: 9), to enable them to undertake the task of the dialogue writer, as is the case in France or Spain, in order to minimize the loss or distortion of information along the various stages of the dubbing process.

Bibliography

Herbst, Thomas, *Linguistische Aspekte der Synchronisation von Fernsehserien. Phonetik, Textlinguistik, Übersetzungstheorie* (Tübingen: Niemeyer, 1994).

Krauss, Helmut, 'Lecture about Dubbing in Germany', (University of Hildesheim, 23 June 2010).

Krueger, Gertraude, 'Roh-Übersetzungen sind eher Blind-Übersetzungen. Über das Synchronisieren von Filmen'. *Zeitschrift für Kulturaustausch* 36/4 (1986), 611–13.

Maier, Wolfgang, *Spielfilmsynchronisation* (Frankfurt am Main: Peter Lang, 1997).

Mälzer-Semlinger, Nathalie, 'Bild-Text-Beziehungen beim Filmübersetzen'. *Lebende Sprachen* 56/2 (2011), 214–23.

Manhart, Sibylle, '"When Words Collide": Betrachtungen über fremde Kulturen im filmtranslatorischen Handlungsgefüge', in Mira Kadric, Klaus Kaindl and Franz Pöchhacker, eds, *Translationswissenschaft: Festschrift für Mary Snell-Hornby zum 60. Geburtstag* (Tübingen: Stauffenburg, 2000), 167–81.

Nöth, Winfried, 'Der Zusammenhang von Text und Bild', in Klaus Brinker, Gerd Antos, Wolfgang Heinemann and Sven Sager, eds, *Text- und Gesprächslinguistik*. Erster Halbband (Berlin: de Gruyter, 2000), 489–96.

Pfister, Manfred, *Das Drama* (Munich: Wilhelm Fink, 2000).

Pisek, Gerhard, *Die große Illusion. Probleme und Möglichkeiten der Filmsynchronisation* (Trier: Wissenschaftlicher Verlag, 1994).

Powrie, Phil, *French Cinema in the 1980s. Nostalgia and the Crisis of Masculinity* (Oxford: Clarendon Press, 1997).

Pruys, Guido Marc, *Die Rhetorik der Filmsynchronisation: Wie ausländische Spielfilme in Deutschland zensiert, verändert und gesehen werden* (Tübingen: Narr, 1997).

Rauh, Reinhold, 'Sprache und filmische Wahrnehmung', in Knut Hickethier and Hartmut Winkler, eds, *Filmwahrnehmung* (Berlin: Sigma, 1990), 95–106.

Remael, Aline, 'Screenwriting, Scripted and Unscripted Language: What do Sub-titlers Need to Know?', in Jorge Díaz-Cintas, ed., *The Didactics of Audiovisual Translation* (Amsterdam: John Benjamins, 2008), 57–67.

Rosenthal, Alan, *Writing Docudrama. Dramatizing Reality for Film and TV* (Newton, MA: Focus Press, 1995).

Seifferth, Veronika, *Die deutsche Synchronisation amerikanischer Fernsehserien* (Trier: Wissenschaftlicher Verlag, 2009).

Troester, Änne, 'Translating Hollywood – The Challenge of Dubbing Film Into German', in Heike Paul and Katja Kanzler, eds, *Amerikanische Populärkultur in Deutschland* (Leipzig: Leipziger Universitätsverlag, 2002), 181–96.

Vanoye, Francis, *La Parole au cinéma* (Paris: Clancier-Guénaud, 1985).

Whitman-Linsen, Candace, *Through the Dubbing Glass: The Synchronization of American Motion Pictures into German, French and Spanish* (Peter Lang: Frankfurt am Main, 1992).

Zabalbeascoa, Patrick, 'The Nature of the Audiovisual Text and its Parameters', in Jorge Díaz-Cintas, ed., *The Didactics of Audiovisual Translation* (Amsterdam: John Benjamins, 2008), 21–37.

DENISE FILMER

Ethnic epithets and linguistic taboos: Offensive language transfer in Clint Eastwood's *Gran Torino*

1. Introduction

Do insults like 'wop' and 'greaseball' carry the same semantic meaning as *mangiamaccheroni* [maccheroni eater]? Is *muso giallo* [yellow muzzle] an adequate translation of 'chink' or 'zipperhead'? More to the point, would a native Italian speaker actually utter such expressions? Do they exist in the linguistic and cultural context of Italy or are they simply the invention of audiovisual translators? Controversial and politically loaded, the issues surrounding racial slurs and ethnic epithets have been the subject of various interdisciplinary enquiries; from sociology (Duane 2006) and discursive psychology (Wetherell and Potter 1992) to the multidisciplinary approach (van Dijk 1998), discourse analysis (Reisigl and Wodak 2001) and linguistic anthropology (Allan and Burridge 2006). Yet, from the point of view of translation studies, this culture-bound lexical minefield remains an underdeveloped area of research.[1]

    This chapter outlines some sociolinguistic and cultural considerations regarding meaning transfer of linguistic taboos in the language pair English/Italian. In a case study of the film *Gran Torino* (Clint Eastwood 2008), racist and taboo language is analysed in the source text (ST), and compared with target text (TT) solutions, examining the techniques and

---

[1]   One important exception, however, is Nobili (2007), who carried out some pioneering comparative research specifically on racial insults in various text genres, including films, newspapers and songs.

strategies adopted in the translation process.[2] A pilot study carried out during classroom investigations with cultural mediation students is included here as a starting point for discussion on the reception and perception of race talk across cultures.

2. Why the film *Gran Torino*?

Gran Torino (2008) was directed and produced by Clint Eastwood who also plays the protagonist, Walt Kowalski, a Korean war veteran, retired Ford worker, and a 'full-blown, unrepentant racist' (Schenk 2008: 6). The plot focuses on the relationship between Walt and his young Hmong neighbour, Thao. As the story unfolds, Walt emerges as an unlikely father figure who ultimately sacrifices his life for the people he initially despised.

There are several reasons why *Gran Torino* was chosen for this study. Firstly, the plethora of racial terms in the ST provides ample material for analysis. There are fourteen different epithets for people of Asian origin alone, while insults to African Americans, the Irish, Italians, Poles, Jews, and Hispanics bring the total to over fifty direct utterances and numerous other pejorative allusions to race and ethnic origin. Secondly, Clint Eastwood is a respected actor, an accomplished film director, and a guaranteed box office hit; his presence in front of and behind the camera assures access to the substantial funding for subtitling and dubbing reserved for high-quality productions. Last but not least, the film deals with controversial issues such as ethnic prejudice, political correctness, old-age, multiculturalism, changing moral values and the like, thus provoking debate among critics and in the media. Adia and Jessie (2009: online) summarizes two opposing points of view regarding the film:

---

2   The expression 'linguistic transposition' rather than translation is preferred by the dubbing director of *Gran Torino*, Filippo Ottoni.

Gran Torino can be viewed as a story of one man's personal triumph over racism and his redemption through his friendship with the Hmong Lors family; and, that certainly seems to be the intention of the film's director, the author of the screenplay, and the interpretation of many critics. Yet, a different reading of the film suggests that the central narrative relies on the intertwining of racialized stereotypes juxtaposed with heroic white masculinity.

This reading of the core narrative of the film highlights the issue at stake as the question of meaning transfer here is not purely a linguistic one. When *Gran Torino* was released in the US it was hailed as a masterpiece yet simultaneously criticized for its politically incorrect language.[3] The film's debut in Italy prompted no such controversy, so was there something amiss in the 'linguistic transposition'? Is there a cultural dimension to political correctness and race talk which also needs to be considered in translation?

3. The question of linguaculture in racial slurs

Ever since the cultural turn (Bassnett 1991: 22), translation scholars have contended with what can or cannot be linguistically transferred from one culture to another. The concept of *linguaculture* (Friedrich 1989; Agar 1994; House 1997; Katan 2004) has been explored in relation to the translatability of culture-bound lexis. The expression was coined by Friedrich (1989: 295–312) in an article where he stated 'language is loaded with culture'.

---

3   Eastwood himself spoke out against the critics, and he is quoted as saying: 'People have lost their sense of humour. In former times we constantly made jokes about different races. You can only tell them today with one hand over your mouth or you will be insulted as a racist. [...] I find that ridiculous. In those earlier days every friendly clique had a "Sam the Jew" or "Jose the Mexican" – but we didn't think anything of it or have a racist thought. It was just normal that we made jokes based on our nationality or ethnicity. That was never a problem. I don't want to be politically correct. We're all spending too much time and energy trying to be politically correct about everything' (*Express* 2009: online).

Schrauf and Rubin (2003: 134) give a more detailed outline of the concept, identifying the three components as linguistic, communicative and cultural competence, and concluding that, 'perhaps the best term for this interwoven linguistic cultural whole in which a person comes to such competence is *linguaculture*'. One may agree or disagree with the concept, but it functions as a convenient umbrella term to denote that point where language and culture meet in order to create meaning. It could be said, therefore, that linguaculture determines the presence, or absence, of ethnophaulisms[4] and the way in which they are received within a language community. Furthermore, it could be argued that racial slurs, racist language, and ethnic epithets are the linguistic manifestation of one culture's attitudes to the Other. Van Dijk (2007: xix) explains: 'Word choice is one of the ways people betray their underlying opinions, social attitudes and ideologies, also because the use of certain lexical items is associated with underlying norms and values'.

From another perspective, Rappaport (2005) suggests that the subversive nature of ethnic epithets can actually combat prejudice with comedy and satire, thus neutralizing offensive overtones. From whichever ideological standpoint, the translator's task is a tricky one. If each linguaculture has its own unique experiences, its own traditions, and therefore its own perceptions, attitudes, and ways of verbally expressing a given reality, can the connotations of a particular slur be conveyed into another language?

Pedersen (2010: 67) notes that 'translators not only transfer the meaning of words [...] they also function as cultural mediators, helping the target language readers gain necessary insight into the source culture'. Nowhere is the need for cultural sensitivity greater than in the field of audiovisual translation (AVT) where the multimodal aspect increases the risk of inaccuracies and where visual evidence must somehow be accounted for. Díaz-Cintas *et al.* (2010: 12) observe: 'As clear evidence of the fruitful marriage between Translation Studies and Cultural Studies, today's AVT authors tend to show an increased awareness of the cultural embeddedness of translation'.

---

4   'A contemptuous expression for (a member of) a people or ethnic group; an expression containing a disparaging allusion to another people or ethnic group' (*OED*: online).

4. Linguistic taboos across cultures

In addition to its cultural embeddedness, the semantics of this field make
the translation process all the more complex, as the perception of what
constitutes a linguistic taboo or verbal offense is not static within a language community (Hughes 1991; Gorji 2007), let alone across cultural
boundaries. Usage, connotations, and even semantic groups can shift, both
diachronically and topographically. As Allen and Burridge (2006: 106–7)
point out when referring to anglophone cultures today: 'blasphemy, religious profanity and religious insults have lost their punch [...] what is now
perceived as truly obscene are racial and ethnic slurs'. In contrast, it would
seem that this shift has not taken place in Italy. Deep-rooted Catholicism, a
male-dominated society and a language which consequently reflects those
patriarchal values ensure that blasphemy and religious insults still rank
the highest in terms of what is considered obscene. The Italian language
contains few explicit racist insults, whereas implicit or indirect forms of
racial discrimination are more common (Polselli 2007: 142).

The scope of this paper does not allow for an in-depth analysis of racist
and taboo language in the respective linguacultures. Suffice it to say that,
from a translation studies perspective, the mere existence of these words
necessitates reflection on their meaning transfer.

5. Research perspective: Theoretical framework

Before turning to the analysis, a brief overview of some theoretical perspectives regarding AVT is necessary in order to understand the research
perspective adopted in this paper. The dichotomy between its conception as
translation proper or adaptation is highlighted by Díaz Cintas and Remael
(2007: 9), who note that the spatial and temporal constraints imposed
by the medium have prompted the preference for the term 'adaptation',

as this 'seems to equate the [translational] process to a *lesser activity* and becomes enough of an excuse to carry out a linguistic transfer that is clearly inadequate but nonetheless justifiable since it is only a case of adaptation' (my emphasis). Díaz Cintas and Remael (ibid.) argue that AVT should be considered as translation proper, but in a more 'flexible, heterogeneous and less static perspective' of translation as a whole, 'that encompasses a broad set of empirical realities and acknowledges the ever-changing nature of the practice'. Italian scholars have also tried to pinpoint the nature of AVT. Pavesi (2005), for example, favours the term 'constrained translation', and Paolinelli and Di Fortunato (2005: 52) state that the only form of translation possible for audiovisual texts is adaptation. These perspectives are counterbalanced by Taylor (2000: 153), who affirms that 'the word is still the anchor for everything'. The comment was made with reference to solutions and strategies adopted in subtitling in the Italian context, but the dictum could equally apply to dubbing and, to some extent, many audiovisual media. It is crucial that Jakobson's 'translation proper' remains the core of meaning transfer in audiovisual products and should be perceived as such by the various operators in the audiovisual field. This work subscribes to the view that, although the intersemiotic and multimodal aspects of film translation cannot be ignored, they must not undermine the importance of the translators, rendering their work as merely instrumental to the overall audiovisual product.

The very fact that approaches to AVT arouse dissent could explain why it is one of the most prolific areas in translation research (Díaz-Cintas et al. 2010). The increase in visual communication in a global context over the last two decades has certainly brought the issue of translation to the fore, and in this sense, Cronin (2003: 6) comments:

> Our narrative imagination, our ability to try to imagine what it is like to be someone else from another language, another culture, another community or another country – it is itself a mere figment of the imagination if we have no way of reading books, watching plays, looking at films produced by others. In other words, if citizenship is seen as no longer exclusively defined by nationality or nation-state (Delanly 2000) then any active sense of global citizenship must involve translation as a core element.

6. Analytical and methodological framework

The methodological and analytical approach sustaining this analysis is part of a multifaceted research methodology that utilizes a combination of analytical tools drawing on Politeness Theory (Brown and Levinson 1978, 1987), Linguistic Anthropology (Allan and Burridge 2006), Discourse Analysis (Fairclough 2003), Ideology in Translation (Hatim and Mason 1997), and Descriptive Translation Studies (Toury 1995).

In an attempt to include the practitioners' perspective in the equation, I contacted the dubbing director of *Gran Torino*, Filippo Ottoni. Having initially agreed to co-operate he subsequently declined,[5] leaving the rationale for certain translation choices to deduction. A further method of assessment focuses on perception and a pilot study was devised to obtain feedback from Italian speakers regarding the rendering of racial slurs from the film in the TL.

7. Fictional slurs and real insults: Examples from *Gran Torino*

Two scenes from *Gran Torino* are examined here. Part of a larger research project with other meaningful examples from the same film, the examination of the clips illustrates how racial slurs and insults perform different communicative functions within the context of the film. They also show that racial insults are the lexical leitmotif running throughout the text and, as such, require special attention in their linguistic transposition.

---

5   Ottoni was contacted on 3 September 2010. He replied on 14 September 2010, with dialogue lists attached. I responded with a list of questions to which he replied that he was unable to help. His motivation for declining was that all the choices made in AVT are dictated by circumstance and would not stand up to 'academic scrutiny'.

Hughes (2006: 150, 177–8) notes that establishing the etymologies of ethnic epithets is notoriously problematic. Lexicographers admit that a melange of historical and sociolinguistic research, folklore and half-truths all come into play to provide insight on their origins; origins that are deeply rooted in the source linguaculture (Green 2010: xiv). Understanding this process is essential to the present analysis as it highlights the culturally specific associations that these derogatory expressions carry. *Racialslurdatabase. com* is a peer-operated website which lists over 500 racial slurs with their supposed origins. Contributions are provided by the general public and therefore it cannot be considered an academically reliable source. However, it does shed some light as to possible origins of slurs which have become part of folklore.

The four terms listed below are just a sample of the many racial slurs in the original script of *Gran Torino*. Three ('wop', 'spook', 'honkey') figure in the examples discussed in this contribution while 'zipperhead' is the most frequently used slur in the film. It is rendered in Italian with *muso giallo* [yellow muzzle] or *mongolo* [mongol], emblematic of how these lexical items lose significant semantic meaning in the transation (see Table 7.1).

Table 7.1 Possible etymology of racial slurs

Slur	Ethnicity	*Racialslurdatabase* and *Oxford English Dictionary* definitions
Zipperhead	Asians	Coined by US soldiers during the Korean War. (1) If Asians were shot in the head with high-powered weapons, their heads would split as if you unzipped them. (2) Vietnam War slang for 'Zero Intelligence Potential', i.e. just kill them, no reason to interrogate. (3) Often, Asians were run over by military Jeeps, the tire tracks on them resembled zippers. (4) Asians part their hair down the middle, in a zipper-like strip.
Wop	Italians	Originated with mass Italian emigration to the US. (1) Stands for 'WithOut Papers' as many entered illegally. (2) 'Working On Pavement'. (3) From 'guappo' (pronounced 'woppo'), Neapolitan dialect meaning criminal, bully or flamboyant, dandy.

Spooks	Blacks	Their dark skin which blends into the night makes them frightening and ghost-like.
Honky/ Honkie	Whites	(1) From the term 'Honky Tonk', a type of country music. (2) Originated as 'Hunky' to refer to Slavic and Hungarian immigrants and became 'Honkey' to refer to all white people. (3) From the African Wolof word 'Honq' meaning red or pink, used to describe white men. (4) From white men honking their horns to call on the lounge singer/ prostitute types in 1920's Harlem.

7.1. Sample one: Pragmatics and parody in the use of slurs

The first sequence shows Walt at the barber's. Friends for years, the two men indulge in some light-hearted verbal sparring. The short, sharp exchange of tongue in cheek insults is used to establish and maintain the power balance between the two characters. Table 7.2 focuses on the lexical items under discussion.

Table 7.2 Comparison of racial slurs in sample one

English ST	Italian translation	Back translation
Doo-wop dago	Impasta pizza. (dubbing) Mangiamaccheroni. (subtitles)	Pizza maker. Maccheroni eater.
What are you, half Jew or something?	Non sei mica diventato ebreo? (dubbing) Non è che sei mezzo ebreo per caso? (subtitles)	Have you turned Jewish or something? You're not half Jew by any chance?
Hard-nosed Polack son of a bitch.	Brutto testone d'un polacco figlio di puttana. (dubbing and subtitles)	Ugly pig-headed Polack son of a bitch.

7.1.2. THE SITUATION

Walt and Martin belong to similar socio-economic groups as they are working class, white males, middle-aged to elderly and probably first generation immigrants to the US. In spite of their different ethnic origins, they have found common ground in their adopted homeland. They use linguistic strategies such as insults and ethnic epithets, not to offend, but to enhance their sense of solidarity, deriving pleasure from their verbal exchange (Azzaro 2007: 74). It is a linguistic code to which they are a party. Outsiders cannot accede unless they, too, have been initiated and accepted (Brown and Levinson 1987: 107).[6] The voice prosody and relaxed body language create an atmosphere of joviality, in spite of the potentially offensive language. In terms of Politeness Theory, this sequence illustrates a face-threatening act and how it is negotiated. Martin cuts Walt's hair and wants to be paid. Having first deployed the positive face strategy of using in-group identity markers to claim common ground, in this case dysphemistic euphemisms, he then makes a bald, on-record request ('That'll be ten bucks, Walt'). In Politeness Theory, 'bald-on-record' is a communication strategy used in those cases where 'maximum efficiency' is wanted even more than the desire to save the interlocuter's face (Brown and Levinson 1987: 95). Walt's reaction to this request could be construed in the light of Goffman's (1955: 213–31) concept of 'ritual' in politeness. He remonstrates with Martin, complaining about the price. From Martin's response ('It's been ten bucks for the last five years, you hard-nosed Polack son of a bitch'), we understand that Walt's objection to paying is all part of the routine, an interpersonal ritual which aids in maintaining the relationship.

6   This is verified by a later scene in which Walt takes Thao to the Barber's and tries to teach him 'how men talk'. Thao succeeds in offending Martin through his indiscriminate use of racial insults, even though he was just imitating Walt.

7.1.3. THE ANALYSIS

Having established the communicative functions and strategies in the ST, we now turn to the TT rendering. Martin launches the first insult, noting that Walt does not come to have his hair cut as frequently as he should, because he is mean with money:

Example 1

MARTIN (the barber, teasing Walt): You shouldn't wait so long between haircuts, you cheap son of a bitch.	
Perché fai passare tanto tempo tra un taglio e l'altro, taccagno figlio di puttana? (dubbing)	[Why do you let so much time pass between one cut and another, you stingy son of a whore?]

The insult 'cheap son of a bitch' has been transferred into the TT with the equivalent expression *taccagno figlio di puttana*, which arguably is even more colourful than the original as *taccagno* [stingy, miserly] has stronger connotations than cheap. However, the use of the translational routine (Pavesi 2005: 53) *figlio di puttana* [son of a whore] is questionable from a sociolinguistic point of view. In the Italian linguaculture, *figlio di puttana* has much stronger implications than its English equivalent in this communicative situation. Even if said in jest, this insult might be hard to brush aside by a man of Walt's generation.

Example 2

WALT (teasing the barber): Yeah. Well, I'm surprised you're still around. I was always hoping you'd die off and they'd get someone in here who knew what the hell they were doing. Instead you just keep hanging around like the doo-wop dago that you are.	
Già. Mi meraviglio che tu sia ancora in giro. Io spero sempre che tu crepi e che finalmente qui prendano qualcuno che sa fare il suo mestiere e invece ci sei sempre tu, con la grazia di quel mangiamaccheroni (subtitles) impasta pizza (dubbing) che sei.	[Yeah. I am surprised you are still around. I always hope that you die and that finally here they take someone who knows his trade and instead you are always here, with the grace of that maccheroni eater/ pizza maker that you are.]

Walt's retort in the ST plays on the classic insults for Italians, 'wop' and 'dago'. He elaborates on them to create 'doo-wop-dago', rendering the potentially offensive 'wop' as simply a component of the expression. With no corresponding term in the TL, the translator's ingenuity was called upon here. The results were *impasta pizza* in the dubbed version, and *mangiamaccheroni* in the subtitles. While both of these fulfil the function of perpetuating the stereotype of Italians as consumers of pasta and pizza, neither expression hints at the underlying meaning of the ST expression (see Table 7.1). Of the two, perhaps *mangiamaccheroni* is the best solution as its alliteration and musicality retain an element of the ST 'doo-wop-dago'. These TT transpositions reflect a more general trend towards adopting terms of abuse based on eating habits (Allan and Burridge 2006: 189), in this particular instance, played for laughs. However in an earlier scene, the overtly offensive 'fucking rice niggers' is translated as *froci mangiariso* [queer rice-eaters]. Such a rendering highlights not only how abusive such expressions can be but, even more disconcertingly, how insidious semantic drifts, in this case a homophobic insult, are added gratuitously. Returning to our analysis, example 3 contains an intertextual reference to the first insult hurled by Martin:

Example 3

WALT (accusing Martin of being miserly): Ten bucks? Jesus Christ, Martin, what are you, half Jew or something? You keep raising the prices. MARTIN: It's been ten bucks for the last five years, you hard-nosed Polack son of a bitch.	
WALT: Dieci verdoni? Cristo Santo, Martin. Non sarai mica diventato ebreo per caso? MARTIN: È dieci verdoni da cinque anni, brutto testone d'un polacco figlio di puttana. (dubbing)	[Ten big green ones? Christ Saint, Martin. You haven't become Jewish, by chance?] [It is ten big green ones from five years, ugly big head (pig-headed) Polish son of a whore.]

Now, it is Walt who accuses Martin of being mean. Interestingly, the stereotype of Jews being miserly is cross-cultural (Dundes 1971: 199) and, hence, rendered by a literal translation. Martin's response concludes with 'you hard-nosed Polack son of a bitch'. The TT has the addition of *brutto* [ugly], making it even more amusing than the ST and much in keeping with the style of Italian insults (Scatasta 2002: 100). A final point, *polacco* in Italian simply denotes a man from Poland, while 'Polack' in English is now considered derogatory (*OED* online).

The closing exchange that follows the previous example includes the insults 'prick', rendered by *scimunito* [stupid], commonly used in Southern regions of Italy, and 'dipshit' with the same scatological reference kept in the TT *sacco di merda* [bag of shit].

7.2. Sample two: Racial slurs as aggressive verbal duelling

In the second sample, racial slurs interlaced with swearwords are used to very different effect in a very different context. Table 7.3 focuses on the key lexical items.

Table 7.3 Comparison of racial slurs from sample 2

English ST	Italian translation	Back translation
Honky	–	–
Spooks	bulli	bullies
white ass	–	–
Nigga	rottinculo	broken arse (homophobic insult)
(super)spade	palle nere	black balls
Ofay	–	–
Paddy	irlandese	Irishman

7.2.1. THE SITUATION

While driving along, Walt catches sight of Thao's sister who is being harassed by three black youths. Reluctantly, he intervenes. The leader of the gang throws the first insult, Walt gets out of the car and the verbal sparring begins. From the outset, a series of face-threatening situations occur in which the real issue at stake is establishing dominance and power. A whole gamut of criteria regarding power relations comes into play regarding age, ethnic origin, gender, sexuality and violence. Bold, on-record and purposefully confrontational, the exchanges in this stretch demonstrate a notion of face as the antithesis to the Politeness Theory (Brown and Levinson 1987). The speakers and addressees have no desire to collaborate in saving each other's face. Rather, they want to demolish it, violating taboos on politeness by being provocative and offensive to achieve their ends. Walt and Monk come from different generations, different socio-economic circumstances and certainly do not share the same sociolect. Although they both use swearwords, Walt's meticulous lexical choices in racial slurs highlight this generational and sociolinguistic distance. In this confrontation, dysphemism is deployed in two ways; on the one hand, it is used in a witty, ironic vein, on the other, as a more sinister weapon to insult, humiliate and degrade. The second of these two aspects is also evident in the voice prosody and kinesics. Monk's opening line 'what the fuck you looking at, old man?' is said in a challenging, derisive and threatening tone, stressing the short, hard word 'fuck'. Walt growls his response 'what the hell you spooks up to?' with the accent on 'hell'. The intonation in both instances is essential to meaning creation, informing the viewers what to expect in the ensuing scene. Monk's body language reinforces his defiant stance. When Walt pulls up to the curb, Monk is loose-limbed and relaxed, cigarette in hand, sure of his territory, but he gesticulates more aggressively on hearing the racial insult 'spooks'. These intersemiotic elements combine to create the tenor of the sequence, one which is full of tension, irony, intertextuality, and coded cultural references. In terms of dysphemisms, there is an almost clichéd insistence on standard swearwords ('fuck', 'shit', 'motherfucker'), which qualify many utterances throughout the scene. While an analysis of their rendering in the ST would also yield some interesting comparative data on linguistic taboo within the linguacultures under discussion, the focus here is on overt and covert references to ethnic origin, age and colour.

Walt is variously referred to as 'old man', 'pops', 'honky', and 'bitch'. He is also told he has an 'old wrinkly white ass'. Ironically, he is even referred to as 'nigga', throwing an interesting light on the current usage of this greatest of all racial taboo words. Walt himself never utters the n-word, his personal idiolect giving preference to outdated slurs like 'spook' or 'spade'. Example 4 throws into relief Walt's idiolect:

Example 4

WALT: (going into the breach): What the hell are you spooks up to? WALT: Spooks? MONK: You better get your ass on, honky, while I still let you. That's what you better do.	
Voi bulli che state combinando? Bulli? È meglio che tiri via il culo, finché te lo permetto.	[You bullies, what are you up to? Bullies? It's better if you get your ass away, while I still let you.]

7.2.2. THE ANALYSIS

The first racial insult, 'spooks', is uttered by Walt. The youths seem more puzzled than offended by this antiquated slur which has been rendered in the TT as *bulli*. In standard Italian, *bullo* denotes an arrogant, belligerent young man who swaggers in an overbearing manner (De Mauro 2000). While it is true that these men behave exactly in this way, it is also true that the term *bullo* has absolutely no reference to race or colour, and therefore loses important semantic value. In fact, the surprised expressions and exclamations of the young men at being insulted in such an old-fashioned way in the ST are not transferred to the TT. Furthermore, the TT question *Voi bulli, che state combinando?* places emphasis on the agents, i.e. the youths, whereas the ST theme position stresses on '*What* the *hell* are you spooks up to?', placing emphasis on *what* is being done rather than *who* is doing it. Monk's retort, 'You'd better get your ass on, honky' has been translated without any attempt to render the slur against whites (see Table 7.3 above). The reference to skin colour has also been omitted in the rendering of 'old wrinkly white ass'.

The foul language comes thick and fast now as another gang member calls Walt a 'crazy motherfucker' in example 5:

Example 5

PREZ: Crazy motherfucker, man. What's wrong with him, man? DUKE: What's wrong with this nigga, man? What the hell ...	
Il rottinculo è matto. Che cazzo vuole fare? Che cazzo fa? È da manicomio.	[The broken ass is crazy. What the fuck does he want to do? What the fuck is he doing? Belongs to a madhouse.]

The highly taboo nature of this obscenity in the Italian linguaculture means it is relayed with what might be considered a 'functional equivalent' but is in fact a very crude insult to homosexuals, *rottinculo*. The appellative 'nigger/nigga' proves equally problematic from a translator's perspective. Much scholarship has been dedicated to its origins, evolution, and the diversity of its uses today (Asim 2007; Azzaro 2007; Kennedy 2002). For our purposes, it is enough to be aware that 'nigger' is no longer a straightforward racial slur, but that its gamut of nuances in modern day interpretations create a veritable hornets' nest in its uses and consequently in its translation (Paolinelli and Di Fortunato 2005: 62). In the example under discussion, the connotation of 'nigga' is most probably closest to the gangster rap tradition. That is, it is used to refer to 'mere ordinary, law-abiding men or to lowlifes unworthy of respect' (Asim 2007: 220). Paradoxically, the black youth uses this disparaging term to refer to Walt, a white man, who until now has been the only character in the film to delight in the irony of racial slurs. The problems surrounding the translation of these semantic inflections have been neatly avoided in the TT and 'nigga' has simply been omitted with no attempt at all to compensate for the loss. Example 6 deals with a different set of expletives:

Example 6

WALT (retaliating): What's all that 'bro' shit, anyway? Want to be Super Spade or something? These guys don't want to be your 'bro' and I don't blame them. Now get your ofay Paddy ass on down the road.

Li chiami fratelli, questi animali? Vorresti avere le palle nere come loro? Questi non ti vogliono come fratello, e fanno bene. Ora vedi di portare a casa il tuo culetto irlandese.	[You call them brothers, these animals? Would you like to have black balls like them? These don't want you as a brother, and they are right. Now see about taking your little Irish arse home.]

The ironic slur, 'Super Spade', a *depreciative* and *offensive* term of contempt or casual reference among white people for a black person (*OED*), has been neutralized with the expression *palle nere* [black balls] in the TT. The last line includes two racial references in the ST, 'ofay' a depreciative name for whites (*OED*) and 'Paddy' a derogatory epithet for the Irish. The TT rendering is bereft of these additional racial connotations.

To summarize, it is clear that the reduced pool of racial insults in the target language leads to omissions. In one particular instance, 'nigga' is omitted in the target text while the cultural taboo of incest referred to in the ST insult 'motherfucker' is rendered in the TL as *rottinculo*, showing how the semantic focus moves from one highly taboo area to another reflecting lingua-cultural mores.

8. Reception and perception of ethnic epithets: The questionnaire

In order to get some feedback on the cross-cultural reception and perception of racial slurs, a sample selection of dubbed translations was taken from *Gran Torino* and a pilot survey was carried out on twenty-one final year undergraduates in cultural mediation from the Faculty of Modern Languages at the University of Catania. Although data gathered from such a small, homogenous group has limited scientific validity, it nevertheless offers some important insights into the ways in which young Italians perceive and respond to racist insults, highlighting divergences between the source and target linguacultures.

8.1. Method

The survey was devised in two parts. The first part consisted of three open questions to establish the students' level of awareness, and/or use of racist expressions in their own language. This was carried out before seeing the clips discussed above, plus another clip which is not discussed in depth here. After viewing the samples, the second part required an evaluation on a scale of one (max.) to five (min.) of how offensive certain expressions were, and on the existence of certain racial expressions in their language.

8.2. Part 1

The first question 'do you know any racial insults in your language?' forced the students to reflect for several minutes before putting pen to paper. They answered with expressions like *Rom* [Rom people], *Marocchino* [Moroccan], and the anachronistic *Abissino* [Abyssinian]. Most of the students included expressions like *extracomunitario* [non-European], *imigrato* [immigrant], and *negro* [nigger]; the latter accompanied by the pejorative adjective *sporco* [dirty], a common collocation in the spoken language (Scatasta 2000: 100). The metonymic expression *vu compra* [you buy?], derived from *vuoi comprare?* [do you want to buy?] was also mentioned. Used to denote street vendors of North African or African origin, according to Beccaria (2006: 144) it is a derisive and pejorative reproduction of their attempts to speak Italian. Regional epithets such as *Terrone*, an insult used by northern Italians to denote Sicilians or people from the south, or *Polentone*, a derogatory term to denote Italians from the north of Italy, polenta being a traditional dish of the north, were also cited, as in Italy 'racism' has long been an internal issue and continues to be so today.

8.3. Part 2

After watching three clips from the dubbed version of the film, the students answered the following questions:

1. Would a native Italian speaker ever use the expression *muso giallo* [yellow muzzle] to refer to someone of Asian origin?
2. Would a native Italian speaker ever use the expression *mangia riso* [rice eater] to refer to someone of Asian origin?
3. Have you ever heard the expressions *mangia maccheroni* [pasta eater] *impasta pizza* [pizza maker] to describe an Italian?
4. Would you be insulted if someone called you *senza documenti* [without papers] or *clandestino* [clandestine, illegal immigrant]?

To the first question seventy-five percent replied that an Italian would indeed use the expression *muso giallo*. However, this was qualified. Some respondents commented that a more common expression in Italian would be *occhi a mandorla* [almond eyes]. Others replied that 'yes', an Italian 'would' use the expression, but added 'I've never heard it'. In the subsequent discussion, students indicated the influence of dubbed US war films and it was suggested that *muso giallo* was a form of dubbese. All replied that the insult *mangia riso* does not exist in Italian, although ninety percent considered that it would be offensive. *Mangia maccheroni* and *impasta pizza* were also unanimously considered invented insults to describe Italians, but the majority of students claimed they would not be offended if they were called by these names. However, they all agreed they would be insulted if someone called them *senza documenti* or *clandestino*. Finally, after watching clip one in the original English language they discovered that *mangia maccheroni* and *impasta pizza* were the TT versions of the ST slur 'wop'. As noted above (see Table 7.1), one of the most common folk etymologies for 'wop' is 'without papers'. The irony was not lost on the students. It was also observed that, in the second clip, a number of racial expressions in the ST had been completely eliminated in the dubbed version.

From this small-scale survey, it appears that the perception of offensive language found in the ST is greatly reduced in the TT, where insults such as 'rice eater', 'maccheroni eater' and 'yellow muzzle' would raise a laugh in the native Italian speaker rather than cause offence. Furthermore, the omission of several racial references from sample two dilutes the impact of offensiveness and compromises the overall meaning of the scene.

9. Conclusion

The two exerpts from *Gran Torino* which have been analysed and the short sample questionnaire illustrate some of the cross-cultural considerations relevant to translating racial insults and taboo words. By using an interplay of analytical tools, the ST and TT have been compared in order to describe the translation strategies employed and to attempt an assessment of their validity. The first sample demonstrates that the meaning of certain expressions has been relayed through literal translations where there is direct correspondence, and dynamic equivalence (Nida 1964: 159) where there is not. For example, the TT solution *mangiamaccheroni* is clearly not a literal translation and neither does it contain any element of the semantic value of the ST 'wop'. However, the stereotype of Italians as pasta eaters could be a pragmatic equivalent in this situation even lending an element of humour. On the contrary, the literal translation of 'son of a bitch', which in the ST functions as an in-group marker, could create a dilemma of intentionality in the TT *figlio di puttana* has stronger connotations in the target culture and would be more likely to cause offence. In spite of this, the overall language transfer could be considered successful. The pragmatic functions of the ST have been met in the TT and although there are some semantic gaps, the intended humour of the ST has been maintained. A final consideration here concerns the question as to whether racial slurs would absolve the pragmatic function of establishing in-groups within the Italian linguaculture. Most forms of verbal abuse between male peers in the target culture tend to cast aspersions on masculinity rather than ethnic origin,[7] whether in the form of ritual insults to signal solidarity (Allen and Burridge 2006: 87) or dysephemistic insults intended to cause offense.

The second sample presented more of a challenge both culturally and linguistically. Several factors contribute to creating a considerably flattened and neutralized TT. It is possible that the change in pragmatic mood has

---

7   For example *cornuto* [cuckold] and *finocchio* [fennel, an insult along the lines of 'ponce', 'faggot', or 'bugger'].

not been fully recognized and insufficient knowledge of ST lexicon could have lead to some expressions being ignored or omitted, while the dubbed speech prosody sometimes conveyed a different meaning from that of the original. These observations would imply that the translator perhaps underestimated the importance of racial content to the overall meaning of the scene and, indeed, in the text as a whole. By disregarding those culture-bound elements, whether for reasons of time constraint, commercial pressure, or purely by choice, the translator has consciously, or unconsciously, censored the TT, causing an impoverishment in lexical variety and shifts in semantic emphasis, at times imposing the target culture's ideologies on the ST. Consequently, the audience is prevented from achieving real understanding and deeper cultural awareness. What appears to be a small issue of a lexical kind, the question of translating racial slurs and ethnic epithets, relates to much larger issues of cultural identity, definition of in-groups and out-groups, and the way in which the boundaries between racism and taboo, the said and the unsaid become blurred or redefined in different cultures. If we consider one of the aims of translation as giving access to another culture, would it not make sense to consider 'abusive' techniques even in dubbing?[8] Should the dominant domesticating strategies adopted in Italian dubbing not be reviewed? Films and other audiovisual materials are by far the most powerful means of mass communication in today's multi-ethnic, global society and translation plays a fundamental role in disseminating stereotypes and in understanding the Other. Racial insults represent one of the thorniest issues in meaning transfer that goes beyond the scope of translation in the narrowest sense to embrace transversal themes such as cross-cultural aspects of race talk and the interpretation of political correctness in different linguacultures.

---

8   For a discussion on abusive techniques in subtitling, see Nornes (2004).

Bibliography

Adia and Jessie, "'Gran Torino," White Masculinity and Racism', Racism Review <http://www.racismreview.com/blog/2009/01/17/gran-torino-white-masculinity-racism> accessed 14 October 2012.

Allan, Keith, and Kate Burridge, *Forbidden Words: Taboo and the Censoring of Language* (Cambridge: Cambridge University Press, 2006).

Asim, Jabari, *The N Word: Who Can Say it, Who Shouldn't and Why* (New York: Houghton Mifflin Company, 2007).

Azzaro, Gabriele, 'Insultare l'altro sugli schermi anglo-americani', in Paola Nobili, ed., *Insulti e pregiudizi: Discriminazione etnica e turpiloquio in film, canzone e giornali* (Rome: Aracne, 2007), 71–127.

Bassnett, Susan, *Translation Studies* (London: Routledge, 1991).

Beccaria, Gian Luigi, *Per difesa e per amore: la lingua italiana oggi* (Milan: Garzanti, 2006).

Brown, Penelope, and Stephen C. Levinson, *Politeness. Some Universals in Language Usage* (Cambridge: Cambridge University Press, 1987).

'Eastwood Slams Politically Correct Culture', *Daily Express* (26 February 2009). <http://www.express.co.uk/posts/view/86571/Eastwood-slams-politically-correct-culture> accessed 24 January 2012.

De Mauro, Tullio, *Il dizionario della lingua italiana* (Turin: Paravia Bruno Mondadori, 2000).

Díaz Cintas, Jorge, and Aline Remael, *Audiovisual Translation: Subtitling* (Manchester: St Jerome, 2007).

——Anna Matamala, and Josélia Neves, eds, *New Insights into Audiovisual Translation and Media Accessibility* (Amsterdam: Rodopi, 2010).

Duane, Ashley, 'What is Racism? Racial Discourse and Racial Politics', *Critical Sociology*. 32 (2006), 255–74.

Dundes, Alan, 'A Study of Ethnic Slurs: The Jew and the Polack in the United States', *Journal of American Folklore*, 84 (1971), 186–203.

Express online, 'Eastwood Slams the "Politically Correct" Culture' (26 February 2009). <http://www.express.co.uk/posts/view/86571/Eastwood-slams-politically-correct-culture> accessed 24 January 2012.

Fairclough, Norman, *Analysing Discourse: Textual Analysis for Social Research* (London: Routledge, 2003).

Friedrich, Paul, 'Language, Ideology, and Political Economy', *American Anthropologist*, 91 (1989), 295–314.

Gorji, Mina, *Rude Britannia* (London: Routledge, 2007).

Goffman, Erving, 'On Face-work: An Analysis of Ritual Elements', *Social Interaction. Psychiatry: Interpersonal and Biological Processes*, 18/3 (1955), 213–31.

Green, Jonathan, *Green's Dictionary of Slang* (London: Chambers, 2010).

Hatim, Basil, and Ian Mason, *The Translator as Communicator* (London: Routledge, 1997).

House, Juliane, *Translation Quality Assessment: A Model Revisited* (Tubingen: Gunter Narr Verlag, 1997).

Hughes, Geoffrey, *An Encyclopedia of Swearing: The Social History of Oaths, Profanity, Foul Language, and Ethnic Slurs in the English-Speaking World* (London: M.E. Sharpe, 2006).

Kennedy, Randall, *Nigger, the Strange Career of a Troublesome Word* (New York: Pantheon, 2002).

Lotti, Gianfranco, *Dizionario degli insulti* (Milan: Orsa Maggiore, 1991).

Nida, Eugene, *Toward a Science of Translating* (Leiden: E.J. Brill, 1964).

Nobili, Paola, ed., *Insulti e pregiudizi: discriminazione etnica e turpiloquio in film, canzoni e giornali* (Rome: Aracne, 2007).

Nornes, Mark Abé, 'For an Abusive Subtitling', in Lawrence Venuti, ed., *The Translation Studies Reader* (London: Routledge, 2004), 447–69.

Paolinelli, Mario, and Eleonora Di Fortunato, *Tradurre per il doppiaggio: la trasposizione linguistica dell'audiovisivo* (Milan: Hoepli, 2005).

Pavesi, Maria, 'Usi del turpoloquio nella traduzione filmica', in Christopher Taylor and Giuliano Soria, eds, *Tradurre il cinema: atti del convegno* (Università degli studi di Trieste, 1996), 75–90.

——*La traduzione filmica: aspetti del parlato doppiato dall'inglese all'italiano* (Rome: Carocci, 2005).

Pedersen, Jan, 'When Do You Go for Benevolent Intervention? How Subtitlers Determine the Need for Cultural Mediation', in Jorge Díaz Cintas, Anna Matamala and Josélia Neves, eds, *New Insights into Audiovisual Translation and Media Accessibility* (Amsterdam: Rodopi, 2010), 67–80.

Polselli, Paola, 'Offese e altre forme di discriminazione all'italiana nei film', in Paola Nobili, ed., *Insulti e pregiudizi: discriminazione etnica e turpiloquio in film, canzoni e giornali* (Rome: Aracne, 2007), 129–76.

Racialslurdatabase, <http://www.rsdb.org> accessed 24 January 2012.

Rappaport, Leon, *Punchlines: The Case for Racial, Ethnic and Gender Humour*. Westport (CT: Greenwood Publishing, 2005).

Reisigl, Martin, and Ruth Wodak, *Discourse and Discrimination: Rhetorics of Racism and Anti-Semitism* (London: Routledge, 2001).

Scatasta, Gino 'Tradurre l'intraducibile. Il turpiloquio', in Romana Zacchi, and Massi-
miliano Morini, eds, *Tradurre l'inglese* (Milan: Bruno Mondadori, 2002), 96–102.

Schenk, Nick, *Gran Torino* (Los Angeles: Warner Bros., 2008).

Schrauf, Robert, and David Rubin, 'On the Bilingual's Two Sets of Memories', in
Robyn Fivush and Catherine Haden, eds., *Autobiographical Memory and the
Construction of a Narrative Self* (Mahwah, NJ: Lawrence Erlbaum Associates,
2003), 121–40.

Taylor, Christopher, 'In Defence of the Word: Subtitles as Conveyors of Meaning
and Guardians of Culture', in Rosa Maria Bollettieri Bonsinelli, Christine Heiss,
Marcello Soffritti and Silvia Bernardini, eds, *La traduzione multimediale. Quale
traduzione per quale testo?* (CLUEB, Bologna, 2000), 153–66.

Toury, Gideon, *Descriptive Translation Studies – and Beyond* (Amsterdam: John
Benjamins, 1995).

Van Dijk, Teun A., *Ideology: A Multidisciplinary Approach* (London: Sage, 1998).

—— 'The Study of Discourse: An Introduction', in Teun A. Van Dijk, ed., *Discourse
Studies* (London: Sage, 2007), xix–xlii.

Venuti, Lawrence, *The Translator's Invisibility: A History of Translation* (London:
Routledge, 1995/2008).

Wetherell, Margaret, and Jonathan Potter, *Mapping the Language of Racism; Discourse and the Legitimation of Exploitation* (New York: Columbia University
Press, 1992).

SERENELLA ZANOTTI

Racial stereotypes on screen: Dubbing strategies from past to present

1. Language varieties in film

1.1. Screen dialects

As Kozloff (2000: 82) explains, one of the main functions of dialect in film is characterization, as language varieties are used on screen 'to sketch in a character's past and cultural heritage, to locate each person in terms of his or her financial standing, education level, geographical background, or ethnic group', thus also contributing to the creation of effects relating to local colour and realism. There is a considerable difference and varying degrees of faithfulness in the filmic representation of dialects. The reasons for such variation are diverse. Departures from linguistic accuracy are often based on 'sheer practicality' (Wolfram and Schilling-Estes 2006: 343), as the need to produce immediately understandable dialogues undermines the possibility of detailed dialectal portrayal. Linguistic manipulation is also carried out to suit artistic purposes, especially when variation is essential to plot development.

Non-standard varieties in films, as well as in other cultural products, tend to be manipulated and stylized, their features being reduced to just a few, immediately recognizable markers. As Taavitsainen and Melchers (1999: 14) point out, this type of linguistic representation is fundamentally metonymic, in that a few (extreme) features are employed for marking a whole social or ethnic group. Neither consistency, nor accuracy is needed, since what really matters is for the non-standard language to 'be sufficiently marked for the audience to grasp that it is non-standard' (ibid.).

The term *screen dialects* has been introduced by Kozloff (2000: 82) to refer
to the immediately recognizable and clichéd non-standard varieties that
are used on screen. Script writers typically 'resort to using a restricted set
of grammatical and lexical features rather than attempting to use a comprehensive set of structures based upon dialectological study' (Wolfram
and Schilling-Estes 2006: 342). For this reason, film dialogue inevitably
lapses into stereotypes.

1.2. Dialect and stereotyping

Stereotyping is described as 'a set of "representational practices" that are used
to represent "difference" by reducing people to a few simplified, reductive
and essentialized features' (Hall 1997: 239). As Dyer (2002: 183) explains,
'stereotypes express particular definitions of reality, with concomitant evalu-
ations, which in turn relate to the disposition of power within society'. As
distinct from social types, that postulate inclusion, social stereotypes are
indicative of exclusion, in so far as they represent those who are outside
a society. In terms of linguistic practice, stereotypes invoke connections
between linguistic and non-linguistic characteristics (Hudson 1980: 213 ff).
They can be defined as 'popular, but imprecise characterizations of speech
as used by social groups', consisting of 'structured and reduced bundles of
markers' (Kristiansen 2001: 132). Every language develops a stock of stereotypical features for the representation of non-standard varieties, which
is part of inherited knowledge. Moreover, each stereotypical variety has
set connotations, which can be more or less negative.

Film has always used linguistic stereotyping as a means for quick
characterization (Grant 2004: 5), often resorting to linguistic features to
generalize the negative characteristics of whole social or ethnic groups.
As Kozloff (2000: 82) argues, 'the film industry has exacerbated negative
stereotypes, and instead of being sensitive to the accuracy of non-standard
dialects, movies have historically exploited them to represent characters
as silly, quaint, or stupid'. Negative linguistic stereotyping participates in
what Lippi-Green (1997) has described as 'the language subordination
process'. According to this model, 'the speech of a socially subordinate

group will be interpreted as linguistically inadequate by comparison with that of the socially dominant group' (Wolfram and Schilling-Estes 2006: 7). Judged against standard language, non-standard accents and varieties are thus 'mystified', 'trivialized', 'vilified' and consequently 'marginalized' (Lippi-Green 1997: 68). It is important to note here that the process of language subordination targets 'not all language varieties, but only those which are emblematic of differences in race, ethnicity, homeland, or other social allegiances which have been found to be less than good enough' (ibid.: 240). As Hickey (2000: 58) explains, linguistic stereotyping results from a conscious manipulation of the prominent features of a language, 'largely to achieve some kind of comic effect'. Its function, thus, often seems to be complicated with irony, satire or parody. In their reliance on trivialization or humour, linguistic stereotypes do indeed demean the language and culture of whole groups of people. Moreover, stereotyping means that certain non-standard features are used as a 'basis for judging not only the content of the message, but also the character and intelligence of the messenger' (Lippi-Green 1997: 41).

2. Representational practices and race: The stereotyping of Blacks on screen

Language variation and stereotyping have been traditionally used in Hollywood films to epitomize racial difference, as demonstrated by 'the broad imitation of Black vernacular allotted to Uncle Tom and Mammy characters in countless American films' (Kozloff 2000: 82). It is true that racial and ethnic caricature is no cinematic invention; in this respect, motion pictures were heirs to minstrel shows – a popular form of entertainment for whites where blacks were portrayed 'in exaggerated, animated characterizations that reinforced prevailing stereotypes' (Ray 2009: 110), including their depiction as 'slow', 'ignorant', 'uneducated', and 'illiterate'. This style of ethnic portrayal was maintained and even extended in film. Movies such as *Uncle Tom's Cabin* (Harry A. Pollard, 1927), *The Birth of a Nation* (D.W. Griffith, 1915), *The Jazz Singer* (Alan Crosland, 1927), and *Gone with the Wind* (Victor Fleming, 1939) 'all dealt extensively with images of race and, for the most part, maintained stereotypic characterizations and themes that had already been established in minstrelsy' (Ray 2009: 110).

According to Bogle (2003), there were five basic stereotypes essential to the characterization of African Americans in film: toms, coons, tragic mulattoes, mammies, and the brutal black buck. They were all used 'for the same effect: to entertain by stressing Negro inferiority' (ibid.: 4). Quite interestingly, as Bogle (ibid.: 17) remarks, while typing affected all minorities in American films, 'no minority was so relentlessly or fiercely typed as the Black man'.

The linguistic counterpart of such typification was a highly marked, stereotypical version of African American speech, which had incorporated stereotypical features from blackface minstrelsy (Green 2002: 202). As stated by Nesteby (in Green 2002: 202), 'Afro-Americans, regardless of class or educational distinctions, were most often expected to speak the least sophisticated forms of black English' and in such a way that was comical to Anglo-American audiences. No matter what their provenance and education, Black actors had to school themselves 'in the slow-and-easy backwoods accent compulsory for every black servant' (Bogle 2003: 63).

As illustrated by Green (2002: 202–4), the linguistic markers of blackness in early mainstream Hollywood films were basically:

- generalization of third person marker -*s* (e.g. *I's, you's, we's*);
- *ain't* as general negator;
- double negation (e.g. 'he *ain't* got *no* three hundred dollars');
- completive *done* (e.g. 'after the buttermilk I *done put* on you all this winter');
- demonstrative *them* (e.g. '*I done put, them* freckles');
- levelling of past tense of verbs (e.g. 'I ain't never *see'd*');
- regularization of reflexive forms (e.g. *hisself* for 'himself');
- pronunciation features such as /θ/ > /f/, /ð/ > /d/, and -*ng* /ŋ/ > /n/.

Early Hollywood films conveyed an image of linguistic segregation, with leading white characters speaking standard or close to standard English, and African American characters confined to speaking a socially and ethnically marked variety. Linguistic variation was thus emblematic not only of differences in race and ethnicity but also, and more importantly, of different power relations.

3. Dialect, race and stereotyping: The translational norms

Translating sociolinguistic variation is a much debated issue among translation scholars.[1] In line with Toury's (1995) law of growing standardization, translators are often tempted to neutralize social dialects for the sake of comprehension. However, as it is standardized in the target language, the ST dialect 'has the disadvantage of losing the special effect intended in the ST' (Hatim and Mason 1990: 41). Alternatively, a particular regional variety can be selected from the target language repertoire (Catford 1965: 87–8), but since its connotation may not be the same as the original, 'unintended effects' may be created (Hatim and Mason 1990: 41). Another possible option for the translator is to modify the standard itself, thus suggesting variation through the non-standard handling of grammar and lexis.

The literature suggests that equivalence should be established functionally: it is important first to 'evaluate the role of the dialectic occurrence' (Díaz Cintaz and Remael 2007:191) and then to operate according to the principle of functional variation. As Hatim and Mason (1990: 40, 43) suggest, the social implicature of the dialect should be relayed along with its discoursal force, so as to allow the speaker's social/linguistic 'stigma' to be brought out.

[1]   Among the recent studies that have tackled the problem of language varieties in film translation, see Assis Rosa (1999), Jäckel (2001), Armstrong (2004), Pavesi (2005), and Bruti (2009).

According to Pym (2000), before entering any discussion, it is first necessary to assess the nature and function of linguistic varieties in cultural products. Pym views the representation of linguistic varieties as oscillating between the poles of *authenticity* and *parody. Parody* consists in 'a functional representation of the variety, shorn to just a few stereotypical elements', the result of which 'is considered amusing' (ibid.: 70), whereas *authenticity* is the representation of a variety 'in so much detail, with such a wide range of finely nuanced accented features, local lexis and faintly non-standard syntax, that the linguistic result gives the impression of being authentic/ real' (ibid.). When confronted with the markers of a variety, the thing to be rendered is not so much the ST variety as 'the variation, the syntagmatic alteration of distance, the relative deviation from a textual or generic norm' (ibid.: 72). Target culture markers will thus be modulated according to the function of the variety in the ST, which will bend either towards authenticity or towards parody. As argued by Ramos Pinto (2006: 3), '[w]hen recreating linguistic varieties, the author, as well as the translator, resorts to sociolinguistic stereotypes which they know to be part of the public knowledge, i.e. those which are associated to a subcode easily understood by the public'. It therefore seems clear that the translator's decisions will be determined, not only by the function of the variety within the text, but also by preconceived notions. This seems especially true with texts where race and ethnic difference are indicated through language.

4. The racial Other in early dubbed films: Variation as racial stereotyping

A pidgin-like language was currently used in early Italian-dubbed Hollywood films to render the speech of African Americans. This type of linguistic portrayal concocted archetypal images of 'servitude, exoticism, and inferiority' (Squires 2009: 2) and clearly stemmed from racist thinking. Often employed in depicting non-white characters in general, it was especially associated with African slaves and servants. In addition, their speech was peppered with ludicrous and exaggerated pronunciations clearly intended to ridicule the speaker.

The dubbed film that proved particularly influential in this respect is *Gone with the Wind*. Released in the US in 1939, the film was first distributed in Italy in 1948 with interlingual subtitles, while the dubbed version was made available in 1950. The enormous success of the film equalled that of the translated novel, originally written by Margaret Mitchell in 1937. The Italian dubbing was clearly dependent on the translation strategies previously set for the novel, where the marking of African American characters' speech was achieved by resorting to a pidgin-like Italian made up of extended infinitives (e.g. *tu mangiare* [you to eat]), generalized third person markers (e.g. *io dice* [I says], *tu mette* [you puts]), and dropping of the definite article (e.g. *tenere scialle su spalle* [keep shawl on shoulders]). In passing from the written to the oral medium, the caricature present in the dialogue was increased by means of exaggerated phonology. Phonological markers were added, such as the voicing of unvoiced dental, plosive, and velar consonants (/t/ > /d/, /p/ > /b/, /k/ > /g/), which belonged to the range of stock features typical of twentieth century racist parodies. The following exchange between Scarlett and Mammie is quite emblematic:

MAMMY: Just *hol* on and suck in.
PRISSY: Mammy, here's Miss Scarlett's vittles.
SCARLETT: You can take that back. I won't eat a bite.
MAMMY: Oh, yes, *maam, you is*! *You's* gonna eat every mouthful of *dis*.
SCARLETT: No, I'm not! Put on the dress, because we're late already.
MAMMY: What's my lamb gonna wear?
SCARLETT: That.
MAMMY: No you *ain't*! You can't show your bosom before three o'clock. I'm gonna speak to your ma about you!
SCARLETT: If you say one word to Mother, I won't eat a bite!
MAMMY: Well ... Keep your shawl on. I *ain't aimin* for you to get all freckled after *de* buttermilk I *done put* on you all *dis* winter, bleaching *dem freckles*. Now, Miss Scarlett, you come on and be good, and eat just a little, honey.

MAMMY: *Reggere* forte. Non *respirare.* PRISSY: Mammy, la colazione di Miss *Rozella.* SCARLETT: Riportala in cucina. Non la voglio. MAMMY: Oh *zi*, tu *mangiare vino uldimo boggone, cabido?* SCARLETT: Ho detto non la voglio! Mettimi il vestito. È già tardi. MAMMY: *Ghe* vestito *ti mette?* SCARLETT: Quello. MAMMY: No, *guello* no! Essere *trobbo sgollato* per *pomeriggio.* Io *andare* dire tua madre! SCARLETT: Se tu lo dici alla mamma, non mangio affatto! MAMMY: Bene ... Però *tenere* scialle su spalle. *Su tua pelle tornare* lentiggini *ghe io fatto sbarire* con crema di latte *guesto* inverno. Ora *tua pelle* molto bianca. Ora Miss Rosella *tu stare buona, mangiare gualche cosa.*	[MAMMY: Hold on. Breathe not. PRISSY: Mammy, here's Miss Scarlett's vittles. SCARLETT: Take it back to the kitchen. I don't want it. MAMMY: Oh yez, you eat to last bite, understand? SCARLETT: I said I won't! Put on the dress. It's late already. MAMMY: What dress you wears? SCARLETT: That. MAMMY: No, not dat! It be too low-cut for afternoon. I go and tell your mother! SCARLETT: If you tell Mother, I won't eat at all! MAMMY: Well ... But keep shawl on shoulders. On your skin freckles come which I bleached with milk cream this winter. Now your skeen very white. Now Miss Scarlett you be good and eat something.]

The language deficit paradigm is also apparent in the dubbing of another legendary film, *Casablanca* (Michael Curtiz, 1942), which was first distributed in Italy in 1945. In the movie, Sam (Dooley Wilson) is 'little more than an updated combination of faithful servant and entertainer' (Bogle 2003:140). Even so, the relationship between him and Bogart crossed normal racial barriers and struck very close at what Bogle (ibid.) terms 'the movie's *huckfinn fixation*', whereby a disillusioned white hero who rebels against society enjoys the friendship of a black man. Sam's linguistic characterization is crafted accordingly, with linguistic markers reduced to just a few non-standard features that are not attributable to minstrelsy nor exclusively to African American English: namely, the use of *ain't* and the double negation (e.g. '*Ain't nothing* but trouble').

Quite interestingly, in the Italian dubbed version, Sam addresses Bogart as *padrone*, which translates as 'master' rather than 'boss'. This lexical choice is a sort of linguistic remainder of a whole film tradition which featured

African Americans solely in the archetypal role of servants. What is more, Sam is dubbed as speaking a non-native variety of the Italian language, characterized by a fictional foreign accent and incongruous syntax and lexis, which signal him as Other, as exemplified by the following exchange of dialogue:

SAM: Boss? ... Boss?

RICK: Yeah?

SAM: Boss, *ain't* you going to bed?

RICK: Not right now.

SAM: *Ain't* you planning to go to bed in the near future?

RICK: No.

SAM: I ain't sleepy either. [...] Please, boss, let's go. *Ain't nothing but trouble* for you here.

RICK: She's coming back. I know she's coming back.

SAM: We'll take the car and drive all night. We'll get drunk. We'll go fishing and stay away until she's gone.

RICK: Shut up and go home, will you?

SAM: No, sir. I'm staying right here.

SAM: Padrone? Padrone?	[SAM: Master? Master?
RICK: Che c'è?	RICK: What's up?
SAM: Non andate *nel letto*?	SAM: Are you not going to the bed?
RICK: Non ancora.	RICK: Not yet.
SAM: Ma presto, padrone, andrete *nel letto*? Non andrete mai *nel letto*?	SAM: But soon, master, will you go to the bed? Will you ever go to the bed?
RICK: No!	RICK: No!
SAM: E allora nemmeno io *nel letto*! [...] *Prego*, padrone, andiamo. Non porterà fortuna aspettare.	SAM: Then I too don't go to the bed! [...] Please, master, let's go. Waiting will bring no luck to you.
RICK: Lei verrà qui, lo so che verrà qui.	RICK: She is coming here. I know she is coming.
SAM: *Prendiamo auto*. Corriamo *tutta notte*. Ci ubriachiamo, andiamo a pescare, stiamo via finché *essa* è partita.	SAM: Let's take car and run all night. We'll get drunk. We'll go fishing. We'll stay away until she's gone.
RICK: Smettila e vattene, capito?	RICK: Shut up and go, OK?
SAM: No, no. *Proprio qui rimango*.	SAM: No, I won't. Right here I'm staying.]

Paradoxically, in a film where all the characters except Bogart and Sam speak English with a foreign accent, Sam is the only one who is dubbed as a foreigner, his racial Otherness thus being signalled and even over-emphasized through language. As the example above illustrates, translators' decisions can modify and even subvert the work's system and meaning. Translators participate in the ideological discourse of their culture, whose system of values they may consciously or unconsciously accept, contributing to their dissemination. As Friedman (1991: 353) observes, films 'are an enormous repository of explicit and implicit information about the projected and perceived racial, ethnic, and cultural identities of individuals and groups'. Therefore, the impact of dubbing translators' choices as regards racial representation cannot be underestimated. Films can be 'powerful perpetrators of stereotypes' since 'stereotypical depictions become normalized through constant repetition within and across texts', thus resulting 'in a vicious circle of negative representation' (Bleichenbacher 2008: 32). Moving from the observation that 'film has been a chief player in race relations, or the lack there of' (Wallace 1993: 258), it seems all the more important to give proper consideration to the ideological implications of the linguistic choices of film translators.

SAM: Boss? ... Boss?
RICK: Yeah?
SAM: Boss, *ain't* you going to bed?
RICK: Not right now.
SAM: *Ain't* you planning to go to bed in the near future?
RICK: No.
SAM: I ain't sleepy either. ... Please, boss, let's go. *Ain't nothing but trouble* for you here.
RICK: She's coming back. I know she's coming back.
SAM: We'll take the car and drive all night. We'll get drunk. We'll go fishing and stay away until she's gone.
RICK: Shut up and go home, will you?
SAM: No, sir. I'm staying right here.

SAM: Padrone? Padrone?	[SAM: Master? Master?
RICK: Che c'è?	RICK: What's up?
SAM: Non andate *nel letto*?	SAM: Are you not going to the bed?
RICK: Non ancora.	RICK: Not yet.

SAM: Ma presto, padrone, andrete *nel letto*? Non andrete mai *nel letto*? RICK: No! SAM: E allora nemmeno io *nel letto*! ... *Prego*, padrone, andiamo. Non porterà fortuna aspettare. RICK: Lei verrà qui, lo so che verrà qui. SAM: *Prendiamo auto*. Corriamo *tutta notte*. Ci ubriachiamo, andiamo a pescare, stiamo via finché *essa* è partita. RICK: Smettila e vattene, capito? SAM: No, no. *Proprio qui rimango*.	SAM: But soon, master, will you go to the bed? Will you ever go to the bed? RICK: No! SAM: Then I too don't go to the bed! ... Please, master, let's go. Waiting will bring no luck to you. RICK: She is coming here. I know she is coming. SAM: Let's take car and run all night. We'll get drunk. We'll go fishing. We'll stay away until she's gone. RICK: Shut up and go, OK? SAM: No, I won't. Right here I'm staying.]

5. Standardizing Mammie: A non-racialized practice

In the cases analysed above, the principle of functional variation seems to be fulfilled in translation, since difference in speech among characters is indeed signified. It has been pointed out that the most common strategy in dubbing African American characters in the past was racial stereotyping, which nevertheless failed to account for complexity in characterization. This type of strategy, however, was gradually dismissed as the perception of race and racial difference changed. After the Civil Rights Movement, film portrayals of racial relations underwent substantial revision and film translators acted accordingly.

The strategy of neutralizing variation was chosen as more adequately representative of the speech of African American characters, even when the original dialogues displayed some dialectic markers. To illustrate this point, I will consider a later redubbed version of *Gone with the Wind*, which was commissioned by Paramount Pictures in 1977. The new dubbing, based on Roberto De Leonardis' translation and directed by Mario Maldesi, intended both to update the language and erase the overtly racist elements of the previous dubbed version. Openly criticized by both critics and audience (Morandini et al. 2009), the new version was never commercialized and only a few very rare copies have survived. The following example shows the alternative translation provided for the breakfast scene already analysed:

MAMMY: Just *hol* on and suck in.
PRISSY: Mammy, here's Miss Scarlett's vittles.
SCARLETT: You can take that back. I won't eat a bite.
MAMMY: Oh, yes, *maam, you is*! *You's* gonna eat every mouthful of *dis*.
SCARLETT: No, I'm not! Put on the dress, because we're late already.
MAMMY: What's my lamb gonna wear?
SCARLETT: That.
MAMMY: No you *ain't*! You can't show your bosom before three o'clock. I'm gonna speak to your ma about you!
SCARLETT: If you say one word to Mother, I won't eat a bite!
MAMMY: Well ... Keep your shawl on. I *ain't aimin* for you to get all freckled after *de* buttermilk I *done put* on you all *dis* winter, bleaching *dem freckles*. Now, Miss Scarlett, you come on and be good, and eat just a little, honey.

MAMMY: Ora reggiti forte. E trattieni bene il fiato.
PRISSY: Mammy, la colazione per Miss Rossella.
SCARLETT: Puoi portare tutto in cucina. Non mangerò un boccone.
MAMMY: Oh, sì che la mangerai. La mangerai senza lasciare niente.
SCARLETT: No che non la mangio! Mettimi il vestito. Siamo già in ritardo.
MAMMY: Quale vestito ti vuoi mettere?
SCARLETT: Quello.
MAMMY: Niente affatto! Non puoi stare col petto scoperto prima delle tre! Vado a dirlo a tua madre, adesso!
SCARLETT: Se dici una sola parola a mamma non mangio un boccone.
MAMMY: Beh ... Questo è il più bel vestito che hai, Miss Rossella. Tieni lo scialle sulle spalle. Non vorrai riempirti di lentiggini dopo tutto quel siero di latte che ti ho messo quest'inverno per mandarle via. Sono brutte. Oh, e adesso, Miss Rossella, deciditi a mangiare qualche cosa.

[MAMMY: Just hold on and suck in.
PRISSY: Mammy, here's Miss Scarlett's breakfast.
SCARLETT: You can take that back. I won't eat a bite.
MAMMY: Oh, yes, you will! You're gonna eat it all.
SCARLETT: No, I'm not! Put on the dress. We're late already.
MAMMY: What dress are you wearing?
SCARLETT: That.
MAMMY: No, you aren't! You can't show your bosom before three o'clock. I'm gonna speak to your mother!
SCARLETT: If you say one word to Mother, I won't eat a bite!
MAMMY: Well ... This is the nicest dress you have, Miss Scarlett. Keep your shawl on. You don't want to get all freckled after all the buttermilk I put on you all this winter to bleach those freckles. Now, Miss Scarlett, please eat something.]

In this version, Mammy is represented as speaking as standard a language as Scarlett does. Characterization is achieved via supra-segmental traits such as voice quality and intonation, with Anita Laurenzi beautifully imitating Hattie McDaniel's style. While in the earlier dubbing, linguistic variation had been translated by resorting to a target culture repertoreme, i.e. the stereotypical black slave speech, in the 1977 dubbing the non-standard variety spoken by the African American characters was standardized, as a consequence of the new, dignified perception of African American people. The negative ideological/sociolinguistic element was thus erased. Furthermore, the Mammy of the 1977 dubbed version stands out as a more realistic and dignified character, which suggests that the dubbed version also responded to an aesthetic demand for greater realism.

Since changing norms in dubbing are indicative of the changing systems of values, the 1977 redubbing of *Gone with the Wind* is to be regarded as the expression of a radical cultural revision. As Tymoczko (2007: 113) argues, translations are forms of representation and, like other representations, they 'are shaped by ideological discourses'. Like all cultural practices of representation, translations have the power of 'creating or constructing a tangible image of the culture represented' (ibid.: 114). The cases discussed above appear to indicate quite clearly that, if translations play a part in establishing and perpetuating stereotypes, they can equally contribute to deconstructing and marginalizing racialized discourses.

6.　Dubbing *Bamboozled*: Between racial stereotyping and new linguistic taboos

The alertness of translators in recognizing racist discourse is apparent in the contemporary practice of film translation. However, dealing with openly racist language today is far from being unproblematic. To examine this further, let us consider the Italian dubbing of the Spike Lee's film *Bamboozled* (2000). In this film, linguistic parody, buffooning and racial stereotyping are used with the intent to expose the subtleties of racism in media discourse. In the following stretches of dialogue, we see two coons in perfect minstrel style who coon and dance in blackface. Their speech is filled both with urban black slang and minstrel-like stereotypes, such as the invariant *be*, *dat*, *I is*, *you is*, *we is*, etc.:

– This here's my best friend Sleep'n Eat.
– This here's my best friend Mantan.
– And we are two real coons.
– We left the hustle and bustle of uptown Harlem ... to return to our roots. Our Alabammy home. That's right. *We is* countrified. *We is sho nuff* Bamas. Here come the Bamas. No more city slickers.
...
– *I seen* a lot of troubles lately.
– Oh? Well, *how be dat*?
– I don't know who I is.
– Well, I'll be a Alabama porch monkey's uncle.
– At least you know *who you is*.
...
– What? *You jivin*!
– *I ain't jivin*!
...
– Holy mackerel! Sleep'n Eat, that *sho is a whopper*!
– You said it, cousin.
– Or *is we*?

– Questo qui è il mio migliore amico Mangia e Dormi.	[– This here's my best friend Sleep'n Eat.
– E questo è il mio migliore amico Mantan.	– This here's my best friend Mantan.
– E noi siamo due veri bifolchi.	– And we are two real coons.
– Abbiamo lasciato il chiasso e il fracasso del nostro quartiere, Harlem ... er ritornare alle nostre radici.	– We left the hustle and bustle of our borough, Harlem ... to return to our roots.
– Per ritornare in Alabama! Perché noi siamo gente di campagna. Perché noi amiamo l'Alabama. Viva l'Alabama. Ne avevamo abbastanza della città.	– To return to Alabama! Because we are countrymen. Because we love Alabama. Long live Alabama! We had enough of the city.
...	...

– Ho avuto un sacco di pensieri in questi giorni.	– I've had worries lately.
– Oh, pensieri? Cosa ti è successo?	– Oh? Worries? What happened?
– È successo che non so chi sono io.	– The point is that I don't know who I am.
– Beh, io so che sono un morto di fame bifolco dell'Alabama.	– Well, I know I'm a half-starved coon from Alabama.
– Almeno tu lo sai chi sei.	– At least you know who you are.
...	...
– Cosa? Stai scherzando?	– What? Are you joking!
– No, non sto scherzando.	– No, I'm not joking!
...	...
– Uh! Porca paletta! Mangia e Dormi, è una storia sconvolgente!	– Uh! Oopsie daisy! Sleep and Eat, that is an upsetting story!
– Puoi dirlo forte cugino!	– You said it, cousin.
– Ma noi siamo cugini?	– But are we cousins?]

In line with current translational norms, neutralization is the translation strategy adopted in the Italian dubbing. In this case, however, the film makes explicit reference to openly racist representational practices of the past, which required the adoption of equivalent discoursal strategies in the target language. Inevitably, the levelling strategy adopted by the Italian dubbers results in a substantial loss of meaning. Linguistic parody and racial stereotyping are used in the film with specific intent: namely, to expose the subtleties of racism and, more specifically, to show African Americans how they 'allow themselves to be used by the media as buffoons who entertain mainstream America' (Green 2002: 206). Quite interestingly, in its lack of stereotypical racial markers, the Italian version seems to perform an unconscious act of repression of the racist discourse of the original, which paradoxically neutralizes its subversive potential.

7. Conclusion

The results deriving from this chronological study allow some considerations to be made on the way dubbing has elaborated, absorbed, come to terms with, and even repressed racist discourse and representational practices. As stated by Hudson (1980: 193), 'language is one of the most important factors by which social inequality is perpetuated from generation to generation'. As a domain where discursive practices are pivotal, the media have a special role in perpetuating racial stereotypes and in framing ethnic prejudice (van Dijk 1989). The issue of racial and ethnic representation in AVT should thus be considered with great attention, especially at a time when 'such blatant forms of verbal discrimination are generally found to be "politically incorrect" [and] much racist discourse directed at dominated ethnic group members tends to become more subtle and indirect' (Cashmore 2004: 352).

Bibliography

Armstrong, Nigel, 'Voicing *The Simpsons* from English into French: A Story of a Variable Success', *The Journal of Specialised Translation* 2 (2004), 97–109. <http://www.jostrans.org/issue02/art_armstrong.pdf> accessed 14 October 2012.
Assis Rosa, Alexandra, 'The Centre and the Edges. Linguistic Variation and Subtitling Pygmalion into Portuguese', in Jeroen Vandaele, ed., *Translation and the (Re)Location of Meaning. Selected Papers of the CETRA Research Seminars in Translation Studies* (Leuven: CETRA Publications, 1999), 317–18.
Bleichenbacher, Lukas. *Multilingualism in the Movies: Hollywood Characters and their Language Choices* (Franke Verlag: Tübingen, 2008).
Bogle, Donald, *Toms, Coons, Mulattoes, Mammies, & Bucks. An Interpretative History of Blacks in American Film* (New York: Continuum, 2003).
Bruti, Silvia, 'From the US to Rome Passing through Paris. Accents and Dialects in *The Aristocats* and Its Italian Dubbed Version', *inTRAlinea*, Special Issue: *The*

Translation of Dialects in Multimedia (2009), <http://www.intralinea.it/specials/dialectrans/eng_more.php?id=760_0_49_0> accessed 15 February 2011.

Cashmore, Ellis, *Encyclopedia of Race and Ethnic Studies* (London: Routledge, 2004).

Catford, John Cunnison, *A Linguistic Theory of Translation: An Essay in Applied Linguistics* (Oxford: Oxford University Press, 1965).

Díaz-Cintas, Jorge, and Aline Remael, *Audiovisual Translation: Subtitling* (Manchester: St. Jerome, 2007).

Dyer, Richard, *The Matter of Images: Essays on Representation* (London: Routledge, 2002).

Friedman, Lester, *Unspeakable Images: Ethnicity and the American Cinema* (Urbana: University of Illinois Press, 1991).

Grant, William, *Post-Soul Black Cinema: Discontinuities, Innovations, and Breakpoints. 1970–1995* (London: Routledge, 2004).

Green, Lisa, *African American English. A Linguistic Introduction* (Cambridge: Cambridge University Press, 2002)

Hall, Stuart, *Representation. Cultural Representations and Signifying Practices* (London: Sage, 1997).

Hatim, Basil, and Ian Mason, *Discourse and the Translator* (London: Routledge, 1990).

Hickey, Raymond 'Salience, Stigma and Standard', in Laura Wright, ed., *The Development of Standard English 1300–1800: Theories, Description, Conflicts* (Cambridge: Cambridge University Press, 2000), 57–72.

Hudson, Richard, *Sociolinguistics* (Cambridge: Cambridge University Press, 1980).

Jäckel, Anne, 'The Subtitling of *La Haine*: A Case Study', in Yves Gambier and Henrik Gottlieb, eds, *(Multi)Media Translation* (Amsterdam: John Benjamins, 2001), 223–35.

Kozloff, Sarah, *Overhearing Film Dialogue* (Berkeley/Los Angeles: University of California Press, 2000).

Kristiansen, Gitte, 'Social and Linguistic Stereotyping: A Cognitive Approach to Accents', *Estudios Ingleses de la Universidad Complutense* 9 (2001), 129–45.

Lippi-Green, Rosina, *English with an Accent. Language, Ideology, and Discrimination in the United States* (London: Routledge, 1997).

Mitchell, Margaret, *Via col vento* (trans. Ada Salvatore and Enrico Piceni) (Milan: Mondadori, 1937).

Morandini, Laura, Luisa Morandini and Morando Morandini, *Il Morandini. Dizionario dei Film* (Bolonia: Zanichelli, 2009).

Nesteby, James, *Black Images in American Films, 1896–1954* (Washington, DC: University Press of America, 1982).

Pavesi, Maria, *La traduzione filmica. Aspetti del parlato doppiato dall'inglese all'italiano* (Rome: Carocci, 2005).

Pym, Anthony, 'Translating Linguistic Variation: Parody and the Creation of Authenticity', in Miguel Ángel Vega and Rafael Martín-Gaitero, eds, *Traducción, metrópoli y diáspora* (Madrid: Universidad Complutense de Madrid, 2000), 69–75.

Ramos Pinto, Sara 'Theatrical Texts vs Subtitling. Linguistic Variation in a Polymedial Context', *MuTra 2006 – Audiovisual Translation Scenarios: Conference Proceedings*, <http://www.euroconferences.info/proceedings/2006_Proceedings/2006_Ramos_Pinto_Sara.pdf> accessed 15 February 2011.

Ray, George, B., *Language and Interracial Communication in the United States: Speaking in Black and White* (New York: Peter Lang, 2009).

Squires, Catherine, *African Americans and the Media* (Malden, MA: Polity, 2009).

Taavitsainen, Irma and Gunnel Melchers, 'Writing Non-Standard English: Introduction', in Irma Taavitsainen, Gunnel Melchers and Paivi Pahta, eds, *Writing in Nonstandard English* (Amsterdam: John Benjamins, 1999), 1–26.

Toury, Gideon, *Descriptive Translation Studies and Beyond* (Amsterdam: John Benjamins, 1995).

Tymoczko, Maria, *Enlarging Translation, Empowering Translators* (Manchester: St Jerome, 2007).

van Dijk, Teun, 'The Role of the Media in the Reproduction of Racism', in Ruth Wodak, ed., *Language, Power, and Ideology: Studies in Political Discourse* (Amsterdam: John Benjamins, 1989), 199–226.

Wallace, Michele, 'Race, Gender and Psychoanalysis in Forties Films', in Manthia Diawara ed., *Black American Cinema* (London: Routledge, 1993).

Wolfram, Walt, and Natalie Schilling-Estes, *American English: Dialects and Variation* (Malden, MA: Blackwell, 2006).

ELENA DI GIOVANNI

Italians and television: A comparative study of the reception of subtitling and voice-over

1. Introduction

Italy is traditionally considered a dubbing country, where the advent of sound in cinema was immediately followed by the setting up of what was to be a prosperous dubbing industry. The latter has been flourishing over the decades, with the Italian population becoming increasingly accustomed to watching foreign films and TV programmes in their mother tongue.

However, over the past decade, Italians have been increasingly exposed to subtitling, through DVDs, film festivals and television. While DVDs and festivals remain an option for Italian viewers, and are not necessarily part of their daily lives, the advent of subtitling through television comes as an interesting 'revolution' and deserves close consideration. If one of the main historical reasons behind the choice of dubbing as a preferred translation technique on a national level has, indeed, been the vast number of viewers and the ensuing possibility of absorbing the high production costs of dubbing, the onset and the first years of broadcasting for groups operating via satellite platforms have been characterized by economic uncertainty and limited budgets. This has led some broadcasting groups, such as Discovery International, to opt for subtitling as a localization strategy across Europe, dubbing countries included.

Despite the poor quality of the subtitles for fiction and non-fiction products which were distributed through the Sky package in Italy in the first years – and which could be ascribed to the lack of well-established subtitling practices – what is most interesting is that the increasing popularity of satellite channels and their programmes has generated a slow but steady trend towards 'increased domestication' as far as translation is concerned. As audiences grew in size and satellite channels saw their revenues boosted, subtitles started to be replaced by voice-over. This tendency has been growing over the past few years on a number of channels broadcasting non-fiction products, with voice-over becoming the norm at least for those channels, or documentary series, which command a fair share of the TV audience. Nonetheless, subtitling remains for channels and broadcasters, which either operate on small budgets or simply wish to remain faithful to this translation mode.

This study aims to explore the stated and unstated preferences of Italian viewers of non-fiction products on television, based on a survey carried out with forty individuals. Before discussing the results, the next two sections will outline the theoretical framework underpinning this experiment, and present an overview of the diachronic and empirical considerations on the habits of Italian viewers.

2. Television, genres and audiences

Television, although increasingly challenged by the ever-growing pervasiveness of the internet, is still the most widespread audiovisual medium, catering for and appealing to mass audiences worldwide. Nonetheless, the very advent of the internet together with the proliferation of new communication channels and entertainment forms have been introducing selectivity into the preference of audiovisual media. Although these preferences vary greatly from country to country, it seems undeniable that the younger generations are more and more inclined to look for entertainment and information in the virtual world (internet-based entertainment and information is particularly popular amongst the young) rather than through the more 'mature' media.

Audience preferences and media proliferation have been accompanied by increased specialization: audiovisual platforms and communication tools are now being generated with specific segments of the audience in mind and this orientation is often the key to success for the platform or tool itself.

Within this never-ending process of development, mature media like television have been confronted with the challenge of renewal and redefinition. Television seems to have developed along a twofold path, with broadcasters either accepting the specialization challenge, with the restructuring and creation of dedicated TV and radio channels, or maintaining their traditional format and appealing to broader, undifferentiated audiences.

The specialization challenge has given rise to a boom of TV channels, most of them made available to viewers as part of the packages provided by private broadcasters. This proliferation has, in turn, yielded a diversification of programmes and formats, in an attempt to meet the needs and tastes of specific sections of the TV viewing population, in terms of age, gender, education, personal interests, time available to watch television, etc. On the other hand, while developing their specialization policies, broadcasters have also embraced what could be defined as the 'simple appeal strategy'. In other words, they have tailored what is on offer by paying attention to maximum approachability and understanding, making their contents simple enough to be appreciated by large audiences. By the same token, the shift from subtitling to voice-over as a preferred translation mode has become increasingly accepted by most Italian viewers.

If TV audiences seem to be so pervasive, ordinary and tangible as to require no definition at all, research aiming to evaluate them, although prolific, has been mostly either ethnographic in nature, and therefore often limited in scope, or generally quantitative, i.e. confined to the counting of viewers for different channels, broadcasting times, genres and programmes. This is due to the fact that, TV audiences are extremely heterogenous and indeed difficult to analyse, especially as television content is mostly consumed within households, in private, thus not implying any socially determined act of sharing (Allen and Hill 2004: 462).

Moreover, the hard-to-grasp nature of television audiences is in line with the nature of the medium itself. As Krivaczek (1997: 25) points out:

> Profound though its social impact may be, television is really not a very intense medium. Unlike the cinema screen, which immerses its audience in a total sensory environment to the exclusion of nearly every other stimulus, the television screen is small, fuzzy, viewed in ordinary light among ordinary surroundings. The set is often not even intended to be the sole focus of attention in the environment.

Therefore, if television audiences and their response to different programmes are hard to evaluate for a number of reasons, mainly due to the idiosyncratic nature of the act of consumption, it seems that television itself, as a medium, encourages a somewhat loose, non-exclusive viewing attitude even when it comes to specialized contents. With reference to translated TV programmes and the case of Italy, this attitude is enhanced by the use of dubbing and voice-over as preferred modes of interlingual transfer. In virtue of their implying the superimposition of an oral, rather than a written, track to the original audiovisual text, neither technique requires any additional interpretive effort on the part of the audience, thus reinforcing the non-exclusive reception which is typical of television viewing.

A fuzzy medium, its hard-to-analyse audiences and the non-exclusive, somewhat loose reception of its contents seem to draw an extremely complex picture of television and its viewers, making them too difficult to be researched. Nonetheless, a number of important projects have been developed over the past few years, across Europe and beyond, to identify audiences for changing media, including television. Some of these projects have been supported by the European Union, mostly focusing on media convergence and its impact on audience composition and redefinition.[1]

With special reference to television, qualitative research on comsumption has also recently witnessed a renewed interest, with emphasis being placed on audience activity rather than passivity (Allen and Hill 2004: 462) and thus focusing on how viewers make meaning in their engagement with television in the context of everyday life.

This is also the aim of this study, namely the unveiling of the processes of meaning-making by Italian TV viewers faced with specialized television

---

1   See, for instance, the ARENA project developed within the Sixth Framework Programme: <http://cordis.europa.eu/fetch?CALLER=PROJ_ICT_TEMP&A CTION=D&DOC=31&CAT=PROJ&QUERY=012a395fe042:88b8:1a71c8b9& RCN=80629> or the Measurement of Interactive Audience project, promoted by The European Interactive Advertising Association and the Internet Advertising Bureau Europe: <http://www.warc.com/Content/News/European_Online_Industry_ Launches__Global_Audience_Measurement_Study.content?ID=694aa699–7280– 4c97-a785-fced122e70e0&q> accessed 20 June 2012.

content, which is made available through different translation techniques. The study yielded surprising results as to the actual understanding of audiovisual texts in translation, especially when the translation technique (voice-over) implies a non-exclusive reception, with the possible expectation of a lower level of comprehension on the part of the audience. However, before describing the actual experiment and its results, we shall briefly focus on documentaries, the audiovisual text type which is the object of this research, and on the impact they have had (and still have) in Italy.

3.   Documentaries and their reception

> Documentary is a form of storytelling. Documentary stories can be about anything: personal tales, accounts of history, predictions of the future, explanations, conflicts, cries of pain or shouts of joy; all share the quality of being stories, arrangements of events in time. And implicit in that quality is the natural response of the audience. Audiences follow stories. For them, the driving force of the story is the question: what happens next?
> — KRIVACZEK 1997: 24

Documentaries have been part of the broadcasters' repertoire for a very long time, traditionally covering a set of topics (sport, nature, science, history) and catering for selected sections of the viewing population. Over the last two decades, Europe and the rest of the world have witnessed an unprecedented growth in the distribution of these non-fiction products. Mostly created by multinational companies and aired by dedicated satellite channels, documentaries have become increasingly sophisticated but also cross-cultural, more structured and less culture-specific. Most significantly, their overall output and distribution have increased thanks to the surge in the variety of dedicated channels and the increasing appeal they exert on their audiences.

One of the reasons for the increasing popularity of specialized, non-fiction products like documentaries lies in their telling true stories and, whether contemporary or steeped in history, these stories meet the requirements of the viewers for further knowledge and real facts. These stories tend to be made accessible to all through the use of coherent structure and clear, catchy images to explain even the most obscure phenomena. Semantic clarity is ensured by the use of strategic language and most documentaries are produced with an international audience in mind, which implies the use of a *lingua franca*, namely Mid-Atlantic English (Luyken 2006).

Documentaries, therefore, seem to be the perfect embodiment of the specialization challenge undertaken by television. Focusing on specific issues, most commonly within the framework of a dedicated channel or series, they follow the 'simple appeal strategy', but they also satisfy the viewers' needs for stories (docudramas) and facts.

In Italy, as in many other countries, documentaries have traditionally been translated for voice-over. This technique, which, at least in Italy, was probably developed with this specific audiovisual genre in mind, allows viewers to hear the original soundtrack, both as a low-volume background track and at the beginning/end of each semantic unit. The retention of the original soundtrack means that the sense of authenticity which the viewers normally expect from, and implicitly attach to documentaries, is preserved, even though the representation of reality which they offer has been defined by several scholars (Orero 2006) as a hyperrealization of actuality. Indeed, retaining the audio of the original soundtrack means that the 'documentary value' of most texts which fall within this genre is preserved (Paolinelli and Di Fortunato 2004: 80), while it also binds the translation to a close adherence to the source text.

As documentaries have long been narrated by a few voices (and largely still are), they have been perfectly rendered through what is widely considered as a sort of simplified version of dubbing, which only requires one or two voices and no lip synchronization. Known as *oversound* by Italian audiovisual translation professionals, voice-over is listed alongside dubbing in the national contract for dubbing professionals,[2] although the fees for both translators and voice talents are lower than they are for dubbing.[3]

When thematic channels first appeared on satellite platforms, it was not without surprise that Italian TV viewers realized that subtitles had replaced voice-over as a translation mode. The partial return to voice-over, as a consequence of increased revenues and viewers, seems to have passed unnoticed, almost constituting a return to normality in terms of the viewing habits of Italian TV audiences. Nonetheless, subtitling has permanently entered the picture and is still being used for non-fiction programmes, even though it tends to be relegated to a marginal position whenever possible, within the context of television.

Besides the differences in production costs, subtitling requires a completely different attitude from viewers, which has not been the object of any investigation in Italy and will be partly profiled thanks to the analysis of the data obtained through our experiment.

4. Italian viewers, documentaries and their reception through different translation modes

> Audiences' different potential pleasures are channeled and disciplined by genres, which operate by producing recognition of the already known set of responses and rules of engagement. [The genre] is a means of constructing both the audience and the reading subject.
>
> — FISKE, 1993: 114

As Fiske puts it, potential audience satisfaction is disciplined by genre. And when audiovisual texts within one genre are translated, an additional

---

2   The latest contract for dubbing, approved by the Italian government, can be found on: <http://www.aidac.it/documenti/ccnl.pdf>.
3   This is due to the greater difficulty of producing lip-synchronized dubbing at all stages: translation, adaptation, and voicing.

disciplinatory role is played by well-known translation practices, themselves producing recognition (of the genre and the text).

As has been illustrated above, the engagement of the Italian TV viewer with documentaries has been traditionally shaped by voice-over. If exposed to a voiced-over documentary track, even in the absence of images, most Italian TV viewers would probably identify the text type and the genre without much difficulty. Thus, in a country like Italy, where documentaries and non-fiction programmes are mostly available through translation, audiences expect a specific translation mode, which in turn moulds their reception attitude. When a variation is introduced, audiences are forced to change their viewing habits and attitudes, but this does not occur without difficulties and explicit rejections.

4.1. The corpus

A variation in the translation mode applied is one of the findings which has emerged from the study presented in these pages.[4] Conceived as an experiment aiming to test the openly expressed preference and the actual audience's comprehension of audiovisual texts translated using the two different translation modes discussed above (subtitling and voice-over), first of all, the study involved recording numerous documentaries broadcast over a three-month period (May–June 2008) by various dedicated channels which form part of the Italian Sky package. A detailed analysis of over fifty documentaries, their content and structure, led to the identification of two which were very similar in nature and represented both translation modes: *The Hairy Bikers' Cookbook*,[5] broadcast with subtitles on RaiSat Gambero Rosso and *Orrori da gustare* [*Bizarre Foods with Andrew Zimmern*],[6] aired by Discovery Travel & Living with voice-over translation.

---

4   The study was designed and supervised by the author of this paper. The experiment was
     carried out by Eleonora Ferretti and reported in her MA dissertation in Multimedia
     Translation, submitted at the University of Macerata in November 2009.

5   *The Hairy Bikers' Cookbook* is a BBC production first aired in 2004 on BBC2.

6   *Bizarre Foods with Andrew Zimmern*, produced for the Travel Channel (USA), was
     first launched on 26 February 2007.

The Hairy Bikers' Cookbook is a documentary series which recounts the crazy culinary adventures of Dave Myers and Simon King. The episode which was selected for this study is the fifth episode in the second series, shot in the Mexican town of Oaxaca. *Orrori da gustare* is a documentary series which follows chef and journalist, Andrew Zimmern, on his travels around the world, in search of culinary secrets and recipes. As with *The Two Hairy Bikers*, Zimmern is interested in unknown, bizarre, often even gross food combinations and recipes. The episode selected for this experiment is the eleventh in the first series, filmed once again in the Mexican town of Oaxaca.

The two documentary episodes were broadcast in May 2008, within a fifteen-day span. After examining them thoroughly, two four-minute clips were selected: one with Italian subtitles and the other one with voice-over. The selection was made based on the similarity in structure and content of the two excerpts: both clips show the protagonists browsing the local food market and discussing the local traditions and dishes, singling out ingredients and occasionally addressing the locals for explanations. All forty participants were asked to watch both clips and fill out a questionnaire.

4.2. The participants

Within the framework of what was conceived as a qualitative, rather than quantitative survey, the research team involved in this project decided to test as wide a variety of Italian TV viewers as possible.

Forty participants were involved to this end: twenty males and twenty females. An equal ratio of males to females (ten plus ten) was selected for the two age groups that had been identified: eighteen to thirty-five and thirty-six to sixty years of age. In terms of education, skills and occupation, no condition was established for this experiment. On the contrary, an effort was made to ensure maximum variation in the personal profiles and characteristics of the participants. This was made possible by setting up the experiment in a public place: the reception area of a large holiday resort in central Italy. The balanced presence of males and females and the differences in terms of age, education, personal interests and backgrounds, helped ensure that the results could be taken as representative of the average

Italian TV viewer, although obviously on a limited scale. Interestingly, despite the variation in terms of individual features, the results of our research questions proved generally homogeneous.

4.3. The questionnaire

In order to obtain detailed information about the participants' preferences in terms of translation modes and to evaluate their perception/comprehension of the two clips, a questionnaire was administered before and after the viewing of each clip. The questionnaire consisted of four sections, all featuring both closed and open questions. Each section was administered at a different stage in the experiment, according to the outline illustrated below:

1. The first set of questions was presented to the participants before the viewing of the clips, with the aim of obtaining general information about the participants (age, sex, education, occupation, interests, knowledge of foreign languages) as well as of enquiring about their viewing habits and preferences. After filling in their personal details, participants were asked whether they preferred cinema or television, if they ever watched TV with subtitles, if their TV viewing included documentaries, and, if so, what genre and at what time of day. These four open questions required short replies and were meant to set the tone of the overall experiment, while also eliciting the participants' general preferences and viewing habits. They were followed by a fifth and final question for this section, which aimed to highlight their instinctive preference for voice-over or subtitling.

2. The second section comprised six questions: four multiple choice and two open. Participants were asked to complete this part immediately after watching the first of the two clips, namely the four-minute excerpt from *The Hairy Bikers* with Italian subtitles. The first five questions aimed to evaluate both their understanding of the verbal information relayed by the subtitles (1, 2 and 4) and their perception of the visual elements on screen (3 and 5). The final open question enquired about

the use of italics in the subtitles and its communicative function, a convention with which most participants proved not to be familiar.

3. The third part consisted of six questions: four closed and two of them open but requiring a very short reply (a number and a body part had to be filled in). Once again, this section had to be compiled immediately after viewing the second four-minute clip, taken from *Orrori da gustare* and voiced-over in Italian. For the purpose of the experiment, four of the six questions (1, 4, 5 and 6) aimed to test the overall understanding of the verbal information conveyed through the translation, whereas the remaining two (2 and 3) focused on the correct perception of important visual information.

4. After viewing the clips and providing answers to the first three sets of questions above, each participant was asked to make an additional effort by replying to a final group of six questions. These were all open and gave the participants the opportunity to reflect upon their experience. These questions and the answers provided by the participants will be analysed in detail in the following section. Questions are numbered from 1 to 4 or 6 for each section of the questionnaire, respectively referred to as 'a', 'b', 'c', and 'd'.

4.4. *The results*

The questionnaire, although fairly long and complex, was completed by all the participants. The overall effectiveness of this experiment is most probably due to the alternate presentation of clips and questions, as well as to the structure of the questionnaire itself, which aimed gradually to draw the participants towards the essence of the experiment. Replies to the first set of questions confirmed the variation in terms of the background and current occupation of all the participants, which ranged from students to bank managers, housewives and factory workers. As for the participants' personal interests, there was a major difference between men and women, with men listing sports among their personal interests, while for women reading was a priority. All women in the eighteen to thirty-five age group listed 'reading' among their hobbies, against a mere 20 per cent of the men.

Thirty per cent of the men in the thirty-six to sixty age group mentioned 'reading' as a preferred activity, whereas women's preference amounted to 70 per cent.

After the personal information, the first set of questions aimed at casting some light on the participants' viewing habits. When asked if they preferred cinema or television (1a), a general preference for television was expressed, particularly by men: in the eighteen to thirty-five age group, six out of ten men declared they preferred television, whereas only three women held this preference (the remaining seven selecting the cinema). In the thirty-six to sixty age group, 80 per cent of the men opted for television, whereas the women expressed an equal share of preferences (50 per cent for TV and 50 per cent for cinema). And if men are keener than women on watching television, they are also much more appreciative of documentaries. When asked 'do you ever watch documentaries?' twelve men out of twenty replied 'yes', whereas only six out of twenty women gave the same reply.

Moving onto the final question of this section (5a), which enquired about the participants' translation habits and preferences, each of them was given a very short presentation of the two translation modes which were going to be tested within the experiment. They were subsequently asked to express their preference for one or the other. As can be seen in Figure 9.1, an overall preference for voice-over clearly emerged from the results, with a significantly larger portion represented by participants aged thirty-six to sixty. This datum seems to prove that the younger generations are generally more inclined to accept subtitles, probably due to the increasing amount of subtitled audiovisual material which is currently available (see section 2). The replies to this question are also reflected, quite strikingly, in the content- and picture-based feedback provided by the participants.

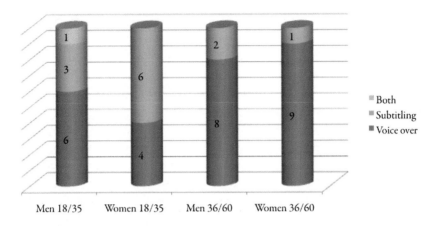

Figure 9.1 Replies to the question 'Which translation mode do you prefer?'

4.4.1. *THE HAIRY BIKERS* AND ITS RECEPTION THROUGH SUBTITLING

After viewing the first clip with subtitles, from *The Hairy Bikers' Cookbook*, the participants were asked to fill in the second part of the questionnaire. As with the third part, which immediately followed the viewing of the second clip, this section comprised both concept questions and picture-detail questions, aiming to test the comprehension of the verbal input and the actual intake of visual information on screen.

The first two concept questions, both closed,[7] scored an average 66 per cent of correct replies (65 per cent for the first and 67.5 per cent for the second). At first glance, it seems that the comprehension of the content relayed by the subtitles was not particularly high, with an average of fourteen individuals out of forty not responding correctly. When analysing the results with reference to the four age/gender groups involved, we

---

7   Question 1b: 'Oaxaca, one of Mexico's culinary capitals, is famous as the homeland of (1) Mescal, (2) Tamale, (3) Mole'. Question 2b: 'What is 'mole'? (1) A type of tortilla, (2) A spicy sauce made with cocoa, (3) A type of cheese'.

discovered that most of the correct answers were provided by the subjects who had expressed a preference for subtitling: 35 per cent of the eighteen-to thirty-five-year-olds replied correctly, followed by the second group of women (thirty-six- to sixty-year-olds) which scored 25 per cent. Men in the eighteen to thirty-five and thirty-six to sixty age groups scored 22 per cent and 18 per cent respectively. These data offer a number of interesting insights. Firstly, it seems that both men and women found it rather difficult to grasp some of the information provided in the subtitles; secondly, it seems that those individuals who had shown a greater acceptance of subtitles responded more positively to these first queries. We need to consider, however, that these two comprehension questions came at the very beginning of the viewing experiment, when the participants still had to become acquainted with the settings, the narration, the tone of voice of the two characters and the issue at stake in the excerpt, since the clip did not correspond to the opening sequence of the documentary episode.

Questions 3 and 5[8] in this section were based on the visual elements and aimed at evaluating whether they were perceived correctly by the forty participants. The first of the two was a closed question, while the second was open. The results are surprising: question 3 scored 80 per cent of correct replies, with thirty-two out of forty individuals selecting the third of the three options provided, whereas question 5 only registered 45 per cent of correct answers. This significant difference should be viewed in relation to the structure of the questions itself: an open question, enquiring about a rather small detail (the picture appearing on a bottle label), is normally more difficult to answer than a closed question about the action performed by one of the main characters. However, other aspects are equally worth considering: (1) the verbal sequence accompanying the images involved in question 3 was quick and complex, with a full two-line subtitle appearing at the same time as the two men eating cheese and talking; (2) while only 45 per cent of the participants provided the correct reply to question 5,

---

8   Question 3b: 'While one of the two hairy bikers explains what *mole* is, what is the other doing? (1) Tasting chocolate, (2) Listening and pointing to the *mole*, (3) Eating cheese'. Question 5b: 'What picture can be seen on the bottle of *Mescal Pechuga*?'

a considerable 47.5 per cent stated that they had not noticed *that* detail, which can be taken to imply that they had followed the visual sequence of information, but had simply neglected small details like the drawing on the bottle label.

Section 2 of the questionnaire ended with a meta-question (6b): participants were asked if they could tell why certain words and expressions in the subtitles were in italics. Interestingly, 77.5 per cent of them provided replies which were accepted as correct, stating that italics are used for foreign words, for local products in a language other than Italian, etc. Most of the individuals who replied correctly were in the eighteen to thirty-five age groups (32 per cent women and 27 per cent men). In general, women provided most of the correct replies to this and the other questions in this section (an average of 60 per cent women against 40 per cent men).

4.4.2. *ORRORI DA GUSTARE* AND ITS RECEPTION THROUGH VOICE-OVER

After viewing the voiced-over clip taken from *Orrori da gustare* participants were asked to respond to six more questions relating to this clip. The first (1c) was a closed concept question, aiming to test their understanding of one of the premises of the whole sequence.[9] Although the question was not particularly specific, the three options provided as possible replies were rather similar and implied an unequivocal understanding of the verbal information. 82.5 per cent of the participants selected the correct option, thus proving that voice-over is indeed easy to perceive and process for the (Italian) brain.

The following two questions (2c and 3c) aimed to test perception of the visual information accompanying the voiced-over track. The first question was open, asking participants to state the correct number of pots of ground coffee which were shown by the guide featured in the sequence. Thirty-nine out of forty individuals provided the right number (3), amounting to an

---

9   Question 1c: 'What kind of specialties can we find in Oaxaca? (1) Colonial dishes, (2) Pre-colonial dishes, (3) Post-colonial dishes'.

impressive 97.5 per cent. This was followed by a second open question,[10] the replies to which were once again generally accurate: 85 per cent of the respondents rightly stated that the women featured in the clip were carrying food trays on their heads, confirming that the visual intake of information is largely accurate when the text is rendered through voice-over.

The following three concept questions,[11] all of them closed, once again yielded generally positive results. Question 4c in this section scored 75 per cent correct replies, with a slight majority of women respondents replying correctly (54 per cent against 46 per cent of men), all of them belonging to the eighteen to thirty-five age group. Question 5c scored an even higher percentage of accurate replies: 90 per cent of the participants (thirty-six out of forty) replied correctly, thus confirming that the verbal information conveyed by voice-over rather than subtitling is more easily grasped by Italian viewers, even when it comes to small details and foreign names or words. The final question in this section (6c) obtained a lower percentage of correct replies: 67.5 per cent of the respondents were able to state that *tlayuda* is a type of tortilla. However, a comparison of the results obtained for the concept questions in this and the previous section of the questionnaire undoubtedly point to a higher accuracy in the replies for the voiced-over rather than the subtitled excerpt.

4.4.3.   SUMMING UP: REACTIONS TO THE EXPERIMENT
AND THE EXPRESSION OF PERSONAL PREFERENCES

The fourth and final section of the questionnaire aimed at eliciting the participants' overt feedback on their reception and comprehension of the two clips. By way of conclusion to the experiment, participants were first

---

10   Question 3c: 'Several women can be seen carrying trays full of food. How do they carry these trays?'

11   Question 4c: 'What is the classification of cocoa (first, second, third choice) due to? (1) The addition of cereals, (2) The cocoa-sugar ratio, (3) The type of chocolate used'. Question 5c: 'What original indigenous dish does Andrew Zimmern get to taste in the clip? (1) Tamale, (2) Tortilla, (3) Gusanitos'. Question 6c: 'What is *Tlayuda*? (1) A type of pepper, (2) A type of tortilla, (3) A type of worm'.

of all asked to comment on their experience: when asked whether they had found the first (subtitled) or the second (voiced-over) clip easier to follow (question 1d), 85 per cent of them firmly opted for the second. As for the remaining 15 per cent, the majority (12.5 per cent) selected the first clip, whereas only one person (2.5 per cent) said it had made no difference. Once again, the eighteen to thirty-five age group proved more 'flexible', with three out of ten opting for the subtitled clip and one stating that both clips had been equally easy to understand.

All the participants were then asked to state whether they thought that it required an additional cognitive effort to process subtitles (2d). This question was clearly guided (they were not asked to state which of the two translation modes implied a greater effort), but the replies were nonetheless unequivocal: thirty-seven out of forty individuals responded that subtitles for them implied an additional cognitive effort.

Among the remaining questions within this final section, the most interesting in terms of its results is the very last one (6d). When asked which of the two translation modes better conveyed authenticity, 55 per cent of the participants opted for subtitles, 37.5 per cent for voice-over and 7.5 per cent stated that both techniques ensured authenticity in the reception of the audiovisual texts. These results are indeed surprising, especially if gauged against the commonly shared idea that one of the main advantages of subtitling lies in its leaving the original soundtrack untouched, thus enhancing authenticity. It seems evident that Italian TV viewers are so accustomed to dubbing and its siblings (i.e. voice-over) that they naturally find authenticity even in a re-voiced, non-authentic audio track. The suspension of linguistic disbelief discussed by Romero Fresco (2009), whereby viewers unconsciously accept dubbed dialogue as if it was authentic, seems to apply to all genres and to be valid for all audiences in dubbing countries. Accustomed to the thorough mediation of dubbing, viewers are happy 'to enjoy the diegetic experience and the genre effect' (Palencia Villa 2002, in Romero Fresco 2009: 68) over the search for true linguistic authenticity.

5. Discussion

The results of this study – the first of its kind to be based on Italian TV viewers concerning their reception of differently translated audiovisual texts – are revealing of audience attitudes, their change in taste and expectations but also, and perhaps more significantly, their overall adherence to the prevailing translation mode. This seems to be a common trend for other dubbing countries, where other translation techniques, although well-known, are still finding it hard to gain ground, especially for the most mature media and their ordinary consumption.

Admittedly limited in the number of participants involved, this study catered nonetheless for a fairly wide variety of Italians, in terms of age, gender, occupation and interests. These factors, along with the general homogeneity of the replies, allow us to venture that these results might be taken as representative of the habits, attitudes and preferences of Italian TV viewers.

One element which needs to be considered, however, is that the order of presentation of the two clips might have had a bearing on the results. Had the subtitled clip been presented after the voiced-over excerpt, and not been affected by a possible 'settling into the experiment' effect, the responses to the concept and picture-detail questions might have proved to be slightly more accurate. However, the effect described above, although not measurable, was probably reduced to a minimum by having a first set of questions administered before the viewing of the clips, as well as by the explanation which was provided by the test administrator (see section 4).

6. Conclusion

On the whole, it seems evident from the findings illustrated above that Italian TV viewers feel more comfortable with voice-over rather than subtitling when viewing documentaries. This attitude, which clearly emerges from the open questions eliciting their preferences, is also visible through the replies to both concept and picture-detail questions in the two central sections of the questionnaire. It should be noticed, however, that within the context of such a guided viewing experience, the non-exclusive, loose attitude to the reception of the voiced-over and dubbed audiovisual texts discussed above (see section 2) has been definitively excluded from the experiment. In other words, differently from the common viewing situation which sees the audience immersed in a multifarious context providing other stimuli besides the television programme, or perhaps engaged in other activities while also following it (since there is no need to constantly look at the screen), the experiment had all participants concentrating on the experiment only, looking attentively at the screen both in the presence and in the absence of subtitles. Moreover, their concentration is very likely to have been high and constant throughout the experiment, considering the limited duration of the clips.

Focusing on subtitles and their appreciation, the experiment confirmed that the younger generations, especially women, are generally more inclined to accept and appreciate subtitled programmes. This increased tolerance and appreciation is generally confirmed by the higher percentage of accurate replies from the younger participants to the concept and picture-detail questions on the subtitled clip. As to the higher proportion of women than men, who expressed their preference for subtitles, replies to one of the opening questions provide a highly plausible explanation: 100 per cent of the younger women selected reading as their hobby, against a mere 20 per cent of men (see section 4.4).

On the whole, it seems clear that further research is needed in the field of audience reception of differently translated audiovisual texts within specific countries, especially Italy. As media change, thus shaping the tastes and attitudes of viewers, a closer investigation of a particular audience's changing or unchanging preferences and reception skills could constitute the key angle in the search and re-search of quality in audiovisual translation.

Bibliography

Allen, Robert Clyde and Annette Hill, *The Television Studies Reader* (London: Rout-ledge, 2004).

BBC Broadcasting Research, *Spoken Translations and Subtitles in Documentaries*. Special report provided by the BBC Written Archives Centre (1985).

Fiske, John, *Television Culture* (London: Routledge, 1993).

Krivaczek, Paul, *Documentary for the Small Screen* (Oxford: Focal Press, 1997).

Luyken, Georg-Michael, 'Lecture given at the Summer School in Screen Translation', University of Bologna in Forlì (May 2006).

Orero, Pilar, 'Voice-over: A Case of Hyper-reality', *MuTra 2006 – Audiovisual Trans-lation Scenarios*, Conference Proceedings, <http://www.euroconferences.info/proceedings/2006_Proceedings/2006_Orero_Pilar.pdf> accessed 10 June 2012.

—— 'Voice-over in Audiovisual Translation', in Jorge Díaz Cintas and Gunilla Ander-man, eds, *Audiovisual Translation. Language Transfer on Screen* (Basingstoke: Palgrave Macmillan, 2009), 130–9.

Palencia Villa, Maria Rosa, *La influencia del doblaje audiovisual en la percepción de los personajes*, unpublished PhD Thesis (Barcelona: Universidad Autónoma de Barcelona, 2002).

Paolinelli, Mario, and Eleonora Di Fortunato, *Tradurre per il doppiaggio* (Milan: Hoepli, 2004).

Romero Fresco, Pablo 'Naturalness in the Spanish Dubbing Language: A Case of Not-so-close Friends', *Meta* 54/1 (2009), 49–72.

PART 2

New perspectives on media accessibility

NINA REVIERS

Audio description and translation studies: A functional text type analysis of the Dutch play *Wintervögelchen*

1. Introduction

Audiovisual translation (AVT) is concerned with rendering the media available to all. As a result, practices specifically concerned with media accessibility for the sensory impaired have come into being, an example of which is audio description (AD). Hyks (2005: 1) defines AD as 'a precise and succinct aural translation of the visual aspects of a live or filmed performance, exhibition or sporting event for the benefit of visually impaired and blind people. The description is interwoven into the silent intervals between dialogue, sound effect or commentary'. Despite this definition calling AD a form of 'translation', and the many characteristics that AD shares with other AVT practices,[1] it remains unclear what place AD occupies within AVT and, particularly, within the wider field of Translation Studies (TS). The fact that AD translates the visual aspect of a text, whereas AVT has been defined by many as a translation of the verbal elements of an audiovisual text, raises the question as to what text type AD belongs, and how it can be related to other text types in (audiovisual) Translation Studies.

This paper aims to provide a tentative reply to this question, focusing on live AD for the theatre. It starts by discussing certain key text type

---

1   For more on the common characteristics of AVT practices, see Gambier (2004). Examples of common characteristics are: the interaction of several semiotic systems, the constraints of the medium and the specific needs of the target text receivers.

concepts derived from TS and their link to AVT. It then applies these text type concepts to a specific case, the Flemish theatre play *Wintervögelchen*, following an interdisciplinary approach that incorporates analysis methods derived from Theatre Semiotics. The focus of this semiotic analysis is to discover how the functions of the play are transferred from the audiovisual source text to the AD. Finally, the article discusses the extent of the findings for this case study.

2. Text types and AVT

Several authors have discussed the place occupied by AV texts in text typologies, although none of these studies specifically mentions AD. Reiss (1976) was among the first to include AV texts in a text typology specifically intended for the study of translation. She introduced a text type called 'audio medial texts', but later abandoned the term, because she concluded that AV texts were not a separate text type, but could fulfil one of the three text functions already defined in her typology: informative, expressive or operative (ibid.: 5–20). It was not until the late twentieth century that Nord (1997) began to emphasize the importance of nonverbal elements in texts, although she never mentioned AVT specifically. Proper research on AVT text types only began in earnest in the twenty first century. Based on Delabastita (1989), Zabalbeascoa (2001, 2008, 2010), for instance, has designed a typology for all text types, audiovisual as well as written, noting that all texts are defined by their medium, i.e. the presence (or absence) and interaction of four semiotic modes: (1) visual verbal, (2) visual nonverbal, (3) audio verbal and (4) audio nonverbal. In its turn, Zabalbeascoa's typology served as the point of departure for Sokoli's (2005) definition of the AV text type.

These approaches draw on two different criteria for classification: the communicative function and the medium. The former is indeed a valid criterion for classification, since it provides insight into the message conveyed by the text. On the other hand, typologies that use the medium as a starting point (Zabalbeascoa 2001, 2010; Sokoli 2005) seem especially appropriate for research on AD, since they address issues typical of multimodal texts. Although a description of any AV text type should include an analysis of both the communicative function and the medium, a third step is still required for a comprehensive analysis of the text type. Indeed, Zabalbeascoa (2001) argues that it is necessary to analyse the presence as well as the relative importance of the four semiotic modes of the medium, though he does not specify what determines the importance of a semiotic mode.[2] This paper regards communicative function as a possible determinant, since a mode is important to the extent that it contributes to conveying the function(s) of the text.

The analysis below is structured around the three concepts of text types mentioned in the previous paragraph. First, it examines the medium of the source text (ST). Then, it discusses the communicative function(s) of the ST. Finally, it assesses the medium-function relation. Before proceeding to the analysis, some more information on the method of how these text type concepts are studied in the case of stage plays and theatrical texts is offered in the following section.

3. Theatre Semiotics for AD

An interdisciplinary approach is required for the analysis of the above mentioned text type concepts in a theatre production. This is because the semiotic modes of theatrical texts and stage plays create an intricate web of meaning, whose deciphering involves a certain degree of personal interpretation.

---

2 Following Zabalbeascoa (2001), in this paper 'medium' is used to refer to the means by which a message is transmitted and the medium can consist of one or more 'modes', i.e. visual and verbal. The term 'mode' should not be confused with 'forms' or 'types' of (AV) translation.

Many AD guidelines stress that it is important not to provide personal views but rather objective descriptions in AD (Ofcom 2000), whereas others, like Elam (1980), claim that objectivity is not possible and, as a result, each AD would necessarily represent one possible interpretation among many. In this respect, Theatre Semiotics can provide a framework for deciphering the meaning of stage plays more objectively. According to this discipline, stage plays rely on six sets of (visual and aural) theatrical signs in order to tell a story or convey a message: (1) proxemic signs (spatial aspects, scenery, lighting and props); (2) kinesic signs (physique, gesticulation and facial expressions); (3) vestimentary signs (costumes); (4) dialogue and tone of voice; (5) music; and (6) sound effects (Pavis 1976; Elam 1980). The six groups of signs together form what is called the 'theatrical code', i.e. a system of rules and conventions used to mediate between actor and spectator in the interpretation of the message or function(s) of the play (Van den Dries 2001: 73). In order to interpret the functions, the manner in which the signs are used needs to be examined: whether they are icons and/or indexes, used in a connotative and/or denotative way. Denotative signs and icons generally refer to the storyline – what Pavis (1976) calls the 'narrativity' of the play. The connotative signs (especially the indexes) refer to the actual performance on stage – the 'theatrality' of the play.[3] A final important concept introduced by Elam (1980: 7) is the 'semiotization' of the theatrical sign: every element on stage is there for a reason and adds to the meaning of the play. In turn, each spectator assigns meaning to the theatrical signs, based on their own insights and background, which increases subjectivity in the interpretation of a play. To date, there is no single, well-defined model for semiotic analysis and the definitions of the above concepts sometimes vary.

---

3   The concepts 'index' and 'icon' are a complex matter and there is no consensus within
     Theatre Semiotics on how to define them. In brief, icons are used to represent objects
     or ideas, whilst indexes are used to refer to them. A short example: a paper crown as a
     prop on stage. As an icon, with a denotative function, it refers to 'a crown' in general
     but as a connotative icon, it refers to 'power'. As a denotative index it refers to 'this
     is a king', and as an index with a connotative function to the actual, paper crown
     one can see on stage. A more detailed account of these concepts can be found in the
     works of Pavis (1976), Kowzan (1976), Elam (1980), and Van den Dries (2001).

The theatre production examined in this chapter is called *Wintervögelchen*, and was created by Jan Decorte, one of Flanders' most renowned theatre makers. Active since the 1980s, Decorte is known for radically breaking away from traditional theatre and for challenging classical forms of representation. In his productions, Decorte performs multiple functions: he writes/adapts the text, conceptualizes and designs the setting and costumes, directs the production and takes part in it as one of the characters. Based on Shakespeare's *A Winter's Tale*, Decorte drastically revised the original play and reduced it to a sixty-minute performance. He also translated the script into a child-like, folkloristic variant of Dutch (Decorte 1991; Decreus 1996; Van den Dries 2001). *Wintervögelchen* was first performed in Brussels, in the autumn of 2008. The AD was performed live by the audio describers, Nina Reviers and Kristien Dubois, in February 2009 during a performance attended by a limited audience of ten visually impaired people at an Antwerp theatre.

4. Analysis of the visual mode

With respect to the proxemic signs in *Wintervögelchen*, they are minimalist and used in a rather unconventional way. The setting is atypical because the off-stage area is visible to the audience and, in the middle of the stage, there is an open wooden box with three walls (two on the sides, one in the back), in which the actors perform. When not performing, the actors sit on chairs placed to the left and to the right of the box, which then becomes the 'off-stage area' where the actors wait and get dressed, even though they are still visible to the audience. A speaker's desk is positioned at the front of the stage, between the wooden box and the audience, from where a narrator relates the story that is being re-enacted in the box. During the performance, the lighting alternates between this narrator and the action taking place in the wooden box. The stage is empty, except for the box, the chairs and a few props on the floor, whose main goal is to indicate which actor is playing which character (for example, a golden crown represents the king and a silver crown represents the queen). The props are not intended to look real, with the crowns made of cardboard and the beards attached with clearly visible strings.

As to the kinesic signs, some actors play several parts, and, conversely, some parts are performed by several actors; men playing women and women playing men. This strategy negates any reference to the actual physique and gender of the actors. What is more, all the actors wear identical, shapeless, blue costumes, which further reinforce the homogenization of the players. Other visual kinesic signs, such as gesticulation, facial expression and movement are generally kept to an absolute minimum, with actors barely gesticulating. When they do express emotion, their gestures are exaggerated and emphasized, as if puppets on a string. Their movements around the stage are similarly minimal and static and, most of the time, the actors stand still and keep a notable distance between each other, rarely touching. When they do touch, it is in a flamboyant and detached manner. Apart from these nonverbal visual signs, there is only one verbal visual sign in *Wintervögelchen*, in the form of the props used to identify the characters: wooden nametags around their necks. Each tag has one name written on the front and another name on the back so that actors can change roles merely by turning the nametag around.

In brief, the visual verbal and nonverbal signs in *Wintervögelchen* are minimalist and unreal – they do not provide any indication of time, place, historical or social context, nor do they bear any resemblance to an existing or fictional world.

5.   Analysis of the aural mode

As mentioned, Theatre Semiotics distinguishes three sets of aural signs: (1) dialogue and tone of voice, (2) music and (3) sound effects. As regards the dialogues in *Wintervögelchen*, these are prominent as the characters talk continuously and the story is conveyed largely through the many dialogue exchanges. In addition, there is a narrator, whose role consists of verbally tying the consecutive scenes together. The language used in the play also merits special attention and some theatre reviewers have described it as childlike. The director of the play also combines different Flemish regional dialects, uses uncomplicated vocabulary and invents words, whereas the actors speak with mistakes. Furthermore, the tone of voice and pronunciation of the actors – slow, emphatic and unnatural – reinforces the strange and artificial nature of the language. Some actors also manipulate their voices to imitate a dog barking or the sound of a horn, or to emphasize the type of character that they are playing (e.g. portraying a young girl and a man by raising and lowering their pitch respectively).

On the contrary, the presence of music and sound effects is limited. Firstly, the production features only two songs, one of which is a German composition with lyrics. The volume of both songs is remarkably high, which suggests an increased semiotic relevance, and while the German song is being played, no other action takes place. Secondly, sound effects are restricted to footsteps and the sound of costumes. Although the actors walk barefoot, the construction of the wooden box reinforces the sound of their footsteps and the plastic-like fabric of the costumes produces a clearly audible rustling sound.

Aural signs represented by the audio verbal mode are prominent in this performance, whereas the audio nonverbal mode is a little inferior in terms of presence.

6. Analysis of the interaction between modes

As discussed, Zabalbeascoa (2010) also underlines the importance of the interaction between the visual and the aural modes in any given text. The analysis of *Wintervögelchen* demonstrates a striking separation and lack of interaction between the visual and aural modes in the play. Indeed, the movements are minimal and the actions in the storyline (e.g. the king locking up his wife, someone dying) are not enacted on stage, and the actors simply render the dialogues that accompany the actions. This emphasis on the verbal mode is reinforced by the presence of the narrator, who links the scenes together by relating the story and the action from behind a pulpit. As a result, the verbal mode dominates and, generally speaking, there are few visual signs bearing a direct relation to what is being said.

There are instances where the following types of relation occur between the signs: (1) complementary, (2) contradictory and (3) redundant.[4] Most often, the relation is complementary, as in the case of the nametags, where there is a strong complementary relation between the visual verbal sign and the audio verbal sign, since without the visual sign it is impossible to know who is talking. In another scene, the audience is expected to finish an actor's sentence: based on the actor's body movement (towards the audience) and facial expression (an expectant look), the audience members realize that a response is expected from them. The histrionic sounds generated by the movements of the actors are another example. When the actors are not in the wooden box, they sit on the chairs next to it, and whenever they have to appear in a scene, they rise, take any necessary props and step into the wooden box. These movements produce audible sounds such as the ruffling of the costumes, the clinking of the iron wire from which the nametags hang around their necks, and their footsteps on the wooden floor. These sounds are complementary, although one could also argue that, in this case, sound and image are redundant, in that the footsteps are very clear and can be interpreted as someone walking, without actually having to see the action.

In other cases, the relation between the signs is contradictory. For example, some actors manipulate their voices, adapting their delivery to the character who is speaking (sometimes a woman speaks with a man's low pitch). Finally, in two scenes, there is a striking redundancy of the visual and the verbal modes. In one such scene, a girl dances round her lover and says *Ik dans rond u om u te bekoren* [I'm dancing round you to seduce you]. In the other scene, the character briefly stops screaming and explains to the audience that he is being eaten by an invisible bear – which the audience can already deduce from the actor's movements.

---

4   Zabalbeascoa (2010) distinguishes five relations in total, including incoherence and separability, which largely correspond with the four interactive relations described in Theatre Semiotics by Pavis (1976).

7. Analysis of the communicative function

The second step in describing an AV text is determining its communicative function(s). As mentioned before, Theatre Semiotics analyses the meaning and function of theatre plays by examining whether theatrical signs are used as icons or indexes, in a denotative or connotative manner. In *Wintervögelchen*, there is a preponderance of connotative indexical signs, because the setting and concept of the play do not refer to the real world or even to a fictional one. Instead, they only refer to the objects themselves and to the fact that they are not real. For instance, the wooden box offers no indication as to where the story is set and the costumes provide no hint as to who or what each character is. Even the movements and facial expressions are so artificial that they do not clearly refer to any particular emotion. Usually, emotions contribute to the storyline, explaining an actor's state of mind. Here, they are either too minimalist or too exaggerated, so that they mainly generate comic effect. In addition, the fact that all the actors wear the same nondescript costumes and play alternate genders erases any link between an actor's physique and his/her character. This is reinforced by the need of nametags, the only clue indicating who is who. In short, the aim of the visual signs is essentially to erase any possible iconic reference to a real or fictional world.

In the scenes that deliberately exploit redundancy between the aural and the visual signs, the connotative indexical function dominates as well. In the example of the dancing girl, by explaining what she is doing, she underscores the idea that, in theatre, all movements and actions are deliberately chosen, what is referred to as the semiotization of the theatrical sign. The aural signs are also connotative indexical, as they do not represent language as one would encounter it in the real world. However, the narrator's and the actors' words do have an iconic and denotative nature, because they relate the storyline (what actions take place, how characters react, and the like).

There are only a few clear icons and denotative indexes in *Wintervögelchen* – nametags, beards and crowns – that clarify which actor plays which character. However, these props are deliberately made to look fake. The crowns

are made of paper and resemble crowns worn by children at birthday parties and the beards are attached with visible strings and often fail to remain
in place. Therefore, the props, combined with the other visual signs, are a
constant reminder that the performance is 'only' theatre and their function
is more connotative indexical than iconic.

The preponderance of the connotative indexical signs means that, in
Wintervögelchen, there is an emphasis on what Pavis (1976) calls the 'theatrality' of the performance. The audience is constantly reminded that what
they are seeing is only a performance – a breaking of theatrical illusion.
This has two intended functions. First, the use of the signs is so unexpected
and often ridiculous that they generate a comic effect. Second, this usage
is intended to make the audience reflect on theatrical traditions, such as
how signs are used to help the audience imagine where and when the story
is set. To some extent, these two functions (humour and reflection) are
more important than the story behind *Wintervögelchen*; a point that is
illustrated by the limited presence of icons and denotative indexical signs
referring to the narrativity of the play.

8.   Analysis of the medium-function relation

The last step in the analysis of the AV text involves determining the relative
importance of the visual and aural modes in terms of their communicative
function. The analysis so far has paid attention to the relationship between
the functions and the different semiotic modes and has highlighted that
even though the visual signs are very limited and minimalist, they play a
crucial role in the emotive function (generating humour) and the evaluative function (reflecting on the nature of theatre). Some visual signs, such
as the nametags and the props, support the referential function although
their evaluative function is more important. By contrast, the aural signs,
such as dialogues and monologues, are very prominent and their unnatural
and comic use contributes, to a certain extent, to the evaluative and emotive functions. Nonetheless, their key role is referential, which, as has been
argued, is less relevant than the other functions.

Assessing the relationship that exists between function and medium sheds an interesting new light on *Wintervögelchen*. Whereas in terms of function the play was defined as having more aural than visual elements, it can now be defined, in terms of the importance of the modes, as a text type in which there are fewer aural than visual elements. This is so because the least important mode in terms of presence, the visual, turns out to be crucial when conveying the main text functions.

9. Relevance of the analysis for the AD text type

The findings of the analysis of the play *Wintervögelchen* are relevant to the AD of the play specifically, and to the AD text type in general. Some translation problems for the audio describer derive from the fact that the visual elements play a crucial role in conveying one of the most important functions of the play: humour. Therefore, the AD of *Wintervögelchen* will have to bear this function in mind if it is to be successful for the blind and visually impaired audience's comprehension of the play. One very important visual referential element is the nametags, which must obviously also be mentioned in the AD.

As the referential function of *Wintervögelchen* is conveyed by the verbal mode, the audio describer can conclude that this function is largely accessible to the visually impaired audience without adaptation. Yet, special attention must be paid to the scenes where there is interaction between the visual and aural signs in the ST, since this interaction is replaced by a new relation between the aural signs and the AD. The following examples illustrate how sounds were taken into account in the AD of the play:

1. The sound of the costumes is mentioned at the beginning of the AD so that the visually impaired can discern when an actor is leaving or entering the stage by following these sounds, which also applies to the sound of the footsteps in the wooden box. It is not necessary to refer to the movements in the AD, or only very briefly, as the visual and aural signs are redundant.

2. To allow the visually impaired to interpret the voices, the AD mentions when necessary that a woman is imitating a man's voice or vice versa.

3. The nametags are mentioned before a given actor speaks or enters the box, so as to clarify who the character speaking is.

These examples demonstrate that it is important to keep in mind the role of the visually rendered signs when writing the AD script, since they need to be transferred to the aural mode.

The analysis in this paper also raises questions on how to define the AD text type more generally. The definition proposed by Hyks (2005) is somewhat incomplete as it only refers to the actual descriptions written by the describer. However, AD is a multimodal text that combines both the descriptions delivered by the audio describer as well as the aural elements of the original ST (such as sounds and dialogue). This understanding of AD takes into account the importance of the sounds, specially when there is a complementary or redundant relationship between the modes.[5] The examples from *Wintervögelchen* illustrate that aural elements are important in the writing process of the AD script as well as during the actual performance of the AD, because the timing of the delivery must be in tune with the other sound elements of the ST.

Haig (2005) suggests that AD cannot recreate all the functions of the ST, due to the different nature of the aural and the visual mode. Although this appreciation requires further scrutiny, for now, let us look at this problem in *Wintervögelchen*. The evaluative function is intended to promote reflection on the use of the visual signs in theatre. In other words, the visual element of the play is the message of the play itself and when the verbal signs of the AD replace these visual signs, it is questionable whether this message can come across to the visually impaired. Will they actually reflect on the nature of the visual signs in the theatre if the signs are rendered to them verbally? This question is also valid for sighted people and

5   Other AVT scholars have discussed the implications of the interaction between visual and aural modes in AV texts, such as Remael (2001) on multimodal translation and Igareda (2012) on music in AV texts and AD.

for all artistic representations, from a painting to a circus performance, as not everybody appreciates Picasso, nor does everyone find clowns funny. Functions can be created in a play by combining the signs in a certain way, but their ultimate impact and effect on the audience cannot be accurately determined. The audience of *Wintervögelchen* is likely to notice and be surprised by the unusual use of signs, but whether this unconventionality elicits laughter and/or reflection on the nature of theatre depends on the audience's readiness and mood. Therefore, in AD the question is not whether one can recreate the same function or generate the intended effect, but rather whether one can transmit the central functions of the ST to blind and visually impaired audiences.

10. Conclusion

The aim of this paper was to look into the nature of AD. By combining certain key text type concepts derived from TS with a semiotic analysis of a specific theatre production, this paper hopes to have illustrated different aspects that are singular to the AD of a play and to have shown how the ST functions are transferred to the TT.

Generally speaking, AD has been identified as a multimodal text, containing audio verbal descriptions of ST visual elements as well as verbal and nonverbal aural elements of the ST. As such, it aims to make the TT accessible to a blind and visually impaired audience by transferring the functions from the original visual to the target audio verbal mode. The analysis has been carried out for one specific live theatre performance relating to a specific genre and the search for a general AD text typology would furnish material for further research.

The interdisciplinary analysis of *Wintervögelchen* has also uncovered certain problems and challenges for the audio describer. The importance of connotations in the play is one such instance. How does one objectively describe an abstract unnatural world with concrete vocabulary? How does one put visual humour into words?

From an analytical perspective, it is interesting to note that the study of key text type concepts such as 'medium' and 'communicative function', and concepts from Theatre Semiotics, can be used for problem identification in the process of describing a theatre performance. In this respect, AD research and traditional TS should aim for more interaction and integration between themselves and for more synergies with other disciplines.

Bibliography

Decorte, Jan, *Portrait de théâtre: 1985–1990* (Amsterdam: Bert Bakker, 1991).

Decreus, Freddy, 'Jan Decorte Regisseert King Lear: Dwarse Behandeling van het Klassieke Repertoire', in Rob Erenstein, ed., *Een Theatergeschiedenis der Nederlanden: Tien Eeuwen Drama en Theater in Nederland en Vlaanderen* (Amsterdam: Amsterdam University Press, 1996), 821–5.

Delabastita, Dirk, 'Translation and Mass-communication: Film and TV Translation as Evidence of Cultural Dynamics', *Babel* 35/4 (1989), 193–218.

Elam, Keir, *The Semiotics of Theatre and Drama* (London: Methuen, 1980).

Gambier, Yves, 'La traduction audiovisuelle: un genre en expansion', *Meta* 49/1 (2004), 1–11.

Haig, Raina 'Verbalising the Visual: the Construction of Meaning in Audiodescription' (2005), <http://rainahaig.com/index.php?id=60> accessed 12 October 2012.

Hyks, Veronika, 'Audio Description and Translation: Two Related but Different Skills', *Translating Today*, 4 (2005), 6–8.

Igareda, Paula, 'Lyrics against Images: Music and Audio Description', *MONTI: Multidisciplinary in Audiovisual Translation* 4 (2012), 233–54.

Kowzan, Tadeusz, ed., *Analyse sémiologique du spectacle théâtrales* (Université de Lyon II: Centre d'Etudes et de Recherches Théâtrale, 1976).

Nord, Christianne, *Translating as a Purposeful Activity: Functionalist Approaches Explained* (Manchester: St Jerome, 1997).

Ofcom, 'ITC Guidance on Standards for Audio Description' (2000) <http://www.ofcom.org.uk/static/archive/itc/itc_publications/codes_guidance/audio_description/index.asp.html> accessed 12 October 2012.

Pavis, Patrice, *Problèmes de sémiologie théâtrale* (Montréal: Les Presses de l'université de Québec, 1976).

Reiss, Katerina *Texttyp und Überzetzungmethode: der Operative Text* (Scriptor Verlag Kronberg/Ts, 1976).

Remael, Aline, 'Some Thoughts on the Study of Multimodal and Multimedia Translation', in Yves Gambier and Henrik Gottlieb, eds, *(Multi)Media Translation. Concepts, Practices and Research* (Amsterdam: John Benjamins, 2001), 13–22.

Sokoli, Stavroula, 'Temas de investigacion en traduccion audiovisual: la definicion del texto audiovisual', in Frederic Chaume, Laura Santamaria and Patrick Zabalbeascoa, eds, *La traducción audiovisual. Investigación, enseñanza y profesión* (Granada: Comares, 2005), 177–85.

Van den Dries, Luk, *Omtrent de Opvoering: Heiner Müller en Drie Decennia Theater in Vlaanderen* (Gent: Koninklijke Academie voor Taal- en Letterkunde, 2001).

Zabalbeascoa, Patrick, 'El texto audiovisual: factores semióticos y traducción', in John D. Sanderson, ed., *¡Doble o Nada! Actas de las I y II Jornadas de Doblaje y Subtitulación* (Alicante: Universidad de Alicante, 2001), 113–26.

——*Research in AVT: Some Insights and Proposals*, paper presented at the Subtitling Symposium *Mij niet gezien!* Ghent, 9 October 2008.

——'Translation in Constrained Communication and Entertainment', in Jorge Díaz-Cintas, Anna Matamala and Joselia Neves, eds, *New Insights into Audiovisual Translation and Media Accessibility* (Amsterdam: Rodopi, 2010), 25–40.

AGNIESZKA WALCZAK AND AGNIESZKA SZARKOWSKA

Text-to-speech audio description of educational materials for visually impaired children

1. Introduction

Audiovisual translation (AVT) is one of the branches of translation studies to have received considerable attention over the last two decades, and the recent flourishing of activity within the discipline is abundantly obvious. These days, rapid developments in the field of media access for people with sensory impairments can be observed throughout the world. One of the fastest growing modes is audio description (AD), which is becoming increasingly prominent as the needs of the visually disabled are beginning to receive more attention, both at European and international levels.

At present, blind and partially sighted people can access information and entertainment in many different ways. Some use modified printed materials, others use Braille. There is also the possibility of using audio information, usually recorded or delivered by another person who reads it out loud (Cryer and Home 2008: 5). However, technological progress has provided yet another alternative: synthetic speech. A wide range of applications, such as 'leisure devices' or 'devices which support independent living' (ibid.), highlight the benefits of synthetic speech for people with visual impairments. With new technological advances on the horizon, the quality of synthetic voices will probably improve in such a way that, in the near future, they may become almost natural sounding, and therefore a more viable and attractive option for accessing products with AD.

2. What is audio description?

Defined by some as 'a type of poetry' (Snyder 2008: 192) or 'the art to speak in images' (Navarette 1997: 70), AD is a spoken account of those visual aspects of a film which play a role in conveying the plot, including the action, the characters, their movements, the scenery and the costumes, to name but a few (Vercauteren 2007, ADI). AD can be provided for television programmes, feature films or websites, but apart from these, there is a large number of other events that can also be described, including theatre, opera, ballet, exhibitions, meetings, dance, tours, parades, circuses, fashion shows, sports events, and even funerals (Orero 2007). In this sense, AD could be considered as a cultural revolution for visually impaired audiences (Hernández-Bartolomé and Mendiluce Cabrera 2004: 267).

3. Audio description for children

As far as guidelines for children's programmes are concerned, there are several issues to be addressed when producing AD scripts (Palomo 2008; Orero 2011). What needs to be considered first and foremost is the type of language and the pace of delivery. As in the case of programmes for adults, sentences should not be complex, but short and simple. Due to short attention spans, young children find it difficult to absorb a lot of information at once. Therefore, descriptions prepared for them should not be wordy, but succinct and to the point (RNIB 2006). The emphasis should be placed on conveying the plot rather than providing the children with all the information they might miss. Vocabulary has to be adapted to suit the needs of the target group. Difficult words should not be used too often, because long passages containing expressions which a child does not know will make the programme hard to follow. Nonetheless, sophisticated vocabulary may sometimes add interest, so that it should not always be avoided. Rhymes, alliterations, and interesting sounding words are advisable as they help to keep the attention of a child (ibid.).

Bearing in mind the differences in age as well as in the background of the youngest viewers, sometimes a more intimate style may be more appropriate in comparison with programmes aimed at adults (Ofcom 2008: 31). Generally speaking, it is recommended that the descriptions should reflect the tone of the programme. Therefore, some productions may require a great deal of sensitivity on the part of the audio describers and other productions, especially those from Disney, will force them to reflect in their descriptions 'the cute aspect of the animations' (ITC 2000: 29).

Sound effects constitute an inseparable part of an audiovisual programme as they not only fulfil the function of entertainment, but also convey action. Young children enjoy listening to them and imitating them (RNIB 2006). The same is true with regard to songs and music. Some children, particularly those with complex needs, might have difficulty understanding a story but, nevertheless, might enjoy listening to a song (ibid.). For these reasons, it is very important not to describe over songs and to keep them intact whenever possible. Last but not least, one of the main functions of AD, both for young and adult viewers, is that it should not be off-putting, but associated with enjoyment and pleasure.

4. Why text-to-speech audio description?

Despite the growing number of audio described products which have been introduced into the market over the last two decades, the availability of AD in Polish still seems to be insufficient. Not enough audiovisual products for viewers with visual impairments are sold on DVD/Blu-ray, there is a limited number of cinema screenings with AD, and the small number of AD screenings are not within the reach of a large audience (Szarkowska 2011: 144). Considering that one of the greatest hurdles to increasing the availability of audio described programmes is the lengthy preparation process and high production costs, a new method of creating AD seems to be needed. One of the solutions that could greatly contribute to an increase in AD output is text-to-speech audio description (TTS AD).

The idea behind TTS AD is quite simple: the AD script is read out by speech synthesis software instead of a human voice talent. TTS systems use a special algorithm that represents rules for combining acoustic properties with pronunciation rules (Papadopoulos *et al.* 2009: 404), thanks to which the text input is converted into a speech waveform. Recent technological progress has significantly expanded the possibilities of producing an effect far more natural than that produced by synthesizers a few years ago (Szarkowska 2011: 144).

What follows is a description of the process of how TTS AD is prepared (Szarkowska 2011). First, the AD script needs to be created. Then, with the use of special software, the script is inserted into a film between the dialogue exchanges, cutting it into chunks to fit certain allocated timecodes. When the timecodes have been synchronized, the resulting text file is ready to be read by a speech synthesis system. If possible, it is advisable to consult with a visually impaired viewer while preparing the script.

In order to watch a film with TTS AD, a film player with a subtitle reader is required (see section 8.1). Read out by the speech synthesizer, the film player menu allows viewers to adjust the settings to their needs, so that it is possible to set the volume or the synthesizer's reading speed. Thanks to recent technological advances, viewers using TTS software can choose from among a variety of different voices. Since there is no single synthetic voice to satisfy all users, it is important for them to be able to select the one they consider to be the most appropriate. Such a variety of voices could also contribute to the readiness of the viewer to accept the TTS system more quickly. Another factor contributing to encouraging the use of speech synthesis software might include the possibility of having TTS AD recorded.[1]

---

1   See examples at: <http://www.youtube.com/user/AVTLAB> or <http://avt.ils. uw.edu.pl> accessed October 2012.

5. Text-to-speech audio description: Benefits and downsides

As with anything, TTS AD has its advantages and disadvantages. Its undoubted advantage is quick access to information for blind and partially sighted people at a fairly low cost. This is because the production of TTS AD, as opposed to conventional AD, does not involve studio recording or reading out of the AD script by an artist or voice talent. With regard to the costs incurred by TTS AD users, they do not seem to be excessive, especially in the case of those users who already have access to speech synthesis software at home, work or school (Szarkowska 2011: 146). Moreover, TTS AD can provide visually impaired spectators with an opportunity to watch audiovisual programmes by themselves, without the help of their sighted friends or family. From this perspective, TTS AD means greater independence.

When discussing the disadvantages of TTS AD, three main points should be made. Firstly, TTS AD requires media literacy, and therefore it excludes those persons with visual impairments who live 'outside modern high-tech information society' (ibid.). Secondly, although of reasonably high quality, TTS software still needs to undergo certain technical improvements if it is to be employed on a wider scale. Issues such as intonation and pronunciation should be addressed and worked on in the future in order for the synthetic voices to become more intelligible and more natural sounding. Thirdly, bearing in mind that in most cases viewing takes place at home, it may be perceived as an experience which does not promote inclusion or integration. In response to this argument, it has to be pointed out that TTS AD is meant to complement, not to replace, conventional AD. Its main goal is to supplement current practices and make AD more readily available for blind and partially sighted people.

6. Study material

An episode from the educational animation series *Il était une fois ... la vie* [*Once Upon a Time ... Life*], dubbed into Polish, will furnish the audio-visual material employed in this study. Directed by Albert Barillé, this programme was originally produced in France in 1987 and then aired in many different countries all over the world. The series is the third out of six seasons of the animation series.

One of the characteristics of the material is the combination of an entertaining storyline with a significant amount of factual information. Every episode tells a story of a different organ or system within the human body. There are, for instance, episodes devoted to the functions of the heart, brain, liver or kidneys as well as to the lymphatic and nervous systems. The episode chosen for the purpose of this study is entitled *Blood* and it is meant to be used as an educational tool in a science class in schools for visually impaired children.[2]

7. Challenges

Overall, the episode was quite well suited to AD, although certain problems were encountered in the process. Some of them were typical of any form of AD, whereas others stemmed from the specificity of the medium used to deliver the message to the audience, namely the speech synthesizer. The major difficulties were related to such matters as the use of terminology or the structure of the AD. Regarding the use of TTS software, the issues requiring special attention concerned phonetics, pronunciation and grammar, as well as the selection of an appropriate voice with which to read the AD script.

---

2   See Krejtz I. et al. (2012) and Krejtz K. et al. (2012) for a study on the application of TTS AD to the education of sighted children.

Taking into account the existing AD guidelines for children's programmes, it was decided that no complex vocabulary would be used in the TTS AD script. The abundance of specific terms and expressions already present in the film itself, such as 'mitosis', 'antibodies', 'interferons', 'granulocytes', 'lymphocytes' or 'macrophages', to name but a few, was another reason to avoid any additional complex words. After consultations with teachers from the schools for blind children where the study was carried out, it was decided to stick to the most basic terminology, such as 'red blood cells', 'white blood cells', 'platelets', because, for some children, especially those with visual impairments accompanied by additional disabilities, the film would be difficult to understand.

The problems connected with the structure of the AD were mainly caused by the limited amout of time available between dialogues for the descriptions to be inserted. In order to convey all the information which was deemed essential to understanding the plot, a certain strategy was needed. The first approach was to mention the characters' names[3] together with the activity in which they were involved, for example 'Professor Globus is talking with Hemo and Globin'. The second approach was to refer to the characters by their function and describe the activity which they were performing, for example 'macrophages are removing the waste of the body'. The third potential approach was to describe the action and the appearance of the characters with no indication of their functions, for instance 'red humanoids are carrying carbon dioxide bubbles in their back pouches'. Bearing in mind the educational role of the film as well as the time constraints, it was decided to name the characters according to their functions and to provide the viewers with a description of what was going on on the screen, for instance 'a white blood cell is sucking in the virus'.

Due to the specific nature of the terminology and the multitude of characters, it was thought that, before the screening of the episode, it would be helpful for the children to hear an audio introduction explaining the details connected with the characters' appearances and the functions which

3   The characters were supposed to have the same names as in *Sekrety ludzkiego ciała* [*The Secrets of the Human Body*], a book published in 1998 by DeAgostini to accompany the Polish version of the programme.

they perform. The idea behind the introduction was to keep it as informative as possible, but at the same time humorous, light and breezy in style. The descriptions concerning the functions of particular elements of the human body were constructed on the basis of comparisons with commonly known professions. The function of red blood cells was, for instance, compared to the work of deliverers or suppliers, white blood cells were called the human body's guards, and platelets were said to fulfil the same duties as plumbers. Since the vocabulary connected with diseases is rather military in character, its tone was also preserved here, the end result being the use of such words as *przyjaciele* [friends] vs. *wrogowie* [foes], *nieprzyjaciele* [enemies], *intruzi* [intruders], *patrol* [patrol], or *dowódca* [commander-in-chief] and verbs like *walczyć* [fight], *bronić* [defend], *atakować* [attack] or *pokonać* [defeat]. The text was constructed in such a way that every difficult or presumed new term appeared at least twice. All these actions were intended to make the film easily comprehensible and unambiguous for children because the issues it covered were deemed to be relatively complex.

Since Polish was the language of the text-to-speech software, the whole AD script was to be read out in compliance with Polish pronunciation rules. However, the speech synthesis system did not always follow these rules. For instance, in such words as *krwinka* [blood cell], *krwi* ([blood] in the genitive case) and *krwionośnych* ([blood-] relating to blood vessels), the consonant 'w' should become voiceless when pronounced. Unfortunately, it did not. In order for the speech synthesizer to read the above mentioned words correctly, in the TTS AD script they had to be changed into *krfinki*, *krfi* and *krfionośnych* respectively. The same happened to words where consonants in the final position had to be voiceless. Therefore, such words as *oraz* [and] or *wirusów* ([viruses] in the genitive case) were included in the script in the forms of *oras* and *wirusóf.*

There were also instances when it was necessary to transcribe the words in order for the speech synthesizer to read them in as natural a Polish as possible. This strategy was adopted when dealing with abbreviations, such as *HLA* (term defining a type of antigens) or *PSI* (name of one of the characters), which had to be rendered as *ha-el-a* and *pe-es-i* respectively. The same was done with foreign-sounding terms like *aparat Golgiego* ([Golgi apparatus]; an organelle found in most eukaryotic cells). In this case, it had to be rewritten in the TTS AD script as *aparat Goldrzjego.*

As to the selection of the appropriate voice used in order to deliver the AD text, it was decided to employ a female voice. This choice was mainly motivated by the fact that the majority of characters which appear in the film are male. Moreover, a voice over narrator informing the viewers about the functions of the blood at the beginning of the film is also provided by a male voice. It was thought that using yet another male AD voice on the top of a number of other male voices already present in the film could prove problematic for the audience to follow. Therefore, it was decided that a female voice would be less misleading to the viewers.

Having completed the preparation process of the TTS AD, it was time for a period of consultation with other viewers. Four sighted persons with qualifications in AD creation expressed their opinions concerning both the script and the introduction. The text also underwent medical consultation, as sometimes the abundance of complex processes touched upon by the episode was quite a challenge to describe. All the remarks were considered and the suggested changes were implemented into the final version of the script as well as into the introduction.

8. Research study

The chief objective of the present study was to examine the acceptability and reception of an educational animation programme with TTS AD by young visually impaired viewers. Thus, the research problems were the following:

1. How to create AD for an educational programme for young viewers.
2. How viable is text-to-speech software to read this type of AD.

The questionnaire completed after the screening was expected to show how this alternative delivery technique is perceived by visually impaired children and whether it suits their needs. It was also hoped to find out whether audio describing this type of film could be of any use for young viewers with visual impairments, and more importantly whether it could prove helpful in their school education and become an additional didactic tool.

What follows is a detailed description of the way in which the study was conducted with a brief account of the software used. Then, a presentation of participants is provided, and finally, the results of the study are discussed.

8.1. Procedure

The screening of the episode took place on different days in three schools for blind and partially sighted children in the following locations in Poland: Laski near Warsaw, Bydgoszcz and Krakow.

Before each screening began, the participants were informed about the procedure that would follow. They were told that they were going to watch the episode entitled *Blood*, from the educational animation series *Once Upon a Time… Life*, accompanied by TTS AD, and that after the screening, they would be asked to provide answers to the questionnaire concerning the content of the film as well as the synthetic voice employed to read the AD.

For the present study the freeware programme BESTplayer (version 2.0), together with the speech synthesizer Ivona Reader and a female Polish synthetic voice named Ewa (manufactured by Ivo Software) were used.

The responses of the participants were collected in three ways. Some preferred to have the questions read out to them by the persons conducting the study or by the teachers. Others chose to write their answers on their Braille writing machines. Some partially sighted children decided to fill in their questionnaires unaided, using large print questionnaire forms.

The first part of the questionnaire aimed to establish the participants' personal characteristics, such as gender, age, type (congenital or acquired) and degree of sight loss (blind or partially sighted). Then they were asked about their previous experience with audio described films as well as their familiarity with speech synthesis software. The second part of the questionnaire was meant to verify whether the respondents could answer any questions concerning the film's content after taking part in the screening. The last part of the questionnaire focused on determining whether the text of TTS AD was clear and intelligible to them, on gathering opinions on the use of the synthetic voice for reading the AD, and on the participants' eagerness to watch other episodes of the series with TTS AD.

A specially prepared questionnaire was also distributed among teachers in order to assess their views and opinions concerning TTS AD and its use in educational programmes intended for visually impaired children. The questionnaire was also designed to ascertain whether it would be possible for such programmes to be used in the future as additional didactic tools during science classes.

8.2. Questionnaire

Table 11.1 reproduces here the questionnaire distributed among young visually impaired viewers.

Table 11.1 Questionnaire

Questionnaire for the Film *'Once Upon A Time … Life'*
Text-to-Speech Audio Description

1. How old are you?

2. You are:
   ☐ a girl
   ☐ a boy

3. Choose the correct option describing your sight loss:
   ☐ I was born with no sight.
   ☐ I lost my sight as I grew up.

4. You are:
   ☐ a blind person
   ☐ a partially sighted person

5. Have you ever watched films with audio description before? (audio description is the additional account of what is happening on the screen, prepared specially for blind and partially sighted people)
   ☐ Yes
   ☐ No
   ☐ Don't know

6. Do you use speech synthesis software at home or at school?
    ☐ Yes
    ☐ No
    ☐ Don't know

7. What new information about blood have you learnt from the film?

8. Red blood cells circulate in your body. In the film, what did they carry in their back pouches?

9. What is the task of white blood cells?

10. Which character from the film did you like the most? Describe it.

11. Which character from the film did you like the least? Describe it.

12. The voice of the speech synthesizer was telling you what was happening on the screen. What was unclear to you in this description?

13. Did you like the voice of the speech synthesizer?
    ☐ Yes
    ☐ No
    ☐ Don't know

14. If you had a choice, which voice would you choose for use in this film?
    ☐ Woman's voice
    ☐ Man's voice
    ☐ Doesn't matter

15. The synthetic voice telling you what was happening on the screen was speaking:
    ☐ Clearly
    ☐ Clearly enough
    ☐ Not clearly
    ☐ Just right
    ☐ Too fast
    ☐ Too slow

16. Would you like to watch more episodes of the series with audio description read by the voice of the speech synthesizer?
    ☐ Yes
    ☐ No
    ☐ Don't know

8.3. Participants

A total of seventy-six children (thirty-five girls and forty-one boys) participated in the study. Of these:

- twenty-two (eight girls and fourteen boys) were pupils from the *Ośrodek Szkolno-Wychowawczy dla Dzieci Niewidomych im. Róży Czackiej* [Róża Czacka Educational Centre for Blind Children] in Laski;
- twenty-seven (eleven girls and sixteen boys) were from the *Specjalny Ośrodek Szkolno-Wychowawczy dla Dzieci i Młodzieży Niewidomej i Słabowidzącej im. L.Braille'a* [Louis Braille Special Educational Centre for Blind and Partially Sighted Children] in Bydgoszcz;
- twenty-seven (sixteen girls and eleven boys) were pupils at the *Specjalny Ośrodek Szkolno-Wychowawczy dla Dzieci Niewidomych i Słabowidzących* [Special Educational Centre for Blind and Partially Sighted Children] in Krakow.

The participants were between eight and seventeen years of age. Three respondents (4 per cent) were not able to state how old they were. Table 11.2 shows the number of participants according to their age.

Table 11.2 Participants by age

Age of participants	Participants	
	By number	By per cent
8 years old	1	1%
9 years old	2	3%
10 years old	7	9%
11 years old	9	12%
12 years old	15	20%
13 years old	10	13%
14 years old	13	17%

15 years old	10	13%
16 years old	5	7%
17 years old	1	1%
Not stated	3	4%
TOTAL	76	100%

With regard to the type of sight loss, out of the seventy-six participants, forty-three (57 per cent) were congenitally blind, nineteen (25 per cent) had an acquired sight loss and fourteen (18 per cent) were not able to specify. With respect to the respondents' visual status, thirty-two (42 per cent) were blind and forty-four (58 per cent) were partially sighted (see Table 11.3).

Table 11.3 Degree of sight loss of study participants

Degree of sight loss	Participants	
	By number	By per cent
Blind person	32	42%
Partially sighted person	44	58%
TOTAL	76	100%

It is worth mentioning here that in modern societies there are, in general, many more partially sighted people in comparison with people with no useful sight at all. Therefore, it was considered to be positive that in the study under analysis these numbers were not equal. Also, it must be pointed out that some participants had cognitive disabilities apart from those connected with visual impairments.

8.4. Results

Both the screening and the questionnaire were greeted with much enthusiasm by the children and also aroused a great deal of interest and curiosity among the teachers. As the aim was to find out how the text-to-speech delivery technique is perceived by young visually impaired viewers and whether audio describing this kind of programme could prove helpful in schools, the questionnaire that was administered after the screening had to be structured accordingly. An analysis of the participants' responses produced the following results.

The responses to the question: 'What new information did you learn from the film?' varied greatly. As many as eighteen participants did not answer the question and nine reported that there was no information which was new to them, while others mentioned that they had learnt about the properties of blood and its functions. Some example responses are listed below:

- 'I learnt how blood circulates round the body.' (Boy, 11 years old)
- 'Blood is needed to live. That was new to me.' (Boy, 12 years old)
- 'I didn't know that blood changes its colour.' (Girl, 12 years old)

The next two questions were aimed at eliciting detailed information concerning the content of the film. First, the participants were asked to state what the role of red blood cells is in the human body. The anticipated answers were that red blood cells carry oxygen, carbon dioxide, or both. The significant majority of respondents (almost 60 per cent) answered the question correctly. Out of the total seventy-six participants, twenty-three replied 'oxygen', eight said 'carbon dioxide' and fourteen enumerated both. Eleven persons (14 per cent) stated that they did not know or could not remember and nine (12 per cent) left the question unanswered.

To the next question, 'What is the role of white blood cells?', almost half the participants (42 per cent) provided the correct answer. Fourteen stated that white blood cells defend the human body against infection, bacteria or viruses, whilst twelve said that white blood cells kill, destroy, or fight with bacteria and viruses. Some children replied with answers such as:

- 'White blood cells tell red blood cells where to go.' (Girl, 10 years old)
- 'White blood cells swallow worms.' (Boy, 11 years old)
- 'White blood cells are responsible for keeping order in our body.' (Boy, 14 years old)

These answers were true according to the content of the film, and therefore also deemed correct. There were two participants who said that white blood cells perform the role of policemen or guardians in our body. Three participants were able not only to describe the role that white blood cells play, but also to enumerate all their different types (lymphocytes, granulocytes, and macrophages).

Fourteen persons (18 per cent) did not know or remember what the role of white blood cells was, whereas twenty-one (28 per cent) left a question mark or a gap in the space provided for the answer. A group of nine participants (12 per cent) gave an incorrect answer to the question, but in most cases this resulted from the fact that they confused white blood cells with red blood cells, reporting that the former were responsible for transporting oxygen in the human body. Table 11.4 summarizes the answers regarding content questions.

Table 11.4 Participants' responses with regard to content questions

Participants' answers	Content of the film			
	The role of red blood cells		The role of white blood cells	
	Number	Per cent	Number	Per cent
Correct	45	60%	32	42%
Don't know	11	14%	14	18%
No answer	9	12%	21	28%
Wrong	11	14%	9	12%
TOTAL	76	100%	76	100%

Such a wide range of answers came as a slight surprise since, when asked whether there was anything unclear in the AD script, the majority of respondents (approximately 70 per cent) said they had understood everything. Some participants commented on the synthesizer's reading speed, which they perceived as being too fast and too blurred. Others stated that the volume of the AD sound was too low, especially when there was loud music, and thus the AD was difficult to comprehend.

Concerning previous exposure to AD, as many as thirty-four respondents (45 per cent) said they had watched films with audio description before. Thirty-nine participants (51 per cent) reported that it was the first time they had had the opportunity to watch audio described films, and the remaining three (4 per cent) were not sure whether they had or not.

The findings of the study also show that many respondents had already had some exposure to synthetic speech. As seen in Table 11.5, forty-three participants (56 per cent) use speech synthesis software at home or at school, thirty-one (41 per cent) do not, and only two (3 per cent) are not sure:

Table 11.5 Participants' experience of synthetic speech

Do you use speech synthesis software at home or at school?	Participants' answers	
	By number	By per cent
Yes	43	56%
No	31	41%
Don't know	2	3%
TOTAL	76	100%

We then asked the participants whether they liked the voice used for delivering TTS AD in the film. A large majority (73 per cent) answered in the affirmative. Fifteen persons (20 per cent) said they did not like it, and five (7 per cent) were undecided (Table 11.6). The negative attitude towards the voice was then examined using different variables, such as its intelligibility, the synthesizer's reading speed, or the participant's degree of sight loss. It turned out that eleven out of the fifteen persons who did not like the voice, reported that they had had problems with understanding what the synthesizer said as, in their opinion, the reading rate was too fast and the text was blurred. Twelve said that they did not use speech synthesis software either at home or at school, out of which six said that they had had no prior experience either of audio described films or synthetic speech. Thirteen participants belonging to this group were partially sighted.

Table 11.6 Participants' opinions on the synthetic voice used

Did you like the voice of the speech synthesizer?	Participants	
	By number	By per cent
Yes	56	73%
No	15	20%
Don't know	5	7%
TOTAL	76	100%

Finally, respondents were asked whether they would like to watch other episodes of the series with AD. As seen in Table 11.7, the vast majority answered 'yes'. Eleven participants responded in the negative, and eight were not sure. Lack of support for the idea of producing AD to accompany the next episodes was mainly expressed by partially sighted persons (almost 73 per cent) and by those who do not use a speech synthesizer either at home or at school (also almost 73 per cent).

Table 11.7 Participants' desire to watch further episodes of the series

Would you like to watch more episodes of the series?	Participants' answers	
	By number	By per cent
Yes	57	75%
No	11	14%
Don't know	8	11%
TOTAL	76	100%

9. Discussion

The study aimed to determine how acceptable TTS AD used in educational films would be to blind and partially sighted children. The overall findings showed a wide range of opinions among respondents, and whilst some were enthusiastic about the idea, others felt that there were no potential benefits to be gained.

It was found that thirty-four children (around 45 per cent) had had some experience of AD. A large majority of them not only liked the voice (76 per cent), but also expressed a desire to watch further episodes with AD (71 per cent). Regarding the answers concerning the content of the film 59 per cent gave the correct answer to question number nine (the role of red blood cells) and 41 per cent to question number ten (the function of white blood cells). The results differed slightly with children for whom this was the first audio described film they had ever seen (51 per cent). Although most of them enjoyed the AD voice (around 72 per cent) and gave almost the same answers in terms of correctness as the previous group (59 per cent and 44 per cent for questions number nine and ten respectively), only five children (13 per cent) said that they would like to watch further episodes of the series using AD.

The acceptability of synthetic speech was also one of the major concerns of the research. A significant finding of the study was that more than half of the participants (around 57 per cent) had already had some experience in using TTS software. Those who declared that they use a speech synthesizer at home or at school were almost unanimous in expressing a desire to watch further AD episodes of the series (93 per cent). Their views on the synthetic voice employed in the film were also positive – 88 per cent enjoyed it. There were also many who, even unasked, provided information on which voices they use at home or at school and which they most prefer. The majority of children (almost 52 per cent), who declared that they had not used speech synthesis software either at home or at school, stated that they did not like the voice reading the AD script. As many as seventeen (55 per cent) out of thirty-one non-text-to-speech users stated that further episodes of the series would be of interest to them. As far as the correctness of the answers was concerned, the responses varied. In the case of TTS system users, correct responses to question nine amounted to 60 per cent and to question ten 47 per cent. Non-text-to-speech users fared less well, with 58 per cent and 35 per cent of correct answers to questions nine and ten respectively.

In view of the above, it can be assumed that the respondents' previous experience using synthetic speech might have a bearing on its acceptability. Those who had already watched films with AD or used speech synthesis software had a wider perspective on the issue and were able to make comparisons. They seemed to be more aware of their own expectations and were more critical. On the other hand, those who had had no previous experience of any audio described audiovisual products mostly enjoyed the film, although their answers concerning the question of the AD employed in the material under analysis, or the synthetic voice used, seemed to be of a rather general nature as they had no basis on which to make any comparisons.

When comparing the group of blind participants (42 per cent) with those who were partially sighted (58 per cent), the answers did not vary much in terms of correctness. In the case of the question on the role of red blood cells, partially sighted viewers performed slightly better than blind children – 59 per cent and 56 per cent of correct responses respectively. To the question concerning the function of white blood cells, the proportion of correct answers was the other way round – 47 per cent of correct responses provided by blind children and 36 per cent by partially sighted children. In terms of voice acceptance and the desire to watch further episodes of the series, the results differed widely. The group of blind participants almost unanimously stated that they both liked the voice and were eager to watch more episodes in the future (91 per cent in both cases). On the other hand, partially sighted viewers were not so keen to watch the series in the future (64 per cent). They did not express as many positive comments on the synthetic voice in comparison with the blind respondents. Only twenty-seven persons (61 per cent) out of forty-four said that they enjoyed it. This might be due to the fact that only 39 per cent of these viewers had had some experience with a text-to-speech system in the past, and only a few more – 43 per cent – said that they had watched audio described films before. As reported by the RNIB (2006), the acceptance of synthetic speech increases with increased exposure to it.

As far as the teachers' opinions on films with TTS AD was concerned, the majority stated that it was a good idea, particularly taking into consideration the simplicity of its use. Some teachers commented on such elements as the quality and speed of the reading voice, but this is considered to be a technical issue which could easily be overcome. When asked about the AD script, the feedback was mostly positive. It was perceived as easily comprehensible and helpful in understanding the content of the film. Regarding the advantages of audio described films, some teachers emphasized that they constituted a far more interesting and clear way of providing essential information to visually impaired children, while others said that they might have a motivating function in terms of learning. Most teachers stated that they had not used films with AD during their lessons, but almost all of them said that, if such films were available, they would definitely include them in their science courses.[4]

It is also worth mentioning that the episodes in the series under analysis were intended as additional didactic tools to be used in science classes in schools for blind and partially sighted children. They were designed to complement lessons and make them more enjoyable. However, it was not possible to achieve this aim fully during the study, as the structure of the school curriculum was not flexible and could not be adjusted to the term of the study. Nevertheless, in the case of those participants who had already covered the topic of blood properties and functions during their classes, the film turned out to be an enjoyable and entertaining form of revising and consolidating their knowledge.

It should be noted that conducting a study among visually impaired children was quite a challenging task. Firstly, a great deal of attention had to be paid to the appropriate construction of the questionnaire and, secondly, the questionnaire had to be properly distributed as most of the children were unable to answer the questions unaided. It required the additional help of teachers or volunteers who had agreed to assist the children taking part in the study. Another difficulty was the stress factor. Some children might have felt slightly uncomfortable when asked questions by unfamiliar people. Lastly, the extent to which the presence of the teacher might affect the children's answers had to be considered. Since this is extremely difficult to measure, it can only be assumed to have had some negative influence in this case.

---

4   In Poland, there are no educational programmes equipped with AD that could be used as additional didactic tools in schools for blind and partially sighted children.

The generally positive results of the study suggest that the use of TTS AD in educational animation films should be considered for future development. Although there is still room for improvement, the feedback from participants seems to provide the motivation for this. Among the comments elicited when conducting the questionnaire after the screening of the film, the following are definitely worth citing:

- 'I'd really like to watch more episodes. Up till now I have watched films without AD. My parents described the action of the film to me. But I prefer films with AD.' (Boy, 13 years old)
- 'I liked the voice and the series is really interesting. If there were more episodes, I would definitely like to watch them.' (Girl, 14 years old)
- 'I want to watch the next episodes, because thanks to them I have a better understanding of what is going on in my body and that is very interesting to me.' (Girl, 15 years old)

Some of the comments were related to the technical aspects of the film, while others touched upon the question of descriptions. All of them are worthy of note and should definitely be taken into consideration when preparing AD for further episodes in the future:

- 'I liked the film very much. There wasn't a single thing I didn't like. The quality could be worked on in the future. But technology progresses, so it won't be a problem.' (Boy, 16 years old)
- 'I'm very happy that there are films with AD. I think this one was faultless. If I didn't know this was a synthesizer, I would think a real person was reading the text. In general, good and clear AD.' (Girl, 13 years old)
- 'Descriptions were clear, I had no problems understanding them, but the intonation could be better.' (Girl, 14 years old)
- 'In general, I liked it. But sometimes the voice was too fast.' (Boy, 14 years old)
- 'The descriptions at the beginning were great!' (Girl, 14 years old)
- 'I liked the film. The descriptions were very interesting.' (Girl, 15 years old)

Although the study was conducted in different locations with a relatively big research sample (seventy-six respondents), its results are not fully representative of the overall population of blind and partially sighted children. Undoubtedly, the findings of the study show the immense potential for TTS AD, but further research still remains to be done.

10. Conclusion

The chief focus of this study was an examination of text-to-speech audio description in an educational animation series designed for visually impaired children. In general, the task was relatively demanding. It required a great deal of sensitivity and creativity on the part of the audio describer in the creation of the AD. It was even more challenging due to the fact that the audiovisual material chosen for the study was not a feature film, but an animation programme designed to enhance the learning process of children with visual impairments.

In general, the results of the study appear to be promising. The overall findings confirm the assumption that the animation series under analysis has the potential to become an educational tool for blind and partially sighted children. Since the majority of participants reported that they had gained new information after the screening of the film, which was in fact the actual intention, it is suggested that the series might be used as a complement to science classes, thus making them more enjoyable. Although the responses related to the use of speech synthesis software were varied, with some negative comments on the speed and intelligibility, a large majority of the participants liked the voice employed and said that they wanted to watch further episodes of the series. Indeed, both learners and teachers expressed enthusiasm for this initiative and its innovativeness.

It is thought that this experience might not only open up a new avenue of university research concerning accessibility, but also provide a possible accessibility mode with the potential for implementation on a wider scale.

It might prove to be a much cheaper and more time-efficient alternative to the traditional form of AD provided by human voices. It is also hoped that the findings of this study might contribute to future research concerning the use of AD in combination with synthetic speech by blind and partially sighted people, and particularly by visually impaired children.

Acknowledgements

We would like to thank the members of the AVT Lab research group from the University of Warsaw for their invaluable help with the preparation of the draft of the AD script and with distributing the questionnaires; the directors and teachers from the schools in Laski, Krakow and Bydgoszcz for allowing us to organize the screenings of the film; and finally, all the participants who agreed to share their thoughts concerning TTS AD with us.

Bibliography

ADI (Audio Description International), 'Guidelines for Audio Description' <http://www.acb.org/adp/guidelines.html> accessed 26 January 2012.

Cryer, Heather, and Sarah Home, 'Exploring the Use of Synthetic Speech by Blind and Partially Sighted People', *Literature Review* 2 (Birmingham: RNIB Centre for Accessible Information, 2008).

Hernández-Bartolomé, Ana Isabel, and Gustavo Mendiluce Cabrera, 'Audesc: Translating Images into Words for Spanish Visually Impaired People', *Meta* 49/2 (2004), 264–77.

'ITC Guidance on Standards for Audio Description' (2000) <http://www.itc.org.uk> accessed 26 January 2011.

Krejtz, Izabela, Agnieszka Szarkowska, Agnieszka Walczak, Krzysztof Krejtz and Zuzanna Kłyszejko, 'Guided Attention. Audio Description in Education'.

ETRA '12 Proceedings of the Symposium on Eye Tracking Research and Applications (2012), 99–106.

Krejtz, Krzysztof, Izabela Krejtz, Andrew Duchowski, Agnieszka Szarkowska and Agnieszka Walczak, 'Multimodal Learning with Audio Description: An Eye Tracking Study of Children's Gaze During a Visual Recognition Task', in *Proceedings of the ACM Symposium on Applied Perception (SAP '12)* (New York: ACM, 2012), 83–90.

López Vera, Juan Francisco, 'Translating Audio Description Scripts: The Way Forward? – Tentative First Stage Project Results', *MuTra 2006 Audio Visual Translation Scenarios: Conference Proceedings* (2006), 1–10.

Navarette, Fernando, 'Sistema AUDESC: el arte de hablar en imágenes', *Integración* 23 (1997), 70–82.

Ofcom, 'Code on Television Access Services' (2008) <http://www.ofcom.org.uk/tv/ifi/codes/ctas/ctas.pdf> accessed 26 January 2011.

Orero, Pilar, 'Sampling Audio Description in Europe', in Jorge Díaz Cintas, Pilar Orero and Aline Remael, eds, *Media for All. Subtitling for the Deaf, Audio Description, and Sign Language* (Amsterdam: Rodopi, 2007), 111–25.

—— 'Audio Description for Children: Once upon a Time there was a Different Audio Description for Characters', in Elena di Giovanni, ed., *Entre texto y receptor: Accesibilidad, doblaje y traducción* (Frankfurt: Peter Lang, 2011), 169–84.

Palomo, Alicia, 'Audio Description as Language Development and Language Learning for Blind and Visual Impaired children', in Rebecca Hyde Parker and Karla Guadarrama García, eds, *Thinking Translation: Perspectives from Within and Without* (Boca Raton: Brown Walker Press, 2008), 113–34.

Papadopoulos, Konstantinos, Athanasios Koutsoklenis, Evangelia Katemidou and Areti Okalidou, 'Perception of Synthetic and Natural Speech by Adults with Visual Impairments', *Journal of Visual Impairment and Blindness* 103/7 (2009), 403–14.

RNIB (Royal National Institute for the Blind), 'Audio Description for Children' (2006) <http://www.rnib.org.uk> *accessed 26 January 2011.*

Snyder, Joel, 'Audio Description: The Visual Made Verbal', in Jorge Díaz Cintas, ed., *The Didactics of Audiovisual Translation* (Amsterdam: John Benjamins, 2008), 191–8.

Szarkowska, Agnieszka, 'Text-to-speech Audio Description: Towards Wider Availability of AD', *The Journal of Specialised Translation* 15 (2011), 142–63.

Vercauteren, Gert, 'Towards a European Guideline for Audio Description', in Jorge Díaz Cintas, Pilar Orero and Aline Remael, eds, *Media for All. Subtitling for the Deaf, Audio Description, and Sign Language* (Amsterdam: Rodopi, 2007), 139–49.

ANIKA VERVECKEN

Surtitles: Types and functions

1. Audiovisual translation: New challenges

Audiovisual translation (AVT) was born out of the need to translate texts that are not merely written or spoken. Source texts in AVT are hybrids: art forms or new ways of communication that combine different semiotic systems. Translating these texts is not only about transposing meaning from one language to another. There are space and/or time limits as well as visual and/or auditory elements that have to be taken into account, and often the target text only fulfils it communicative function when combined with the source text (ST). These new challenges not only provide a reason for the existence of AVT studies, but they also define the different forms of AVT.

This paper begins by comparing the difficulties in producing surtitles with those posed by some related forms of AVT in an attempt to uncover the unique challenges that define surtitling. It then discusses the different types of surtitling available today, a typology based on the performance they accompany. The third chapter discusses the displays and the technology used to make surtitles visible. Finally, the different functions of surtitling are addressed.

2. Related types of AVT

2.1. Surtitling versus standard subtitling

The terminology surrounding titling may be confusing. The term 'surtitling' did not merely emerge because these titles are shown above the stage
during the live performances or events they translate. As the analysis in this
chapter illustrates, both terms refer to two distinct forms of AVT. Though
the etymology of the prefixes 'sub' and 'sur' is clear, in this article they do
not refer to the place where the titles are shown, but rather to specific sub-
disciplines of AVT. The term 'surtitles' thus refers to titles that accompany
live performances and have been translated beforehand but still need to
be synchronized live.

When comparing surtitling and subtitling, it becomes apparent that
they share many characteristics, the most significant similarity being that
they both translate a multimodal text. Sur- or subtitles do not constitute
the translation of a script, but rather the translation of a performance
(Griesel 2007: 21), movie or TV programme as a whole (Díaz-Cintas and
Remael 2007: 45). This form of translation takes into account verbal and
nonverbal auditory signs, as well as visual elements. It is important to keep
in mind that any form of translation is inevitably an interpretation and
that the same words can have completely different meanings depending
on the context. In order to produce a good translation, one needs to know
the intentions of the producers of the ST. In this respect, surtitlers are in
a slightly better position than subtitlers as they are often able to talk to
directors to find out what their general intentions are, or even specifically
what interpretation they favour for certain ambiguous sections. But, even
though surtitlers may be at an advantage due to their proximity and access
to the director, they are often confronted with the same prejudice as subtitlers, as the importance of the work they perform is often underestimated.

As mentioned before, subtitles and surtitles are limited in time and
space. The audience has only a short period available in which to read the
titles at the same time as following the action. In subtitling, the spatial

restriction is related primarily to the width of the screen whereas in surtitling this limitation is less problematic. Nevertheless, there is always a spatial restraint related to the assumed reading speed of the audience as only a certain amount of characters can comfortably be read in a specific amount of time. Therefore surtitlers and subtitlers attempt to convey what is being communicated in the ST in a concise manner. Selectivity of information is an absolute necessity (Carlson 2000: 84) thus sur- and subtitles apply frequently the reduction strategy. Reduction is mostly achieved by finding concise formulations and eliminating repetitions or elements that are conveyed via other communicative channels (such as images, body language or sound effects). Conciseness is also desirable so as to limit as much as possible the distraction from the primal point of focus, i.e. the audiovisual ST.

For surtitling, however, this limitation in time is much more problematic. This is due to several reasons. Firstly, the exact timing is unknown when the translation is produced, which makes conciseness even more important so as to ensure that the audience will have enough time to read the surtitles, even when the performers speed up.[1] Furthermore, the distance between the action and the projected translation is greater in surtitling and often the audience has to move their heads to read the surtitles. Therefore it is assumed that reading surtitles requires more time and is more distracting than reading subtitles, though, to date, no research has been conducted on how (quickly) the audience reads and absorbs surtitles.

The greatest difference between subtitling and surtitling lies in the synchronization of the ST and its translation. In conventional subtitling this is handled before or during translation. Since a subtitler works with a finished product, for which the timing will never change, synchronizing the titles can be done with a high degree of precision. In surtitling, synchronization is partially completed before translating, as the script or libretto is segmented into portions of text that will then be translated into one surtitle, based on the rhythm and speed of the performance. The actual

---

1　In rare cases does the opposite problem arise, when a performer slows down and the surtitles are too concise.

synchronization, however, needs to be achieved live during the performance by a cue master,[2] who is responsible for rendering every single surtitle exactly when it is vocalized on stage. Needless to say, live synchronization is much more problematic than pre-prepared subtitles.

In short, subtitlers and surtitlers share a number of challenges, the most significant ones being the translation of multimodal texts, the trivialization of their work as well as spatial and temporal constraints. Nonetheless, what really distinguishes each discipline is the manner in which synchronization is done.

2.2. Surtitling versus live subtitling

Superficially, there appears to be a close similarity between surtitling and live subtitling. However, when examining the obstacles faced by these two forms of AVT, it becomes clear that they do not have much in common, particularly when we look at the production process. The following descriptions have been simplified, but they will hopefully provide an understanding of how these forms of AVT are produced. There are several methods available for live subtitling: respeaking (Romero Fresco 2011), stenography, velotyping and multiple typing (Rander and Looms 2010). The translation (or reformulation in the case of intralingual subtitles) is produced in real time and appears on screen with a slight delay.[3] Depending on the method and technology used, the subtitler may be able to determine where one subtitle ends and a new one begins, but the synchronization is difficult to control. For surtitles, however, the translation is prepared in advance of the live performance. This process consists of two stages. First the ST is segmented according to the rhythm and speed of the speech (based on

2   A cue master only performs the synchronization; a surtitler prepares the cue list and translates but may also assume the role of cue master.
3   Though the timing in live subtitling will always be problematic, the gap can be virtually eliminated by delaying the actual broadcast by five to seven seconds. Though this practice is regularly used to manipulate the content of programmes (to cover up swear words for instance), its application in order to improve the reception of surtitles is still rare.

attendance at rehearsals or on a recording of the performance). Every segment is then translated and becomes one surtitle, ensuring that the level of reduction is relative to the time the audience has to read the surtitle. During the performance, the cue master synchronizes the surtitles with what is being vocalized on stage. Provided there are not too many unexpected changes to the text or rhythm, a talented and experienced cue master may attain nearly perfect synchronization, particularly as the number of performances of the same play increases with time. In live subtitling this is virtually impossible.

When defining surtitling according to the challenges posed in the production process, it could be argued that the main obstacle is translating an unfinished product. A surtitler receives a script, but this text may still change. The performers, director and/or playwright may alter the original script for a number of reasons throughout the pre-production, rehearsal and performance process. And it is not uncommon for them to 'forget' to update the surtitler. Moreover, during the performance itself, the actors may skip a sentence or entire section and later return to something they have omitted, or they may suddenly change the text or improvise. Furthermore, there is another essential element which is not available to surtitlers, namely the exact speed of the speech and rhythm of the performance. Although, as mentioned before, a video recording or access to rehearsals is provided as a basis for segmenting the text, the rhythm and pace is never exactly the same and may change significantly with each performance. A surtitler needs to take this into account while segmenting, translating and, especially, cueing.

A live subtitler, on the other hand, does not often receive much information beforehand, with the exception of some partial scripts as in the case for the news, for example. Unlike surtitlers, live subtitlers have no time to ponder the best solution, since they have only a split second in which to translate or transcribe. The challenge facing live subtitlers involves the extreme time pressure under which they work.

Though surtitling and live subtitling share a live dimension the challenges faced by the professionals involved differ significantly. Nevertheless, the application field of surtitling is expanding and some of the new uses of surtitling, for instance, incorporate the translation or transcription of unscripted material (see 2.3). When that is the case, we can speak of (partial) live surtitling,[4] which bears all the characteristics of live subtitling. Though there are some differences in the practical application, the production process and specific challenges are virtually identical in live sub- and surtitling.

2.3. Surtitling, a unique challenge

As already mentioned, one of the challenges that most distinguishes surtitling from all other forms of AVT is that a surtitler receives an unfinished product to translate (Vervecken 2012).

There is one more characteristic of surtitling that is quite unique. It is not uncommon for people to think that, once the list of surtitles (the cue list) has been created, it remains constant for the entire run of the production. However, the live performance which the cue list accompanies is different every night and, depending on how significant these changes are, the surtitles may need to be adapted each time. This is especially important in theatre, where the rhythm and pace are constantly evolving and the target text will be different every night, if only because the timing will never be exactly the same. Regrettably, the practice of fixing the cue list is quite common in the profession.

3. Some types of surtitle

3.1. Opera surtitles

The first type we will address is surtitling for the opera, since this is the field where surtitles were first used in the early 1980s (Mateo 2002: 54;

---

4 Partial live surtitling, where most of the titles have been preprepared and some are produced live, should not be confused with partial live subtitling, where the text has been prepared beforehand as is often the case for news programmes (a practice very similar if not identical to surtitling).

Sisk 1986: 50). Although surtitling opera presents specific challenges, it is also the art form to which surtitles seem to adapt most easily. Technically speaking, the use of surtitles in opera is the most straightforward because the rhythm and pace are dictated by the music. Therefore an opera surtitler has less difficulty in deciding how to segment the text and changes to the cue list due to changes in rhythm are not often required. Unexpected changes to the text are also rare as opera singers are less likely to skip a line, thus simplifying the job of the cue master significantly.

There seems to exist a misconception that surtitles for the opera are easier to produce as the text is stretched out over the music and therefore less, or even no reduction, is required in the translated text. Of course, this is not always the case, but on those occasions when a phrase or even a single word are stretched out over quite a long time, or repeated, the surtitler will have to decide whether to keep the surtitle up the whole time or not. Opera presents another challenge that is rare in other forms of surtitling, namely that several people sing different lyrics concurrently. When, as is the case in Verdi's *Falstaff*, they sing at a considerable pace, the surtitler faces a complex task.

Translating an opera production as one complete entity, as opposed to translating a libretto, poses an additional difficulty because, in opera, disparities between what is being said and what is being done are not uncommon. When this occurs, there are two possibilities: to ignore the disparity and maintain the literal meaning of the libretto with the risk that it might distract and annoy the audience; or to downplay these disparities as much as possible, thus avoiding confusion. Ideally, the choice is made in conjunction with the director.

Since the use of surtitles has become virtually standard in opera, more directors are beginning to recognize the importance of this translation process on their work. Today, opera directors are more willing to take the time to discuss a general strategy as well as any problematic passages with the surtitler. That being said, for some directors, surtitles are still not part of their *Gesammtkunstwerk*.

3.2. Theatre surtitles

The definitive challenge in theatre is that, unlike in opera, the rhythm and pace are in constant flux and unexpected changes to the text are not uncommon.

The rhythm of an actor's speech influences where blank cues are required and how the surtitles are segmented. It is very important in dramatic or humorous sections that certain information does not appear in the surtitles before the actor has actually uttered the words. To read the punch line to a joke before the actor has actually vocalized it would undermine the performance. In some styles of theatre, actors constantly play with the rhythm, which makes the job of the surtitler more challenging. And even when actors claim to adhere to a specific rhythm, this rhythm will inevitably evolve over time. This is why theatre surtitles are most effective when the cue master, or someone else involved in the production, takes notes during the performance, marking where the rhythm has changed.

Actors who unexpectedly change their pace can be problematic, since the level of reduction in the translated text is generally based on the expected pace. A dramatic increase in the pace might cause the surtitles to disappear before the audience has been able to read them. A dramatic decrease, on the other hand, may leave the audience frustrated, wondering: 'is that all he said?'

Unforeseen changes to the source text occur quite often in theatre as actors may skip a line or entire paragraph, then realize their mistake and attempt to return to the missed dialogue. This is where the surtitling software comes into play since only a few surtitling programs enable the cue master to respond effectively to leaps in the text without the audience noticing. It goes without saying that this also requires a skilled cue master. A more problematic, unforeseen textual modification is improvisation. When it only concerns one short remark or phrase, some software allows the cue master to insert a new title quickly by manually typing it. In this case there will inevitably be a delay. However, when the improvisation exceeds one or two phrases, then regular surtitling practices can no longer be used and live subtitling techniques, such as respeaking, will be required. To date, however, technology combining both translation methods has not yet been developed.

Live theatre was probably the first performing art in which surtitles surpassed their mere translational function and were used to communicate information that had little or nothing to do with, or even contradicted, what was being said on stage. In fact, Bertolt Brecht used placards with text long before surtitles as we know them today existed. He considered the explanatory or instructive placards a device to stimulate an 'exercise in complex seeing' (Brecht 1978: 44). The artistic function of surtitles is further discussed in section 5.

3.3. New uses

The days when surtitles were only used in opera and were projected with an analogue slide projector, which allowed no flexibility whatsoever, are long gone. Today, technology enables surtitlers to be much more accurate, flexible and creative. It is not surprising that live events now turn to surtitling, either to improve accessibility, or for creativity purposes.

Some musicians have started using surtitles during their concerts, both for practical as well as for artistic reasons. Artists may use this form of translation for performances in countries where they do not speak the language so as to translate what is said in between songs. Usually, these texts are prepared beforehand, though there may be a certain degree of improvisation. Sometimes texts are projected during the songs, which may or may not be translations of the songs.

Surtitles are also becoming more common at professional and academic gatherings. The use of conference interpreters is still prevalent, but intralingual surtitles are sometimes employed for the purposes of accessibility for the deaf and the hard-of-hearing.[5] When surtitling is used, the captions only display the translation or transcription of the papers that were available beforehand, leaving out introductions or deviations from the written paper. The opening ceremony of the Paralympics in Vancouver in 2010,

---

5   One contributing factor is that, in some countries, the organizers of conferences are legally required to provide live transcription when a deaf or hearing impaired person requests it.

for instance, featured surtitles, albeit only during the speeches. On the other hand, when live sub- or surtitling techniques are applied, all that is said will be included in the captions, in which case stenographers are often employed. On these occasions, there will be a delay, the readability and required reading speed of the titles will be more difficult to control and the chance for errors, both human and technical, increases dramatically.

Most of the new uses of surtitling involve a mixture of scripted and unscripted text. When conventional surtitling techniques are used, the improvisational or unscripted aspect tends to be left out. This may change when software is developed that allows surtitlers to combine conventional surtitling (preparing a list of surtitles based on the scripted material) with live subtitling techniques (creating new surtitles live). As the industry is quickly evolving and accessibility is increasingly demanded, this type of software might soon become reality. This could mean a drastic change in how live events are transcribed or translated by offering a viable new option, in which the quality of the translation might be significantly increased and resources spared, as the advantages of both techniques are combined.

4. Technology

In the previous sections, different types of surtitles have been discussed on the basis of their field of application. Another means of examining surtitling is to analyse how the translated works are displayed. The two most popular methods of presenting surtitles are by projecting them or by displaying them on a Light Emitting Diode (LED) or other type of screen. Both methods are used in all types of surtitling. And while each method may offer some advantages, it cannot be argued that either approach is superior to the other. Ideally, both approaches would be considered and the most suitable option for each specific production chosen. Many venues, however, will have one system in place, which they always use. A relatively new option is an individual screen for every audience member. In the following sections, each of these approches to displaying the translated text are discussed, including the software used to operate the modes of display.

4.1. Projection

In the 1980s, analogue slide projectors were used to display surtitles. These have now long been replaced by digital projectors that project either onto the back wall, another part of the décor or a panel suspended above and, at times, placed at the sides of the stage.

The use of projection is practical, in the first instance, because virtually all venues possess the hardware required: a video projector. This is why it is a popular choice for theatres which only use surtitles once or twice a year, as it does not require a significant capital investment. This mode of display is also popular for productions which tour extensively since, for companies bringing their own equipment, a beamer and a canvas screen are easier to transport than a large digital LED-screen. Perhaps the major advantage of using projection is the versatility of this medium. There is no limit to the size, font or colour that can be used. The surtitled text can be animated so that it moves about and can be further augmented by illustrations, photographs and videos. The surtitles can also be displayed at several different places either synchronously or alternating between the different displays. This can be realized by using several projectors but can also be achieved with a powerful projector and good software. Only the sotware operating it limits the many creative possibiblities of this method of display.

Nevertheless, interference from light or special effects, such as a stroboscope or smoke, may not always be compatible with the use of a projector, although this problem can be overcome by utilizing more powerful projecting equipment. The beam of the projector can create aesthetic interference in the form of light pollution, for example when the borders of the projection space are visible when the stage is very dark. Often there is a simple way to solve these problems though this does require creativity and preparation time.[6] Another disadvantage of using projectors is that

6 *Sportivo Teatral* from Argentina performed *La Pesca* in Antwerp at theatre deSingel in 2008. At the beginning of the play, the stage was completely dark and the actors talk while coming down a long flight of stairs. The director did not like the square of the projection that remained during silences. As his request for this problem to be solved only came at the last minute, the theatre technicians placed a little flag in front of the beamer that the surtitler could move up and down. This flag, however,

they can overheat and shut off in the middle of a performance. This may happen if the projector has been left on too long, if the ventilation vent has been blocked, or when too many hot items such as lamps are placed close to the beamer. Sometimes, the machine has simply worn out. The ventilator of a projector also creates a slight noise, though this is rarely an issue as the projector is often placed far beyond the ears of the audience.

The popularity of projectors to display surtitles is not surprising, as this method is relatively inexpensive and allows a high degree of flexibility and creativity. Nonetheless, it is imperative to consider the technical requirements.

4.2. LED monitors

There is a misconception that the use of Light Emitting Diode or LED monitors is limited to displaying boxy fonts, in some five colours, as with the scrolling LED screens used in shop windows. This may be true for some of the first generation LED screens produced for surtitling in the late 1980s, but today the possibilities are vast. Naotek (www.naotek.com), for example, is a French company producing LED monitors which are capable of 16,384 colour tones, in numerous fonts, of which the brightness can be individually adjusted. Sometimes LED panels are preferred for aesthetic reasons, as they produce brighter, more vibrant colours than projectors and without light pollution. Interference with other light sources or special effects is rare. LED displays do not reflect light as a Liquid Crystal Display (LCD) screen may. Other reasons to choose this mode of display are that, once installed, the chance of sudden technical failure is very slim and LED screens are also virtually silent. Though these screens are expensive, they are a good investment when used continuously, as they are more likely to be replaced due to obsolescence rather than wear. Thus, LED screens are a practical solution for fixed installations at opera houses and other similar venues.

---

made a robotic noise and was quite distracting so, in the end, the director decided the projection square was less intrusive than the noise (Vervecken 2009: 74–5).

Nevertheless, LED screens are large and heavy, making them more difficult to transport. The fixed size of LED displays restricts the way in which they can be integrated into the décor of the production and poses further limitations on how creatively they can be applied. A common installation plan involves several LED screens used to display surtitles in different locations simultaneously. For example: one screen is mounted at the proscenium and two smaller panels are placed to the sides of the stage. This layout is intended to ensure that all spectators have a good view of the surtitles. However, there is less flexibility for displaying the surtitles in different locations throughout the production/venue as this requires several screens and locations to mount them.

LED displays are a better long-term investment and are, arguably, more reliable than beamers. These screens also possess a certain aesthetic quality which projection cannot offer. The drawback is that these types of screen are expensive and not the most versatile or flexible medium for displaying surtitles.

4.3. Individual screens

The latest development in the display of surtitles is the use of individual screens by each audience member. Two varieties exist: back seat screens very similar to those deployed on commercial airplanes, and hand held devices. The former are used at the Liceu in Barcelona and the Metropolitan in New York, for example. The latter are used at the Shaftesbury Theatre in London.

The larger LED screens are marketed as having a very wide angle of visibility. Most of the individual screens, however, are designed to be visible only to the person sitting directly in front of the monitor (or holding the hand held variety), to avoid distracting neighbouring audience members. Individual screens allow each audience member to decide whether or not they want to use the surtitles. It must be noted, though, that individual screens are often offered in addition to surtitles displayed for the entire audience. Furthermore, individual screens may permit the viewer to choose from different languages as well as surtitle adaptations intended for audience members with specific needs.

4.4. Surtitling software

Any mode of display still requires software to manage and render the actual surtitles. Most of these computer programs have been developed specifically for one display mode, though some software developers claim that their product will function for both LED screen and projection standards. The importance of using the right software is often underestimated. It is not uncommon for large theatre companies or opera houses to use *PowerPoint* in combination with a projector, simply because it is the cheapest solution. *PowerPoint* is a wonderful tool for presentations, but it was not designed for surtitling.

Many opera houses and surtitlers have developed their own software for rendering translated texts. This explains the abundance of computer programs used in spite of the relatively small application field. Unfortunately, many of these applications are just a small step up from *PowerPoint* in terms of functionality. There are, however, some companies that have developed software which is more in keeping with the needs of surtitlers. Some of these software developers have begun to market their products on a larger scale: Supertitles (www.supertitles.gr) from Greece and Naotek in France are some European industry leaders in the field.

Describing all the desired features for surtitling software would be a substantial undertaking, worthy of an independent article. For the sake of brevity, the following are some essential considerations:

- The ability to import and export texts easily.
- The ability to manipulate and edit texts after they have been imported.
- The ability to see both source and target text while cueing.
- The time required to set up the hardware and software.
- Compatibility with projectors as well as LED screens.
- Potential for creativity in rendering colours, fonts, sizes, movement, etc.
- Flexibility in using more than one screen or projection layout.
- Ability to monitor reading speed.
- Ability for the cue master to jump in the text when actors skip lines.

5. Some functions of surtitling

5.1. Translation and transcription

The principal function of surtitles is translation as in the case of the sur-titler who translates Italian dialogue into German, for instance. But the surtitler may also convert operatic Italian into written Italian; or present an auditory experience as captions for the deaf and the hearing impaired. Surtitles translate the vocal, but also some visual and non-vocal elements to a concise, written vernacular that needs to make sense in combination with its ST (Griesel 2007: 13). Though surtitles are often perceived as a 'neutral, clarifying device' (Carlson 2000: 84), they are interpretative and suggestive and, like subtitles, their influence on the perception and reception of the production should never be underestimated.

5.2. Artistic expression

Some artists use surtitles in ways that surpass their informative function and take on an expressive function. When surtitles display ideas that have never been uttered on stage or even contradict what is being said, they become an independent channel of communication. In Shakespeare's *Julius Caesar*, as performed by the Dutch theatre company *Toneelgroep Amsterdam*, the character of Lucius only exists in the surtitles and Brutus appears to be talking to a phantom.

Surtitles may transcend their original function when their presence is acknowledged by the performers. Even though this does not entail a disparity between the surtitles and what is being said, the surtitles are no longer something that is added to the performance to aid comprehension. Rather, they have become *part* of the performance as a metatextual device.

Surtitles can also be expressive in terms of their physical appearance. The international theatre company *Needcompany* has experimented with different fonts, sizes, colours, and surtitles that move, become larger and smaller, etc. Carlson (2000: 88) provides a very interesting analysis of the use of surtitles in their production of *King Lear*.

5.3. Accessibility: Surtitling for the deaf and the hard-of-hearing

One of the current trends in surtitling is to produce titles to overcome a disability rather than a language barrier. Where audio description allows the visually impaired access to a performance, surtitling for the deaf and the hard-of-hearing (S^{r}DH) provides support for the hearing impaired. S^{r}DH is generally offered for one specific performance such as a matinee, where they will be visible to the entire audience. The matinee is often chosen because it tends to be popular with senior citizens and many of them suffer from hearing problems. S^{r}DH may also be available on individual screens for the entire run of the production.

Before discussing what distinguishes S^{r}DH, one should understand who uses this medium. There are three main groups within the hearing impaired: (1) the hard-of-hearing; (2) the physically deaf, who were born hearing and became deaf later in life; and (3) the culturally Deaf who were born deaf or became deaf at a very early age. Not having had access to spoken language (which is essentially the basis of our written language), the culturally Deaf will often prefer to have sign language interpreters translate the performance, since sign language is their native language and a vital part of the 'Deaf' culture. Therefore S^{r}DH is often primarily intended for the hard-of-hearing and the physically deaf.

Unfortunately, it is not uncommon for theatres, festivals or opera houses to claim that they provide S^{r}DH, while in reality all they offer are intralingual surtitles. The differences, however, are vast. Like subtitling for the deaf and the hard-of-hearing (SDH), S^{r}DH should also indicate who is speaking when appropriate. In SDH this is often achieved by utilizing different colours, particularly on TV. But experience has proved that this approach is not practical for live performance and is very distracting for the hearing-able audience. Therefore S^{r}DH tends to resort to labels, as in SDH for DVDs, and display the names or initials of the person speaking. This is essential, since the hearing impaired are often unable to distinguish voices. Moreover, due to the distance between the audience and the stage, it is difficult to distinguish the performers' faces and establish who is speaking or singing. It should be borne in mind that the majority of the hard-of-hearing are elderly people, many of whom also have diminished vision.

S^{r}DH also need to incorporate nonverbal auditory signals, which are essential for the audience to understand what is happening on stage. This includes non-vocal sounds, as well as nonverbal vocal sounds. Non-vocal sounds may include music and/or sound effects that attempt to create a certain atmosphere, such as rain. The sound of cutlery clinking may be used to indicate that a particular scene is taking place in a busy restaurant. Other non-vocal sounds can be those that are created by an action, such as a creaking door or a slap in the face. On the other hand, nonverbal vocal sounds are audio cues produced by the actors and relate to *how* they say something, as opposed to *what* they say. When someone hesitates, for example, a hearing person would hear this pause whereas for the hearing impaired, this nuance will be lost unless the 'ums' are included in the surtitles.

Translating these auditory signals into written language is done in various ways. Sometimes mannerisms in speech can be incorporated into the actual text or the surtitler may add descriptions between brackets, in a different font or capitals to distinguish them from the transcriptions. Due to the restrictions in space and time, adding more text may be problematic, thus making the job of a S^{r}DH surtitler even more challenging. Some surtitlers use symbols such as emoticons to overcome these hurdles.

One option which was tested by Karam et al. (2009) is the use of a chair that translates sound into vibrations. In this way, the viewer can feel variations in volume and rhythm and even the pitch is taken into account. The use of this chair or other vibrating cushions is still in its experimental phase and it has yet to be determined how much meaning the deaf can derive from such devices. One immediate observation is that these vibrations might be very efficient at translating some of the sounds that are intended to provoke an emotional reaction; for instance, a sudden harsh vibration would be quite effective at recreating the impact of an unexpected gunshot, more powerful than a descriptive BANG in the surtitles. In order to boost accessibility, venues may also want to distribute programme guides to the hearing impaired audience members, in which the use of music or the characters' voices and speaking mannerisms are explained.

Describing auditory subtleties is a balancing act. When too few are included, the hearing impaired may not understand why certain things are said or done. Including too much information in the surtitles may distance the audience from the performance because they must focus on the surtitles most of the time. Clearly, not every single sound can be included and a careful analysis is needed to determine what, and how much information the audience needs in order to understand what is being communicated. SᵗDH tends to be in a more difficult position than SDH because, unlike in the cinema or TV, there are no close-ups to reveal emotions and other nonverbal messages. The hearing population often does not appreciate the greater reliance that the deaf have on deducing nuance and meaning from facial expressions, gestures, or other visual indicators. In a theatre, however, distance makes the ability to present these indicators more difficult.

The evolution towards more SᵗDH is definitely to be encouraged. Yet, the need for quality should be stressed, as poorly produced SᵗDH is more likely to drive the hearing impaired away from theatres and might actually discourage them from trying it again.

5.4. Accessibility for minorities

The use of surtitling for minorities is certainly not common, but nonetheless very interesting. The theatre department of the University of British Columbia (UBC) in Vancouver, Canada, has experimented with providing surtitles in the languages of some of its large immigrant communities. In 2009, UBC provided Korean surtitles for a production spoken in English and, in 2010, they produced a performance spoken/sung in Cantonese and English with surtitles in both languages. In the future, graduates of the directing programme will be encouraged to provide surtitles for two of the ten performances of their theatrical productions. This type of surtitling allows people access to aspects of culture and society to which they would otherwise not have access.

5.5. Language acquisition

Like subtitles, surtitles are sometimes used for purposes of language acquisition. Usually, the surtitles are not designed with that purpose in mind, but audience members may decide to use them for that reason. Sometimes schools will take students to a performance in a chosen language so as to expose their students to this language in a different setting. The surtitles thus serve as an aid to confirm that the foreign dialogue on stage is correctly understood.

Intralingual surtitles, such as S'DH, may also be helpful for people who are new to a place and want to further their understanding of the local language, as they reinforce from a written perspective what has been presented in an audio context.

5.6. Political issues

When there is more than one language or culture at play, politics is likely to be involved to some extent. Surtitling makes no exception.

Political involvement in the translation of performing arts is most apparent in multilingual countries or regions. Surtitling, or other forms of translation, may be encouraged in order to promote more exchange between the different communities. At times, accessibility for both language communities is taken into account in applications for public funding. In other regions, politics seems to work as an impediment and appears to favour a separate cultural community for each language. Brussels is a very interesting example in this respect. According to Jan Goossens, the artistic director of the Royal Flemish Theatre (KVS), it is easier to receive public funding to produce surtitles in a co-production with a company from Senegal than for a production where the Flemish and Walloons are intended to work together (van der Kris 2007). Though this may not be the motivating intention, using surtitles has become a political statement in Brussels (Demeyer 2007). In 2008, the multilingual promotional material of the KVS even became the subject of debate in one of the commissions of the Flemish Parliament (Vervecken 2009: 47).

5.7. Commercial function

Surtitles with a commercial function are shown at the beginning or end of a performance or, occasionally, at the intermission, but never during the performance itself. These titles show the names of the partners who have sponsored the production, or advertise other productions by the same company or theatre. Surtitling companies may also display their name or logo and the name of the translator/surtitler at the end of the performance, much as one would see in some movie credits. This practice is not as prevalent as in subtitling and is rare when in-house personnel produce the surtitles. It is not uncommon for surtitlers to go completely unaccredited, not receiving any mention in the programme or surtitles, even when the translator who translated the script or libretto for the performance is credited.

6. Conclusion

The aim of this article has been to provide a detailed account of the current practices in surtitling. It is hoped that the reader has a better understanding of the challenges facing the surtitler as well as the variations in the types and functions of surtitles. Though this was not the primary focus of this article, it may also have given the reader an insight into the future of this field. To enable surtitling to provide more qualitative translations and expand into other application fields, two developments are needed: more research and improved technology.

Further research should help determine effective practices, may establish how surtitles are received by the audience and, among other things, may also show audience preferences. This knowledge would allow surtitlers and producers of live performances to adjust to the needs of their audience, thus allowing them to appreciate the performance better.

The knowledge uncovered by research can also be used to improve the existing software and develop new tools that could broaden the application field of surtitles significantly. The success of surtitles not only depends on a qualitative translation but also on good synchronization and for that, talented, engaged cue masters with well developed software at their disposal are needed.

Thus the present and future success of surtitling, as in many other areas, is very much dependent on improving software functionality and providing the research and information that will enable professionals to reach their full potential.

Bibliography

Brecht, Bertolt, *Brecht on Theatre*, ed. and trans. John Willet (New York: Hill and Wang, 1987).

Carlson, Marvin, 'The Semiotics of Supertitles', *Assaph* 16 (2000), 77–90.

Demeyer, Paul, 'Franstaligen en Vlamingen Slopen Onderlinge Muren', *Het Nieuwsblad* (24 February 2007) <http://www.nieuwsblad.be/Article/Detail. aspx?articleID=grg18qijp> accessed 4 February 2012.

Díaz Cintas, Jorge, and Aline Remael, *Audiovisual Translation: Subtitling* (Manchester: St Jerome, 2007).

Griesel, Yvonne, *Die Inszenieruing als Translat, Möglichkeiten und Grenzen der Theaterübertitelung* (Berlin: Frank&Timme, 2007).

Karam, Maria, Frank Russo and Deborah I. Fels, 'Designing the Model Human Cochlea: An Ambient Crossmodal Audio-Tactile Display', *Ted Rogers School of Information Technology Publications and Research*, 20 (2009), <http://digitalcommons.ryerson.ca/trsitm/20/> accessed 4 February 2012.

Mateo, Marta, 'Surtitling Today: New Uses, Attitudes and Developments', *Linguistica Antverpiensa*, 6 (2000), 135–54.

—— 'Los sobretítulos de ópera: dimensión técnica, textual, social e ideológica', in John Sanderson, ed., *Traductores para todo. Actas de las III Jornadas de Doblaje y Subtitulación* (Alicante: Universidad de Alicante, 2002), 51–7.

Rander, Anni, and Peter Olaf Looms, 'The Accessibility of Television News with Live Subtitling on Digital Television', *EuroITV '10 Proceedings of the Eighth International Interactive Conference on Interactive TV&Video* (2010), <http:// portal.acm.org/citation.cfm?doid=1809777.1809809> accessed 4 February 2012.

Romero-Fresco, Pablo, *Subtitling through Speech Recognition. Respeaking* (Manchester: St Jerome, 2011).

Sisk, Douglas F., 'Surtitles ... Surtitles ... Surtitles', *Theatre Crafts*, 20/50 (1986), 50.

van der Kris, Jeroen, 'Bruxelles, Brussel, Brussels', *NRC Handelsblad* (27 October 2007) <http://vorige.nrc.nl/nieuwsthema/belgie/article1851746.ece/Bruxelles,_Brussel,_Brussels> accessed 4 February 2012.

Vervecken, Anika. *Surtitles, The Making of*, unpublished Master's thesis (Antwerp: Artesis University College, Antwerp, 2009).

—— 'Surtitling for the Stage and Director's Attitudes: Room for Change', in Mary Carrol, Pilar Orero and Aline Remael, eds, *Audiovisual Translation and Media Accessibility at the Crossroads* (Amsterdam: Rodopi, 2012), 229–47.

TIA MULLER

Subtitles for deaf and hard-of-hearing people on French television

1. Introduction

One day, most of us are likely to experience a certain degree of hearing loss due to advancing old age. The medical term 'presbycusis' refers to this type of hearing impairment which affects up to 90 per cent of individuals aged eighty and over, worldwide (Shield 2006: 32). It has been predicted that, as a result of the continuing increase in life expectancy, the number of hearing impaired people in Europe will grow from eighty-five million to over 100 million by 2025 (ibid.). In 2002, this group represented nearly 10 per cent of the population in France, amounting to some six million people. Díaz Cintas et al. (2007: 12) note that in such circumstances, 'it is only fair that [...] media, including more traditional ones, be made fully available and accessible to all citizens'.

This paper presents an overview of the state of affairs concerning subtitling for the D/deaf¹ and the hard-of-hearing (SDH) on French television at the end of the first decade of the twenty-first century. In the opening sections, the French audiovisual landscape and the historical and legislative contexts of SDH in France will be established, followed by a discussion of SDH conventions. In the final part, a sample of SDH output on French television selected from four days over 2009 and 2010 will be analysed.

---

1   Deaf written with a capital letter refers socially to the Deaf community, for whom sign language is generally the mother-tongue; deaf written with a small letter refers to the medical condition.

2.   The French audiovisual landscape

In this first section, aspects of the French audiovisual landscape will be outlined, including its multiple channels, the body that regulates audiovisual media, the switchover from analogue to digital terrestrial television (DTTV) and the funding of broadcasting companies.

2.1. A multitude of channels

According to the European Commission (Harmann and Kevin 2010), there are 297 television channels in France. The Conseil Supérieur de l'Audiovisuel (CSA), the country's audiovisual regulatory body, recognizes a further thirty-six regional and local television channels, bringing the total number to 343.

In its classification of channels, the CSA identifies six distinct criteria: transmission from or outside France; the mode of transmission (terrestrial digital, analogue, or satellite network); coverage (national, regional or local); ownership (public or private); accessibility (free or fee-based); and programming (generalist or thematic). Varying combinations of these characteristics define each channel. For example, TF1, the channel with the highest annual audience share,[2] which transmits from France through a terrestrial (digital and analogue until the end of 2011) and a satellite network, is national, privately owned, free, and generalist.

2.2. The regulating body

Established by law in 1989, the CSA is composed of nine elected members whose mission is to guarantee and promote the freedom of audiovisual communication in France (CSA 2010b). The President of the Republic,

---

2   In 2009, TF1 had an annual audience rate of 26.1 per cent. In second position came the TV channel France 2 with 16.7 per cent and in third France 3, with 11.8 per cent (Dubner and Maurice 2010).

the President of the Senate and the President of the National Assembly each elect three of these individuals for a period of six years. Two of the CSA's missions are of particular interest to this study: making television accessible to all, especially the hearing and visually impaired, and ensuring that national operators comply with laws and regulations, penalizing those who violate them.

2.3. DTTV

According to the Observatory of Home Television Equipment (CSA 2010a) by mid-2010, 85.8 per cent of households with a television set received digital transmission either via DTTV, cable, satellite or ADSL via the internet. The shift to DTTV started in France in March 2005 and was completed with the national shutdown of analogue television at the end of 2011. This switch has been organized as a progressive, region-by-region process. For example, while Alsace underwent the switchover on 2 February 2010, the region of Languedoc Roussillon, the last one to switch, was not due to make the change until 29 November 2011.

With the launch of DTTV in 2005, thirteen free national channels were created, adding to the nation's five long-established ones: TF1, M6, France 2, France 3 and France 5. Between 2005 and 2010 an additional nine free regional or local channels and nine fee-based national ones were authorized by the CSA to broadcast on DTTV.

2.4. Funding of public service channels

France Télévisions is a broadcasting corporation forming part of the nation's public audiovisual services. It is the only state television company in France and the French government is its sole shareholder. It encompasses seven national free channels: France 2, a generalist channel with the second highest annual audience share; France 3, a generalist channel that has timeslots allocated to the airing of twenty-four local channels corresponding to the twenty-four French regions; France 4, a generalist channel aimed at a younger audience; France 5, a general channel focusing on documentaries, current affairs programmes and live debates; France Ô, intended for French nationals living overseas; Arte, a channel owned equally by the French and German governments; and La Chaîne Parlementaire, a thematic channel on which parliamentary and political news are discussed daily. Of these, France 2, 3 and 5 form part of the quantitative analysis of SDH output provided in the last section of this article.

France Télévisions is financed through two distinct sources: public funding raised through an annual licence fee, and commercial revenue secured through the sale of televised advertising time. The licence fee is a tax levied yearly per household – not per television set – and, in what has been described as 'an iniquitous situation' (Charpillon 2002: 22), most deaf and HoH who own a TV have to pay this fee, though exemptions may be granted for people with a recognized incapacity for work. The money collected through this tax constitutes up to two thirds of France Télévisions' budget. The fee is reviewed annually by the Parliament and has been indexed to the rate of inflation since 2009. For example, in 2010, the fee was fixed at €121, while in 2005, it cost licence payers €116 (Direction générale des médias et des industries culturelles 2005).

The remaining third of the funding required by France Télévisions is raised through commercial sources. The length of time occupied by advertising on state channels is strictly regulated by the government and controlled by the CSA. Since January 2009, state channels are no longer allowed to air advertisements between 8pm and 6am and their total duration cannot exceed two hours and sixteen minutes per day (Braganti 2010).

2.5. Funding of private channels

Just a few telecommunication companies own the majority of private channels. Created in 1935, TF1 is the first and oldest channel. Originally publicly owned, it was privatized in 1986. It is a free, generalist channel that belongs to the Groupe TF1. M6 is a free, generalist channel that, amongst other programmes aimed at a younger audience, airs the most recent series from the United States. It was created in 1987 and belongs to the Groupe M6. These two channels form part of the quantitative analysis of SDH output provided below.

The funding for private channels comes primarily from revenue generated by the sale of advertising slots. It can also come from sponsorship deals and teleshopping and, for the fee-based channels, from membership charges. The average daily length of time allocated to advertisements on private channels is also regulated by the government and controlled by the CSA. It is limited to three hours and thirty-six minutes per day of broadcasting (Braganti 2010). However, unlike state-owned channels, the time of day at which they can be aired is not restricted.

3. Historical and legal contexts of French subtitling for the D/deaf and the hard-of-hearing

The French teletext information service first used the Antiope (*Acquisition Numérique et Télévisualisation d'Images Organisées en Pages D'écriture – Digital Acquisition and Remote Visualization of Images Organized into Written Pages*) system to broadcast its pages and subtitles on terrestrial television. Created in 1976 and only used in France, the Antiope system was abandoned in 1994. Ceefax, a system developed by the BBC in 1974 and more widely used across Europe, replaced it.

When the Antiope system was launched it required a separate decoder to be plugged into a television set in order to read teletext pages. By 1985, these decoders were integrated into new sets enabling direct reading, first, of the Antiope system and, later, of Ceefax. In France, the first teletext programme to be broadcast was a weather forecast on France 2 in 1979 (Mousseau and Brochand 1982: 177). By 1983, the same channel started subtitling a weekly news magazine. In 1984, France 3 and TF1 followed suit and introduced limited SDH of their programming using teletext (Charpillon 2002: 9).

At this point, no laws had been passed to regulate SDH and state-owned channels were the first to start adding clauses about accessibility to their mission statements from 1984, although they did not stipulate the number of programmes they aimed to subtitle (Brochand 2006: 646).

Charpillon (2002: 8–10) states that during the 1980s, 1990s and the early years of the new millennium, no French channel subtitled more than 10 per cent of their annual programming. He goes on to compare France's subtitling output with other European countries, such as England, noting that by 2002, BBC1 was offering SDH for 76 per cent of its airtime, while ITV and Channel 4 provided 73 per cent and 74 per cent respectively (ibid.: 22).

In 2000, an existing law on communication liberties, originally passed in 1986, was amended, in a first attempt to oblige both public and private channels in France to make their programmes accessible to the D/deaf and the hard-of-hearing. However, these amendments did not stipulate minimum annual quotas of material to be subtitled. Thus, TV companies increased their SDH outputs only slightly until 2005, when the French Parliament passed the *Equal Rights and Opportunities, Participation and Citizenship of People with Disabilities Act* (No. 2005–102). Article 74 of this law requires all channels with an annual audience share of 2.5 per cent or above to use adapted subtitles or sign interpretation in order to make 100 per cent of their programming accessible (with the exception of advertisements) by 12 February 2010. This article applies to all channels transmitting via analogue, digital, satellite, ADSL or cable networks.

However, at the beginning of the second decade of the twenty-first century, the positive impact of this law remains limited in a number of ways and for a variety of reasons. Firstly, it only applies to those channels that enjoy at least 2.5 per cent of the annual audience share. Consequently, in 2010, a mere seven national channels were affected: public France 2, 3, 4 and 5, and private TF1, M6 and Canal+. Secondly, the term 'adapted subtitles' is not defined in the law and is therefore open to interpretation. This phrase can potentially result in a confusing range of SDH formats and marked variations in quality. Thirdly, the law states that special dispensations may be granted for certain types of programme and yet it fails to specify the exact nature of what might be exempt.[3] Fourthly, the law

---

3   In an attempt to provide clearer guidelines, the CSA (2009) has specified that the following areas may be exempt: multilingual services such as the channel Euronews; mentions of sponsorship; announcements and trailers for forthcoming programmes

stipulates that local channels may be totally exempt from making their programmes accessible to the D/deaf and the HoH people. This is possibly due to the cost involved, though this is not made clear. Finally, the law does not lay down any penalties for those channels that do not respect its terms. Instead, it is the role of the CSA to penalize channels in breach of the law. However, Christine Kelly, the chairwoman of the CSA's working group on accessibility, has explained that, due to the economic difficulties caused by the current global financial crisis and to the investment required for the channels to be able to adhere to the 2005 law, no penalties were envisaged for the year 2010 (in Pellerin 2010).

The CSA asked DTTV channels with an annual audience share of under 2.5 per cent to indicate in their mission statements that they intended to make 40 per cent of their programmes accessible by 12 February 2010. This figure was reduced to 20 per cent for TV companies whose frequencies had not been assigned by the CSA. However, as these mission statements are not legally binding, the channels cannot be penalized if they do not comply. Moreover, the CSA has declared that, until 2012, interlingual subtitles broadcast in foreign films can be counted as part of these percentages, a concession that effectively further reduces the channels' target level of SDH output.

4. Conventions of French subtitling for the D/deaf and the hard-of-hearing

For physical reasons, the target audience for SDH has reduced, little, or no access to aural information. Therefore, SDH aims to compensate for the absence of sound. Elements such as music, sound effects, paralinguistic information and character identification and localization need to be

---

or films; live singing and/or instrumental music; coverage of live sporting events broadcast between 12pm and 6am; and pay-per-view services.

incorporated within the subtitles to compensate for this loss (De Linde and Kay 1999: 12). Conventions need to be agreed upon prior to engaging in the production of subtitles in order for these various components to be easily recognizable for the D/deaf and the HoH audiences.

The current practice in France is to assign one colour to music, a different one to sound effects and another four to indicate the various types of voice that can occur in a programme.[4] This colour code, which can be found on all channels for every type of programme, differs from other European countries. For example, in England and Spain, it is more common to assign different colours to specific characters and to use different fonts and/or backgrounds to indicate the other elements. An explanation of the colour code for SDH in France can be found on page 880 of the French teletext.

White is only used for on-screen dialogue, whether the mouths of characters on screen are visible (voice-in) or not visible (voice-through). Thus, if a group of people is talking on screen, white will be assigned to all of them. However, in cases when characters are off screen (voice-out) yellow is used in the corresponding subtitles.

White and yellow are also assigned to voices heard through machines and when an on-screen character with a voice-in or a voice-through speaks through a megaphone or a telephone, the subtitle is in white but preceded by an asterisk (*) to indicate that their words are mediated by a machine. In turn, when characters are off screen and their voice can be heard through a television or an intercom, the subtitle appears in yellow and is preceded by an asterisk.

The colour cyan (light blue) is used for characters' interior monologues and for narrators (voice-offs). Cyan is also used in news reporting, where the voice of a correspondent is treated like that of a narrator.

---

4   Carmona (1996: 107–9) distinguishes the following five different voices: (1) voice-in of an on-screen character whose mouth is visible; (2) voice-through of an on-screen character whose mouth is not visible; (3) voice-out of an off-screen character; (4) voice-off used for interior monologues or for the narrator, whether diegetic (as in a flashback) or non-diegetic (as in documentaries); and (5) voice-over, which is recorded over the original audio track and can be heard in the background.

Green is applied when a character speaks in a foreign language. The colour is used to emphasize the fact that the original language is not dubbed into French.[5] Green subtitles either specify the name of the foreign language or provide a translation of the words in French.

Finally, red is used for any type of sound effects, while magenta (pinkish purple) is employed for music-related subtitles. The latter includes all types of music, from background (extra diegetic) to that which forms part of a programme (diegetic). Titles of songs, lyrics and names of singers are rarely given in subtitles in France.

The origin of the code is unclear. Whereas Boutet (2007: 6) writes that France 2 created it before the year 2000 in collaboration with SDH viewers and Deaf organizations, Charpillon (2002: 11) mentions that all television companies agreed a harmonization of SDH norms in spring 2001. Furthermore, it remains uncertain whether or not channels that started subtitling prior to 2001 employed this code. Nevertheless, by 2012, this use of colours for SDH has become the standard practice across all television channels, for broadcasting corporations and for all types of programming. It can also be found on (the very few) DVDs available with French SDH.

5. SDH output

Every year, channels must send data about their SDH output to the CSA. Following this, the regulating body compiles an annual report comparing the figures provided with what the television companies had previously agreed to and stated in their mission statements. The CSA further analyses progress made in terms of the quantity and genre of programmes

---

5   Although France is a dubbing country *par excellence*, soundtracks are not always altered. The original language of many documentaries is left in place, more often than not, for financial reasons; the same happens in news interviews, for authenticity and/or lack of time; and, in some films where, for geographical reasons, several languages are spoken.

subtitled. The CSA (2010c) publishes these reports on their website, usually in November of the following year, where they remain for twelve months.

In the following sections, the quantity of SDH between 2000 and 2010 on five long-established channels (TF1, F2, F3, F5 and M6) will be examined. As, at the time of writing, the annual reports for 2009 and 2010 has not yet been circulated, data on the same channels was collected over a period of four days (two in 2009 and two in 2010, including 12 February 2010) in order to analyse the developing trends in the level of SDH output.

5.1. SDH output: 2000 to 2008

Médias Sous-titrés (<http://www.medias-soustitres.com>), an independent French association devoted to providing SDH-related information, produces a comprehensive overview of the yearly figures published by the CSA. Table 13.1 shows the annual subtitling hours for the five aforementioned channels from 2000 to 2008. A channel broadcasting twenty-four hours for 365 days transmits a total of 8,760 hours annually. The annual percentages correspond to the annual quantity of SDH available to viewers out of the total annual broadcasting time.

Table 13.1 Hours of subtitling per year per channel

Channels	2000	2001	2002	2003	2004	2005	2006	2007	2008
TF1	1,322	1,816	1,752	1,841	1,845	2,275	3,838	4,727	5,641
France2	1,521	1,712	1,792	2,261	2,642	3,569	4,225	4,814	5,189
France3	806	884	1,390	1,838	2,296	3,439	4,849	5,117	5,699
France5	16	84	897	1,216	1,468	2,004	2,546	3,862	5,146
M6	–	–	213	412	694	1,116	1,582	2,757	4,114
Annual output	5,665	6,497	8,046	9,571	10,949	14,408	19,046	23,284	27,797
Annual percentage	8%	10%	14%	17%	20%	28%	39%	49%	59%

As can be seen, the quantity of accessible programming has been steadily improving over the years, with a sharper increase from 2005 onwards. In 2000, channels were subtitling an average 8 per cent of their total airtime. Since 2005, the yearly percentages have grown exponentially, reaching 59 per cent of airtime by 2008.

It should be noted that the information on SDH output collected by the CSA on an annual basis is compiled directly by the channels themselves. No verification is carried out and it is only the channels' intention to broadcast SDH that is taken into account. In other words, if, for example, a channel plans to subtitle a programme but, due to technical failure, is unable to do so, the SDH airtime will nonetheless be added to the channel's annual figures.

5.2. SDH output: 2009 to 2010

The weekly national French television listings magazine *TéléPoche* was used for the data analysed in this section. Most national and local television magazines use the international symbol for deafness

to show that a programme is subtitled. Others use a

T

for teletext. Although these magazines are under no legal obligation to do so, the CSA strongly recommends that they advertise those programmes that will be subtitled in a visible manner.

Although *TéléPoche* is available throughout the French territory, its listings are regional. This analysis focuses on Alsace, the second region to experience the switchover to digital television on 2 February 2010 (Tous Au Numérique 2010). In 2009, *TéléPoche* in Alsace published listings for analogue television; by February 2010 the magazine listed only programmes for DTTV.

As noted previously, advertisements are not subtitled. Therefore, their airtime was deducted pro rata and per channel from the daily number of subtitles. Indeed, this calculation was necessary because the magazine did not publish the schedule or the length of advertisements.

The following sample from 2009 and 2010 encompasses two weekend days and two week days: Sunday 24 May and Tuesday 26 May 2009 (Table 13.2), and Sunday 7 February and Friday 12 February 2010 (Table 13.3). In order to draw comparisons with SDH outputs from 2000 to 2008, the data relates to the same five channels.

Table 13.2 Subtitled output for two days in 2009

Channels[*]	Sunday 24 May 2009		Tuesday 26 May 2009	
	Subtitled output	Percentage of subtitled output	Subtitled output	Percentage of subtitled output
TF1	16h05	67%	16h30	69%
France 2	13h40	57%	13h17	55%
France 3	18h34	77%	18h52	79%
France 5	12h36	63%	12h46	56%
M6	09h55	50%	12h02	59%

[*]   On analogue television in 2009, the public channel France 5 and the private channel M6 broadcast for only twenty hours at the weekend and twenty-two hours and twenty-one hours respectively on the week day under study. The daily percentages of SDH take this into account.

The results show that the amount of subtitling for all five channels totalled seventy-one hours on Sunday 24 May 2009. This represents an average of 63 per cent of the daily airtime across the channels. For Tuesday 25 May 2009, the total was seventy-three hours, representing 64 per cent of their daily airtime.

Table 13.3 Subtitled output for two days in 2010

Channels*	Sunday 7 February 2010		Friday 12 February 2010	
	Subtitled output	Percentage of subtitled output	Subtitled output	Percentage of subtitled output
TF1	16h17	68%	17h38	73%
France 2	14h38	61%	14h20	60%
France 3	17h03	71%	20h04	84%
France 5	17h49	74%	14h29	60%
M6	19h37	82%	16h39	69%

*   On DTTV France 5 and M6 broadcast for 24 hours, 365 days a year.

For Sunday 7 February 2010, the total number of hours of SDH was eighty-five for the five channels, representing an average of 71 per cent of their daily airtime. For 12 February 2010, the amount was eighty-three hours, representing 70 per cent.

In order to draw comparisons with previous years, the daily outputs studied for 2009 and 2010 can be extrapolated to annual figures, thus showing (Table 13.4) that the annual average percentage of subtitled output would be 63 per cent for 2009 and 70 per cent for 2010. The estimated average for 2010 seems to suggest that there may have been an increase of 10 per cent in SDH output since 2008. In this sense, channels seem to have steadily increased their amount (daily and annual) of SDH.

Table 13.4 Annual output for 2009 and 2010

Channels	2009		2010	
	Output	Percentage	Output	Percentage
TF1	5,943	68%	6,187	71%
France 2	4,915	56%	5,286	60%
France 3	6,832	78%	6,771	77%
France 5	4,629	60%	5,895	67%
M6	4,003	54%	6,619	76%
Annual	26,323	63%	30,757	70%

A more detailed analysis of the data shows that some channels have a greater SDH output than others. It seems that, since 2006, France 3 has been providing a larger percentage of SDH than any of the other channels. With an average of 78 per cent of subtitled programming in 2009 and 77 per cent in 2010, the state-owned channel France 3 offers the most. On Friday 12 February 2010, 84 per cent of its programming (20 hours) was accessible to the D/deaf and the HoH. Out of the four non-subtitled hours, over two hours were occupied by advertisements, while the remaining time was taken up by a consumer programme, a lottery game and two short sports programmes.

After France 3, the private channel TF1 has offered the second largest SDH output. M6 comes third with a 20 per cent increase between 2009 and 2010. On Sunday 7 February 2010, M6 subtitled nearly twenty hours of its total airtime. Just like France 3, half of the hours not subtitled were occupied by advertisements while the remaining time was occupied by teleshopping and two short sports programmes. France 5 is fourth, while France 2 comes last. Although France 2 was the first channel to broadcast SDH in 1983, in 2010 it seems to have been the channel with the lowest output. For each of the days under assessment, approximately ten hours were not subtitled.

Analysis of the data indicates that, in 2009 and 2010, the majority of channels were more accessible on week days than at the weekend. The only exceptions in 2010 were France 5 and M6, which had substantially more SDH available on Sunday 7 February than Friday 12 February. The data also reveals that SDH is not as prevalent on public service channels as it is on private ones. Indeed, two of the France Télévisions channels (France 5 and France 2) provided less than 65 per cent of subtitled programming over the two years. However, despite these findings, the data does indicate that the overall quantity of SDH is increasing every year and that some channels seem to be close to attaining the 100 per cent mark.

6. Conclusion

Since 2003, designated as the European Year of People with Disabilities by the European Commission, the French government has modified the law in a first attempt to compel both state-owned and private channels in France to make their programmes accessible to the D/deaf and the HoH. However, the fact remains that only a small fraction of France's large audio-visual landscape is required to provide SDH. Furthermore, TV channels are not subjected to independent and external assessments to evaluate whether or not the set annual output is being met. For those who do not comply with the law, no penalties are envisaged, at least for the near future.

This article has focused on producing a broad survey of the French audiovisual landscape, the third largest in Europe after the UK and Italy (Harmann and Kevin 2010) and the place of SDH within it. Due to the complexities surrounding subtitling conventions and their impact on the D/deaf and the HoH, this area needs to be held up to greater academic scrutiny.

The conventions currently used by French channels providing SDH for every programme have been described. However, there remain uncertainties surrounding the origins of these conventions along with questions about how unique they are in comparison with those in other countries.

In terms of the quantity of SDH currently provided in France, the overview and basic analysis given above provides a starting point for future research. Of particular interest is the fact that the data seems to indicate that two out of the three public service channels that have been offering, albeit restricted, SDH, for nearly thirty years, are currently providing the least.

The basic relationship between disability and accessibility to the media was not considered an obvious one by most broadcasting companies until recently. However, this question is now being increasingly emphasized by lobbying associations, academics and governments. More specific analysis, such as that suggested above, should and must follow in order to achieve equal access for all.

Acknowledgements

I would like to thank Jen Rutherford for her linguistic revision of the text. The research of this article is supported by the grant from the Spanish Ministry of Science and Innovation FFI2009–08027, Subtitling for the Deaf and Hard of Hearing and Audio Description: objective tests and future plans and also by the Catalan Government fund 2009SGR700.

Bibliography

Boutet, Lucie, *Télévision, DVD, Internet, cinéma: État des lieux du sous-titrage sourds et malentendants en France*, unpublished Master's thesis (Institut Supérieur de Traducteurs et Interprètes, Brussels, 2007).

Braganti, Nicolas, 'FAQ – Réglementations', *SNPTV* (2010) <http://www.snptv.org/generalites/faq.php?theme=1> accessed 3 June 2010.

Brochand, Christian, *Histoire générale de la radio et de la télévision en France: Tome III 1974–2000* (Paris: La Documentation Française, 2006).

Carmona, Ramón, *Cómo se comenta un texto fílmico* (Madrid: Cátedra, 1996).

Charpillon, Jacques, *L'Adaptation des programmes télévisés aux personnes sourdes et malentendantes* (Paris: Ministère de la Culture et de la Communication, 2002).

CSA, 'Présentation du baromètre piloté par l'observatoire de l'équipement des foyers pour la réception de la télévision numérique' (2010a), <http://www.csa.fr/actualite/communiques/communiques_detail.php?id=131977> accessed 16 December 2010.

—— 'Que fait le CSA?' (2010b) <http://www.csa.fr/conseil/role/role_csa.php?rub=4> accessed 13 October 2010.

—— 'Toutes les actualités' (2010c) <http://www.csa.fr/actualite/actualites.php?rub=3> accessed 20 December 2010.

De Linde, Zoé, and Neil Kay, *The Semiotics of Subtitling* (Manchester: St Jerome, 1999).

Díaz Cintas, Jorge, Pilar Orero and Aline Remael, 'Media for All: A Global Challenge', in Jorge Díaz Cintas, Pilar Orero and Aline Remael, eds, *Media for All: Subtitling for the Deaf, Audio Description and Sign Language* (Amsterdam: Rodopi, 2007), 11–20.

Direction Générale des Médias et des Industries Culturelles, 'À quoi sert la contribution à l'audiovisuel public (Anciennement Redevance Audiovisuelle)?', *Ministère de la Culture et de la Communication* (2005), <http://www.ddm.gouv.fr/article.php3?id_article=796> accessed 13 October 2010.

Dubner, Nelly, and Isabelle Maurice, 'Médiamat annuel 2009', *Médiamétrie* (2010) <http://www.mediametrie.fr/television/communiques/mediamat-annuel-2009.php?id=178> accessed 22 April 2010.

Harmann, Florence, and Deirdre Kevin, 'Growth of the Number of Television Channels and Multi-channel Platforms in Europe Continues Despite the Crisis', *The European Audiovisual Observatory* (2010) <http://www.obs.coe.int/about/oea/pr/mavise_end2009.html> accessed 19 April 2010.

Mousseau, Jacques, and Christian Brochand, *Histoire de la Télévision Française* (Paris: Fernand Nathan, 1982).

Pellerin, Marc, 'Le CSA sera plus strict avec les chaînes d'info', *Aujourd'hui en France* (12 February 2010).

Shield, Bridget, *Evaluation of the Social and Economic Cost of Hearing Impairment: A Report for Hear-It* (Brussels: Hear-it AISBL, 2006).

Tous Au Numérique, 'Où et Quand ?' (2010) <http://www.tousaunumerique.fr/ou-et-quand/> accessed 20 November 2010.

Pennsylvania, the University of Paris VII, Brown University, and Imperial College London. She is a professional translator specializing in videogame localization, which she researches as a side project.

MARIAGRAZIA DE MEO is a researcher in English language and linguistics at the University of Salerno, Italy. She holds an MA in Translation Studies from the University of Warwick, UK, and teaches English at the Faculty of Scienze della Formazione. Among her publications is a book on phraseology and corpus linguistics. Her other areas of interest are sociolinguistics, pragmatics and language teaching. More recently her research has focused on audiovisual translation and subtitling.

ELENA DI GIOVANNI is Lecturer in Translation at the University of Macerata, Italy, where she is also Director of the Language Centre. She holds a degree in specialized translation from the University of Bologna at Forlì and a PhD in English and audiovisual translation from the University of Naples Federico II. She has taught audiovisual translation theory and practice in several MA programmes at the universities of Bologna/Forlì, Parma, IULM (Milan), Autònoma de Barcelona (Spain), and Roehampton (UK). She is the director of the recently launched, international MA programme in Accessibility to Media, Arts and Culture at the University of Macerata. Her research interests include translation as intercultural communication, translation and postcolonialism, and audiovisual translation. She has published extensively on subtitling, dubbing and audio description and has been working as a professional audiovisual translator for over twenty years.

DENISE FILMER worked for Cosmopolitan Magazine in London before moving to Italy in the early 1990s. She obtained a first-class honours degree in Communications and Modern Languages at the University of Catania in 2007, where she worked as an English language assistant. Her undergraduate dissertation was the trigger for her interest in cross-cultural meaning transfer of culturally contingent ideologies. In 2011 she completed a part-time MA by research at Durham University on translating racial slurs and taboo words, published in 2012. Awarded a Durham Doctoral Studentship, Denise is currently investigating the translation and representation of Berlusconi's politically incorrect discourse in the British Press.

Notes on Contributors

VERONICA BONSIGNORI holds a PhD in English Linguistics and has carried out her research at the Department of English studies at the University of Pisa. Her research interests are in the fields of pragmatics, sociolinguistics and audiovisual translation. She has contributed in national and international conferences and has published various articles on audiovisual translation, focusing on the study of linguistic phenomena pertaining to orality in English filmic speech in comparison to Italian dubbing.

SILVIA BRUTI, PhD in English from the University of Pisa, is Associate Professor of English language and linguistics at the University of Pisa. Her research interests include text linguistics, discourse analysis, (historical) pragmatics, corpus linguistics and translation. She has published widely in these areas and contributed to national and international conferences. She is the (co-)editor of several collections of essays, on reformulation and paraphrase (2004), on lexicography and translation (2009, with Cella and Foschi Albert), on translation (2011, with Barone, Foschi Albert and Tocco). She has recently conducted research on intercultural pragmatics and audiovisual translation, e.g. the translation of compliments, terms of address and conversational routines in interlingual subtitling and dubbing.

ALICE CASARINI is a PhD student in audiovisual translation and a liaison interpreting instructor at the University of Bologna in Forlì, Italy. Her research focuses on the perception of American adolescent culture through the dubbing and fansubbing of television series aimed at teenagers (1990–2010), the evolution of the Italian audience, and the impact of the new media on television production and consumption. She holds a BA in Foreign Languages and Literatures (2005), an MA in European Languages and Philologies (2007) and an MA in Screen Translation (2008), all from the University of Bologna. She has also studied at the University of

ANNA JANKOWSKA graduated with an MA in Spanish Philology from the Jagiellonian University in Krakow, Poland. She is currently a lecturer at the UNESCO Chair for Translation Studies and Intercultural Communication of the Jagiellonian University, where she teaches audiovisual translation, including audio description. She is also an active audiovisual translator, audio describer and president of the 7th Sense Foundation, which promotes and delivers audio description and SDH for institutions, film festivals, theaters, DVD distributors and television broadcasters. She is a member of ESIST and STAW (Polish Association of Audiovisual Translators).

NATHALIE MÄLZER teaches Film Studies, Theatre Studies and Comparative Literature at Freie Universität Berlin and Sorbonne Nouvelle Paris. Having completed her PhD with a thesis titled *The Transfer of French Literature to Germany between 1871 and 1933*, she has been teaching at Universität Hildesheim, Germany, since 2009, where she has developed an MA pro-gramme in audiovisual translation. Her research interests are audiovisual translation, dialogue and orality, transmedial narratology, and literary translation. She has translated over thirty novels and non-fiction books from French into German, for which she has obtained many grants and been awarded the Stefan-George-Prize.

TIA MULLER holds an MA in Audiovisual Translation from the University of Roehampton (UK). She is currently working on her PhD at the Universitat Autònoma de Barcelona, Spain. Her research topic deals with subtitling on television for the D/deaf and the hard-of-hearing people in France. She is a member of the research group TransMedia Catalonia & CaiaC. She has presented her work at the international conference s Media for All 3 (2009), Media for All 4 (2011) and Languages & the Media (2012). She is currently working as a quality control manager in the dub-bing agency Audioprojects.

NINA REVIERS has a degree in Translation and a European Master in Conference Interpreting from Artesis University College, Antwerp, Belgium. She wrote her Master's dissertation on Audio Description in the theatre and has collaborated with several theatre groups and organi-zations in Belgium as a freelance audio describer for the past three years.

She also works as a research assistant at Artesis University College, with a scholarship granted by the University of Antwerp, on a project on Audio Description in Dutch: introducing corpus analysis in multimodal translation. She is a member of the TransMedia Benelux Research Group.

AGNIESZKA SZARKOWSKA, PhD, is an assistant lecturer at the Institute of Applied Linguistics, University of Warsaw. She is the founder and head of the Audiovisual Translation Lab (<http://www.avt.ils.uw.edu.pl>). Her research interests include audiovisual translation, especially subtitling for the deaf and the hard-of-hearing (SDH) and audio description. Her recent research projects include an eyetracking study on SDH, multilingualism in subtitling, audio description in education, text-to-speech audio description and audio description of foreign films. She is a member of the European Association for Studies in Screen Translation and an honorary member of the Polish Audiovisual Translators Association (STAW).

ADRIANA TORTORIELLO has been a translator, subtitler and lecturer for many years and is at present a part-time lecturer at Imperial College London, where she teaches audiovisual translation and translation theories. Her doctoral research focuses on the relationship between verbal and nonverbal codes and the consequent issues related to semiotic cohesion in subtitling.

ANIKA VERVECKEN has always had two passions: performance and language. She studied acting and music before commencing her studies in translation in her native Antwerp. During her MA in translation she was able to combine both passions in her research on surtitling. This investigation, and the enthusiasm with which it was received, sparked Anika's interest in research. Today, Anika lives in Vancouver, Canada, where she is the in-house surtitler for the Vancouver Opera. She also works as a freelance surtitler, researcher and guest lecturer. Her future aspirations include improving accessibility to performing arts in Vancouver and initiating a doctoral research project.

AGNIESZKA WALCZAK holds an MA in Applied Linguistics from the University of Warsaw. Her research interests include audiovisual translation with special focus on audio description for the blind and the partially sighted as well as subtitles for the deaf and the hard-of-hearing. She currently works as an audiovisual translator, specializing in audio description.

SERENELLA ZANOTTI is Lecturer in English language and translation at the Department of Linguistics, Roma Tre University, where she teaches English linguistics, audiovisual translation and subtitling. She has a PhD from the University of Rome 'La Sapienza' and an MA in English from Goldsmiths College, London. From 2005 until 2010, she taught at Siena University. Her main interests are in the areas of audiovisual translation (ethnic varieties in AVT, intralingual dubbing, children's TV programmes, redubbing, censorship and manipulation, fansubbing), English sociolinguistics (youth language, conversational narrative) and literary translation (authorship in translation, polysystemic approaches, translation history).

Index

NEW TRENDS IN TRANSLATION STUDIES

In today's globalised society, translation and interpreting are gaining visibility and relevance as a means to foster communication and dialogue in increasingly multicultural and multilingual environments. Practised since time immemorial, both activities have become more complex and multifaceted in recent decades, intersecting with many other disciplines. *New Trends in Translation Studies* is an international series with the main objectives of promoting the scholarly study of translation and interpreting and of functioning as a forum for the translation and interpreting research community.

This series publishes research on subjects related to multimedia translation and interpreting, in their various social roles. It is primarily intended to engage with contemporary issues surrounding the new multidimensional environments in which translation is flourishing, such as audiovisual media, the internet and emerging new media and technologies. It sets out to reflect new trends in research and in the profession, to encourage flexible methodologies and to promote interdisciplinary research ranging from the theoretical to the practical and from the applied to the pedagogical.

New Trends in Translation Studies publishes translation- and interpreting-oriented books that present high-quality scholarship in an accessible, reader-friendly manner. The series embraces a wide range of publications – monographs, edited volumes, conference proceedings and translations of works in translation studies which do not exist in English. The editor, Dr Jorge Díaz Cintas, welcomes proposals from all those interested in being involved with the series. The working language of the series is English, although in exceptional circumstances works in other languages can be considered for publication. Proposals dealing with specialised translation, translation tools and technology, audiovisual translation and the field of accessibility to the media are particularly welcomed.